Karl August von Hase

Miracle Plays and Sacred Dramas

A historical survey

Karl August von Hase

Miracle Plays and Sacred Dramas
A historical survey

ISBN/EAN: 9783337394622

Printed in Europe, USA, Canada, Australia, Japan

Cover: Foto ©ninafisch / pixelio.de

More available books at **www.hansebooks.com**

MIRACLE PLAYS AND SACRED DRAMAS

A HISTORICAL SURVEY

BY

Dr. KARL HASE

TRANSLATED FROM THE GERMAN
BY

A. W. JACKSON

AND EDITED BY

THE REV. W. W. JACKSON
FELLOW OF EXETER COLLEGE, OXFORD

LONDON
TRÜBNER & CO., LUDGATE HILL
1880

CONTENTS.

CORRIGENDA.

Page 26, last line, *for* "the authors, priests, or troubadours," *read*, "the authors, whether priests or troubadours."

Page 38, last line but one, omit "and."

Page 56, line 4, *for* "*Heiliger*," *read* "*Heiligen*."

Page 90, last line, insert reference to note (65).

MIRACLE PLAYS AND SACRED DRAMAS.

LECTURE I.

THE MYSTERIES OF THE MIDDLE AGES.

THE new birth of our poetry and art is due to the Church of the Middle Ages: they were but touched by some faint memories of the splendour of classical antiquity. The same may be said of their highest expression, the drama, which once before had originated in the religious rites performed at the altar of Dionysos the Liberator. It was, however, the very circumstance of this origin, added to an Oriental horror of all imitation of the human form, which caused the Church—the Church of the martyrs— to regard the theatre, with its alluring portraiture of the whole sensuous life of the old world, as a place consecrated to the service of the evil one. It was so regarded even when the arrogance of Imperial Rome only mocked in humorous representations the lust and greed of the old gods.

In the end of the second century one of the Fathers of the Church wrote a special treatise against plays (Tertullian, *De Spectaculis*), in which he asks those who will not renounce them whether the God of truth, who hates all falsehood, can be willing to receive into His kingdom those whose features and hair, whose age and sex, whose

A

sighs and laughter, love and anger, are all feigned ? He promises them a tragedy of their own, when, in the day of judgment, they shall be consigned to everlasting suffering. He was able to appeal to the two great lawgivers of Greece: Lycurgus would tolerate no theatre in Sparta, and Solon is reported to have said, on seeing the car of Thespis, surnamed the Founder of Greek tragedy [1]— "Are you not ashamed to tell so many lies?" Athens showed no accordance with this remark, although Plato, face to face with Greek tragedy in its high moral beauty, resolved to exclude the drama from his ideal republic, because it represented passion, in its unbridled, tempestuous display, as beautiful and worthy of imitation. The intellect of his great scholar, on the contrary, did not scorn the task of unravelling the laws of the drama from the rich mass of the inherited treasures of Greek genius, while he placed the moral significance of tragedy in the purification of our emotions.

The Church encountered on the one hand the intoxicating performance of paid actors, to whom Roman custom, even more than Roman law, denied the rights of citizenship, on a stage on which the burning of Hercules was once represented in earnest, and on which an early Christian empress was not ashamed to enact the part of Leda with the swan. On the other hand, she saw the sanguinary realities and harsh indifference to human life displayed in the Roman amphitheatre, on whose arena heroic Christians were often constrained to act a part in strife with the beasts of the wilderness.[2] For a long time she threatened to expel any of her members who would not relinquish their love of the theatre, and she refused to admit actors except on condition of renouncing their profession. These last, nevertheless, obtained a patron saint, if one but dubiously recognised, in St. Genesius. He had been baptized on the stage in mimicry of Christian baptism, and was so impressed by the solemnity of the act, that he considered himself really baptized, and in the persecution under Diocletian he received the baptism of blood.([3])

But Christianity, although victorious over the Greek gods, proved at length powerless to resist Greek culture. Its influence even gave rise to a tragedy, the *Passion of Christ*,([4]) which was assigned by early tradition to St. Gregory Nazienzen, the celebrated orator, whom his contemporaries esteemed the great lyric poet of the Greek Church. It is undoubtedly a work of the age in which the pious Apostate made a last vain effort to arrest the Church's career of conquest by prohibiting Christian teachers from expounding the heathen classics in their schools. Julian was of opinion that a Christian, if instructed in the Bible only, would be no better than a barbarian.

It was then that learned Christians rather hastily undertook to form a literature at once classical and Christian by fusing the new Christian material in the old classic moulds. About a third of the verse of the *Passion of Christ* was borrowed from different tragedies of Euripides, in order that the new Hero of Tragedy might be celebrated in the familiar classic phraseology. Perhaps also there already existed some trace of the idea, prevalent at a later period, of representing the Attic poets as unconscious heralds and witnesses of Christ. The prologue certainly makes no secret of the debt; it commences—

> " Thou who hast verses heard with pious soul,
> And now a pious tale in verse would hear,
> With willing ear incline to me who sing,
> After the manner of Euripides,
> The pangs of Him who saved mankind from bale."

Very few of the lines recall the noble tragedy of Æschylus, the *Prometheus Bound*. The Christianity of the fourth century had not yet attained the breadth and freedom of thought which would allow it to recognise a type of the crucified incarnate God in the suffering demigod chained to his cross, the rock of Caucasus, with his secret of the destruction which awaits the dynasty of the old gods.   In the Passion of Christ, the chorus, in antique style, but without any special poetic exaltation, manifests its sympathy in the overwhelming tragedy, advises and moderates.   The action takes place principally behind the scene, and is only announced by messengers.   The principal medium is the Virgin Mother; the sorrows of her Divine Son are almost entirely represented through their reflection in her; the sword goes through her soul until the risen Christ appears with His greeting from the other world.   There is throughout no deficiency of genuine human, maternal sentiment : she addresses the body of her beloved Son—

> " Thou liest again, enfolded in thy shroud,
>   As once in swaddling clothes, upon thy mother's lap."

Her lament is not devoid of some most pathetic touches, but the alien verses often do not readily serve the new subject, and thus cause an interminable diffuseness ; while at the same time the agony of the mother's soul, which naturally arises from the contradiction of the circumstances, is by the poet's treatment increased to despair. It is especially for this reason that later Catholic research has ascribed the poem to a lesser author than Gregory, as this despair is inconsistent with an insight into the necessity of the Redeemer's death and with the assurance of His coming resurrection.   The Virgin is comfortless, and yet she does not believe in the capacity for suffering and death of the Deity whom she has so marvellously borne.   Like many an early church which is built on the ruins of an ancient temple and adorned with its columns, the Passion of Christ, the first Christian drama, has its foundation on Attic tragedy and is constructed from its fragments.   It already contained in germ the various legends of the Virgin Mother and the dogma of the

Incarnation. It was not intended for representation, but for the schools. On the Passion plays of the Middle Ages, whose elements it comprised in a freer and yet more artistic form, it had little influence.

The Christians of the Roman Empire nevertheless loved the theatre. St. Augustine acknowledges that during his wild youth at Carthage he was fascinated by the imaginary joys and sorrows of the stage, and that he himself was one of the rival poets in a dramatic contest.(5) St. Chrysostom declaimed zealously against members of his flock, who learned in the theatres witty and unseemly songs, and afterwards sang them in their houses or in the streets, while they could hardly chant a single psalm.(6) He reproached his hearers with having amused themselves even on Good Friday with the frivolous representations of the stage. The Church deemed it necessary about this period to threaten excommunication in case of attendance at theatres on holy days.(7) It was partly on account of her disfavour, but still more through the prevailing distress of the age, that the handsome structures for all kinds of amusements were allowed after the fifth century to fall into decay.(8) Later they were used as quarries for the feudal castles and the cathedrals of the Middle Ages. Actors never entirely disappeared, but as players, *jongleurs*, mummers—degenerate offspring of the Roman actors, and perhaps also of the Celtic bards—they held exhibitions of all sorts of mummery in the open streets, or were present at great festivals, at one time richly rewarded, at another driven forth as outcasts. In German charters they were allowed no public rights, but the learning of the Church sometimes took them under its protection.(9) Yet in a synod of the time of Louis le Debonnaire it was decreed that priests and clerks should not remain during the representation of any play, either on the stage or at a marriage feast, but before the players entered should rise and go out.(10)

The culture of the ancient world was nearly lost to the

West during a long period of frightful disturbance.([11]) It surprises us to find that in the tenth century, especially termed the dark or starless, the comedies of Terence were diligently read in a Saxon cloister. In order to do away with this scandal, a nun, Hrosvitha,([12]) the "loud voice from Gandersheim," devised six Latin comedies, which show the influence of the semi-Greek culture of the Imperial House of Saxony. They are in servile imitation of Terence, and consist of legends in the form of dialogues —mere rhymed prose, which has for its theme martyrdom and the glorification of chastity.([13]) The pious sisters of Gandersheim may perhaps have found edification and amusement in the representation of these comedies— although the exhibition of supersensuous modesty may have demanded for its illustration some rather vivid pictures of the opposite quality. This is certainly the case with the subject of two comedies [*Abraham* and *Paphnutius*], which depict the repentance of an erring woman, and even the corpse of a noble lady needs a miracle to save it from the passionate lover whom she died disdaining. Only one of these dramas corresponds in some measure with our received ideas of a comedy; it has a burlesque scene in juxtaposition to the martyrdom of three virgins. Their persecutor, a high official under Diocletian, who wishes to wrong the already imprisoned maidens, is made to appear as if struck by sudden insanity. In the dark he embraces dripping pans and all sorts of cooking utensils, and at last, as he is returning home, as black as a chimney-sweep after his imaginary gratification, he meets with ill-usage from his own soldiers, who take him for a devil.

These erudite comedies remained confined within convent walls. The new popular drama originated in the very midst of the Church, from her Liturgy at the altar of the Son of God, the Redeemer. The Church of an incarnate God, who was accounted actually present in the Eucharistic feast, could not fail in time to free herself from the Jewish dread of all visible and artificial representation of human or divine beings.

From the time of Gregory the Great the mass itself became an almost dramatic celebration of the world-tragedy of Golgotha. It embraced the whole scale of religious emotion, from the mournful cry of the *Miserere* to the jubilee of the *Gloria in excelsis*. It was for this reason that it afterwards so readily served as a text-book for majestic symphonies.([14])

During Passion Week, the custom, which once prevailed in old Roman churches, is still retained in the Chapel of the Vatican. After the Old Testament psalms and prophecies, on the morning of Good Friday, the Passion from St. John is sung with voices arranged as in an oratorio: Christ is tenor, Pilate bass; there are choruses of the priests, of the soldiers, of the people, interspersed with the evangelical narrative in recitative.([15]) Thus the Passion-music of Sebastian Bach, which is usually esteemed a fruit of the religious worship of Protestant Germany, belongs in some sense to the early Church. At any rate, it is in unconscious agreement with her practice, of which it is merely a grand Protestant development.

In the processions which were held by the towns, according to immemorial custom, either on the day of the death of their patron saint, which was regarded as the day of his birth to everlasting life, or in commemoration of some great deliverance—also later in the pageantries of Corpus Christi Day—the priests and friars in their picturesque costumes, and the guilds and corporations in their festival robes, with their tapers and banners, formed a spectacle in themselves. In addition, we find all kinds of pious mummeries: Adam and Eve carrying between them the Tree of Knowledge; St. John the Baptist as a herald, with the banner of Christ and a lamb; Judas bearing a bag of money, followed by the Devil with the gallows; St. George on his war-horse, training after him the slain dragon; with other saints, represented according to their varied individuality. In the yearly procession at Messina, the principal part is still assigned to a camel, or rather to its skin, in which are stuck two lusty youths. The legend relates that once during a famine the Madonna sent a camel laden with corn to the relief of the city. At Orleans, on the anniversary of its deliverance, the triumphal procession was headed by a lad in the knightly-armour of the maid. At Quedlinburg it was not considered that the Bishop of Halberstadt had usurped any undue honour when he rode into the town as the representative of the Saviour, while priests, people, and children cried Hosanna, and strewed the ground before him, not perhaps with palm-branches, but with willow-boughs and branches of fir.

At Christmas-tide the shepherds of the Abruzzi, the *Pifferari* so dear to our young artists, come to Rome principally that they may adore the Mother of God by kneeling before her images at the corners of the streets and piping in old-fashioned style a hymn to the Madonna. In Germany, many a long year ago, Knecht Ruprecht and Santa Claus, in strange confusion with the Virgin and our Lord Himself, wandered about on Advent evenings, frightening and admonishing the children, and then, as now, consoling them with Christmas gifts. At the root of the mummery lay harmless jest, and perhaps also some forgotten legend of the wanderings of the old Teutonic gods. In Germany, also, the early years of this century still witnessed the journeying of the Wise Men, those three holy kings whose kingdom has never cost either blood or tears. They were certainly more in the habit of receiving small gifts "from the honoured goodman or the beloved goodwife," than of bringing gold, frankincense, and myrrh. In front the King of Morocco carried the Star on a long stick. In Thuringia they sang—

> " The holy Three Kings with their star,
> They loved the Lord, they came from far.

When Herod's house before them lay,
They heard him from the window say :

" ' Oh, good wise men, come in and dine ;
I will give you both beer and wine,
And hay and straw to make your bed,
And nought of payment shall be said.'

" ' Oh, no ! oh, no ! we must away,
We seek a little Child to-day,
A little Child, a mighty King,
Him who created everything.' " (16)

Even in worldly and rural festivities the Church had her share. Froissart, the chronicler of departing chivalry, recounts what he witnessed in the year 1389, on the magnificent entry of the mischievous Queen Isabella into Paris. Above the gate of St. Denis, God the Father sat in majesty, with the Son and the Holy Ghost, surrounded by choristers dressed as angels, who sang very sweetly. As the Queen's litter passed through the gate, a small door opened, and two of the angels floated down, and placed a crown of gold and jewels on the head of the Queen of the Fleurs-de-lis.(17)

The feast of the expulsion of winter or the casting forth of death, which was usually held on Mid-Lent Sunday, and which in Silesia and Lusatia existed almost up to our own time, was founded partly on an old Sclavonic spring festival, and partly on a dim popular tradition of the casting forth of the images of the old gods, which were in like manner burned or thrown into the water when the spring of the Gospel dawned on our ancestors.(18)

It scarcely needed the wish for some counter-charm and equivalent of the old heathen gaieties at the spring or Eostra festivals and the Yule feasts—respectively correspondent in time to our Easter and Christmas seasons—to induce the early Teutonic Church to attempt some visible representation of the purport of these her greatest festivals. This attempt was at first a very simple one.(19)

On Good Friday a crucifix was laid in a sort of grave

beneath the altar, and on Easter Day it was taken out
and elevated amid solemn singing.[20]   A synod held at
Worms in 1316 decreed that the elevation should take
place with closed doors in the presence of the priests only;
as, in consequence of a superstition that none who beheld
it would die that year, the people had disturbed the ceremony by their tumultuous crowding.[21]   Occasionally
the Three Maries, who came to anoint the body of the
Lord, were represented with the angel who announced to
them the glad tidings of the resurrection.   At first the
priests wore their festival robes, and the dramatic effect
was given simply by their coming and going, and their
part-singing of the words of the Evangelist.   But how
easy it then became to realise the scene by giving to
acolytes or choristers women's dress or angel's wings, while
the risen Christ came forth in living form !

Such was the origin of the Easter play, which appears
to have been the first, as it was certainly the most fully
developed, of the miracle plays: continuing as it did through
the descent into hell,[22] which the Church had already
begun to regard as the period of the conquest of Satan and
the admittance of the saints of the Old Testament from
Hades into Paradise—onward to the Ascension, and in
every case to the Last Judgment.   It also seemed fitting
to go backwards a little, and to represent our Lord at the
Judgment-seat, with the rest of the tragedy of the Passion.
Then through the feeling that the true significance of all
these events lay in the redemption wrought by the life as
well as by the death of our Lord, scenes of the former were
introduced, especially those in which it was easy to trace
a token or emblem of His work.   Such were the first
miracle of the change of Water into Wine, and the
miracle of the Feeding of the Five Thousand, with their
great complement, the Last Supper.   We also find the
healing of the man who was born blind and the Raising
of Lazarus, these last being symbols of the power of the
Dispenser of light and life.[23]

In pursuance of the same line of illustration the Old
Testament and the antique world were introduced. The
play then commenced with the prophets who prophesied
of the Saviour, and with the " heathen people " as they
appeared in the history or the legends of the Church.
Balaam, on the ass which spoke, beheld the Star which in
the far-away future should arise out of Jacob ; Virgil was
added, because he predicted the renovation of the coming
ages through a virgin and a scion of heavenly race ; [24]
also the Sybil who pointed out to the Emperor Augustus,
as greater than himself, a Child in the heights of heaven
in the arms of His Virgin Mother.[25]   Eden and the
expulsion from it were included, the Tree of Knowledge
being taken as the type opposed to the Tree of the
Cross.   The legend was sometimes introduced in which
the dying Adam, in order that he may be restored to
health, sends Seth to Paradise for a fruit of the Tree
of Life.   The cherub at the gate gives him a twig, which
is both to cure his father and to bestow on him everlasting life.   When Seth returns, Adam is already buried,
so Seth plants the twig on his grave, and from it grows
the Tree of the Cross.[26]

At last, an earlier beginning was sought than even the
creation, and the action commenced with the fall of Lucifer
and his angels ; so that the work of redemption was pictured through the entire course of its majestic story.

Sometimes from this large whole single groups would
be detached to suit narrower measures of time or ability,
or in order that they might receive a fuller individual
development.   Such a group is the mourning of the Virgin,
in the pathetic tones of whose lament—which is rather
lyric than dramatic—we trace the echo both of the mourning psalms of the Old Testament and of the lamentations
for the dead in the German heroic poems.[27]

The Christmas play arose out of that most simple exhibition which still, as the illuminated Bethlehem, amuses
children on Christmas Eve in many old-fashioned patri-

archal families. Its subject, the birth of the Divine Child,
is in its source, the Gospel narrative of St. Matthew and
St. Luke, already rich in poetic elements. For the services
on Christmas morning a manger was erected in the church,
and in the inventories of many old churches we find the
pictures of an ox and an ass—just as in the inventories of
many old schools we find small figures of these animals,
to be used as admonitory ornaments for children who
were supposed to resemble them. When the contemporaries of St. Francis of Assisi relate as a novelty his erection
of a manger in the woods, the only remarkable point is the
full substantial realisation of the scene through the presence of real animals and real herdsmen. The Adoration
of the Shepherds was fitted for congenial popular representation, and the simple, hearty accents of their song are
still heard among the rustic population.([23])

In Flanders, the common people, as shepherds, brought
cheese and eggs, while at the great houses the noble
families, in the guise of the Three Kings, presented their
gifts to the infant Christ. A beautiful memorial of this
custom has been preserved to us in a picture of the school
of Van Eyck in the Munich collection, which represents
the Dukes of Burgundy, Philip the Good, and Charles the
Bold engaged in this regal office.([29]) Worldly pomp also
found an opportunity for display in the representation of
the Three Kings and of Herod. With such pomp English
bishops, during the Council of Constance, brought on the
stage before the Emperor Sigismund, a Christmas play,
which closed with the tragic scene of the murder of the
Innocents, the emblem of the future crucifixion of the
Son of God.([30])

It was possible to begin the Christmas play, no less
than the Easter play, with scenes from the Old Testament, such as the prophetic announcement of the Branch
out of the Root of Jesse. Moreover, as the Church regarded
the assumption of our human nature by the Son of God
as in itself a redemptive act, Paradise was given as the

prototype of the stable of Bethlehem, with Eve as the sisterly emblem of the Virgin; then followed Rachel weeping for her children, the harbinger of the mourning of the Holy Mother. It was only that the bitter Christmas season proved unfavourable to a lengthy development of the theme; and in spite of this we find an old French Christmas play which commences with the creation of man, and passing beyond its natural limit, the birth of our Saviour, ends with the flight into Egypt and the divine command to return.([31]) Another drama in old Norman-French of the twelfth century, which was found some years ago at Tours,([32]) is apparently part of a Christmas play, though the discoverer rather hastily entitled it *Adam*, on account of its first section. It contains three acts: the Fall of Man; the first bloody fruit of the Fall of Man, and the Old Testatment prophecies of the Redeemer. The language is sustained, solemn, and liturgic, but the motive of the scenes is often supplied by the study of character, with which the authors of such pieces have elsewhere not concerned themselves. For instance, in the Temptation, the devil first tries to rouse Adam's curiosity and to make him discontented and envious, and is rebuked by the words, " Get thee behind me; " but he understands how to incite Eve's vanity by his sly flatteries.([33])   It is at first sight surprising to find that in this piece not only Cain, but also Abel, with the patriarchs and prophets, when they have finished their speeches, are carried off in iron chains to hell by the devil; Abel alone, as we learn by the stage directions, being treated with more leniency than the rest. Yet this quite agrees with the common representation by the Church of Hades and hell as one; so that the saints of the Old Testament, till freed by Christ, were imprisoned in the lower world in subjection to the devil. The intentional prominence, nevertheless, which is given to this point, seems one of the strongest proofs that in this play of *Adam* only a fragment has been discovered; for holy men who loved God could never have

been condemned to so fearful a fate before the very eyes
of the spectators, unless they were afterwards to be
delivered.

The musical character of these pieces was determined
by their growth out of the worship of the Church. At
first they consisted merely of chant and recitative, but by
degrees separate speeches were introduced. The music
was probably in the style of the Gregorian chants, but the
notes which remain are to us in great measure hiero-
glyphics. We find many fragments of the Liturgy of the
Romish Church, and at the close, or in some solemn pause,
the choir comes in with well-known Church hymns.
The words spoken by God Himself are sometimes set for
three voices, bass, tenor, and alto, to signify His threefold
nature. Single scenes of the Old Testament, as prefiguring
the Passion, and the visions of the Apocalypse are introduced,([34]) to use the modern term, as *tableaux*, or else
with silent pantomimic movement. Generally, however,
each actor, in speech or song, declared what he represented, with a simplicity which reminds one of the scrip
which in old pictures we see proceeding from the mouth
of each figure. At first the representations took place in
church, and the actors were priests or acolytes, who spoke
their parts in Latin, the universal domestic language of
the Church, after the repetition of the mass, and sometimes
after a sermon also.

The first recorded development of the miracle play which
has yet been discovered occurred in France in the eleventh
century, but soon all German and Latin nations shared the
same impulse.([35]) With the exception of some Epiphany
plays, which we have only as fragments, but which were very
highly esteemed, and were still wholly entwined with the
worship of the Church,([36]) the *Rise and Fall of Antichrist*, an
Easter play of the twelfth century found in the convent of
Tegernsee in the Bavarian Highlands, is the first great
miracle play of German origin which we possess. It has
one special peculiarity : it appears to have been written

partly in adoration of Christ, and partly to celebrate the
succession of Germany to the imperial sovereignty of
Rome; for to the nation under the Hohenstaufen their
rule seemed world wide.([37])   From the careful specification of the very simple *mise-en-scène*, we gather that it
was a musical play and intended for representation.   It
may perhaps have been acted before the great hero-
Emperor Frederic Barbarossa.([38])   The scenery is given:
in the background to the east, the Temple of the Lord;
and in front of it, at specified points of the compass, the
thrones of the principal personages, surrounded by their
respective armies.   The intercourse between the princes
sitting on the thrones is carried on only through messengers,
and the space is supposed to be large enough to represent
the distance between Germany and Jerusalem, and to
allow of the delivery of sundry battles.

Allegoric personages open the play, Paganism ([39]) and
the Jewish synagogue being represented as women.   The
former extols the devout polytheism which accords due
reverence to all heavenly powers, while the latter opposes
the One God to all who put their trust in created beings
who cannot help themselves.   Then the Church comes
forward in regal crown and armour, having on her right
hand Mercy with the olive branch, on her left Justice with
balance and sword.   Against those who are of another
faith than hers she pronounces eternal damnation.([40])
She is followed on the right by the Pope and clergy, on
the left by the Emperor and his hosts.([41])   The kings of
the earth bring up the rear.

In the first part the Emperor appeals to his historic
rights, and sends heralds to the kings of the earth to
demand their submission: " As historians relate, the whole
world paid tribute to Rome; the might of our ancestors
collected it, but the indolence of their descendants has
forfeited it."([42])   The King of France gives the defiant
answer that the imperial rights rather belong to himself;
that his ancestors once held them; and it is not till he is

subdued in battle that he consents to become the vassal
of the Emperor. The kings of Greece and Jerusalem
willingly admit the German sovereignty. When all the
kingdoms of the Church have submitted,([43]) the King of
Babylon unites with Paganism in an attempt to crush
Christianity in the very land of its birth as an upstart
superstition. The King of Jerusalem sends for aid to the
Emperor as the defender of the Church. He immediately
comes with his army, and when he has subdued the enemy,
he lays the crown and sceptre of Babylon in the Temple
of the Lord.

In the second part the hypocrites assemble at Jerusalem,
bowing low before all men in feigned humility, in order
that they may obtain the approbation of the unlearned.
In their midst is Antichrist, that strange ideal personification of the powers inimical to Christianity. He wears a
shirt of mail hidden beneath his wings, and he has on his
right hand Hypocrisy and on his left Heresy. The hypocrites greet him with the cry, "Long hath religion been in
danger; long hath the Church given herself unto vanity;
God loveth not worldly prelates." Relying on the favour
of the laity,([44]) they erect the throne of Antichrist in the
Temple, and the Church, conquered and humiliated, is
driven for refuge to the Papal See. Antichrist wishes
to abolish all that is ancient and to found a new kingdom.([45]) He sends ambassadors to demand the homage of
the world for himself, the ruler and the Lord predicted in
the Scriptures. The kings kneel before him, and he in-
scribes on their brows the first letter of his name. The
King of Germany, perhaps as the son and heir of the
apparently forgotten Emperor, he endeavours to win by
gifts, as it would not be prudent to engage in a struggle
with the "furor Teutonicus."([46]) The King, however,
penetrates the delusion; he dismisses the ambassadors
with contempt, delivers battle, and subdues the army of
Antichrist. The latter then works miracles, heals a cripple
and a leper, and restores to life a man who has feigned

himself dead, so that even the Germans are persuaded to acknowledge him. By their help he conquers the King of Babylon, and he gains the synagogue by the persuasive assertion of himself as the true Messiah. His earthly kingdom thus extends beyond the former kingdom of Christ. But by the manifestation of Enoch and Elias to the synagogue, the Jews are won to recognize the crucified Saviour, and they renounce Antichrist, who causes them to be persecuted. All kings come to worship him, and he promises peace to the whole world. At that moment a sound is heard from above, Antichrist falls, the hypocrites flee away, and the rest return to the true faith, while the Church sings—" Behold the man who took not God for his strength ; as for me, I am like a green olive-tree in the house of the Lord." Then she receives her own again, and sings—" Praise ye the Lord."

The speeches and chants are in rhymed verse ; every speaker says what he has to say without any dialogue properly so called, and the heralds repeat word for word, with epic brevity, the messages delivered to them. Thus also, in different parts of the piece, the three allegoric personages repeat their sacred war-songs. Everything is very clear, and, in spite of the Latin, in accordance with simple, popular conceptions—only the end is too gravely majestic and not illustrated, as might have been expected, by the return of Christ.

The common people generally knew the tenor of these plays, as they were taken from the Bible or from popular legends, so that they understood the pantomime, and were able to enjoy the splendour or the fancifulness of the representation. Still we find some very early instances of a lapse into the vulgar tongue. The earliest known piece, which as we have seen belongs to the eleventh century, the *Wise and Foolish Virgins*, is all in Scriptural Latin, Christ speaks, or rather sings, in the words of the Latin Bible, but He then repeats what He has said in Provençal verse, which is also used by the Virgins.([47])

B

From the thirteenth century the miracle play, in its gradual severance from the Church offices, was confounded by the Pope, some bishops and their synods, with other less spiritual amusements, and banished from the churches.([48]) At the same time, almost universally, the people ascended from the place of the spectators to the stage, so that the priests thenceforward only directed the action, or retained the individual rôles of pre-eminently sacred personages.

With the acting of the people the transition to the vulgar tongue became absolute, although the stage directions were still commonly in Latin, and old Latin hymns were sung in the established language of the Church. Well-known sentences of Holy Writ were also introduced, followed by a translation into the vulgar tongue, or sometimes by an allegoric explanation. Thus in the Sterzing Passion play of 1496, Christ stops on His way to Calvary at the usual stations to sing the *Lamentationes;* ([49]) and on the cross He sings the *Sitio,* after which He says :

> " I deeply thirst for man's salvation,
>   And for it bear much tribulation :
>   Mankind to-day redeemed shall be,
>   And comfort find for aye in Me."

Occasionally Lay Brethren devoted themselves to the pious work. In Antwerp the Brethren of St. Luke, a brotherhood consisting principally of artists and artificers, acted the old Flemish pieces ; and in Paris the *Confrèrie de la Passion*, a body of artizans, received from Charles VI., in 1402, a charter for the exclusive performance of miracle plays in the town and suburbs. In Rome, the Fraternity *del Gonfalone* represented in Passion Week the sufferings of Christ on the arena of the Coliseum, once consecrated by the blood of so many martyrs, shed in combat with wild beasts. In York, on the introduction of the Feast of Corpus Christi, every guild had to exhibit some scene from the Holy Scriptures, and the procession passed through the midst of the spectacle, till, on the application of a pious mendicant friar, the Town Council in 1426 decided to have the play on the previous day, in order that the procession for the attainment of the Great Indulgence might alone take place on the divine festival. ([50])

If a whole town undertook a play, a solemn trumpet-call (*le cri du jeu*) summoned all who wished to join in the representation for the honour of Christ or the good of their souls. Such persons had to place in the hands of an officer of justice a signed paper, in which they swore, on pain of death or the forfeiture of their goods, that they would carefully study the rôle they undertook, and that they would appear on the day fixed for the performance. As the common people found many suitable parts—for instance, those of the Israelites in the wilderness, or the Jewish spectators at the entry into Jerusalem, at the judgment-seat, and during the crucifixion—great numbers flocked to offer their co-operation. Sometimes nearly half a town acted, while the other half looked on, in company with the people from the surrounding districts.

We may here remark that generally no entrance-money was paid, only sometimes voluntary gifts were received to provide for the expenses incurred. The same had been the case in the churches where offerings had been accepted. As regards in particular the Parisian Brotherhood of the Passion, a prologue exists which may be taken either for or against the question of a fee—

"Now will we hold an Easter play,
Tis merry, and there's little to pay." ([51])

The pieces were not divided into acts, but the larger ones were portioned into days; as sometimes the performance was carried on unwearyingly through all the principal points of the revealed narrative from the Creation of the World to the Judgment-day; and the entertainment lasted, with some interval for the noontide meal, from morning until evening, or not unfrequently, like the feasts of the good old times, for several successive days.

Such great popular plays could only be performed in the open air, and we hear of prayers for favourable weather, and of interruptions on account of rough weather. In the play found at Tours (see page 13), the scene of the heavenly Paradise is laid in the church, and God the Father comes out whenever He wishes to speak to Adam. The earthly Paradise appears to have been so arranged outside the great western door, that space was still left to represent the world beyond Paradise, into which there was a descent of a few steps. We are hence led to suppose that in the drama of *Antichrist*, the Temple of the Lord in the background to the east may have been a real church. Later many other spots, conveniently situated for a spectacle, were not disdained.

The great number of actors, and the desire for a complete illustration of the scene of important events, while the art of shifting the scenes was still unknown, necessitated a very large stage, on which the different places, whether towns, houses, or woods, were fenced off, sometimes with the names affixed on a scrip. In the middle a sort of common ground was always required for the mass of actors, and for the representation of events which demanded less definite scenery. [52]

As the action of the miracle play extended beyond this world into the upper and lower worlds as well, we find in France a stage of three stories. The topmost represented Paradise, and in it were the Trinity, the saints and angels. It was carefully adorned with tapestry, and shaded by trees, of which it is incidentally remarked that they were green, and that they appeared to blossom and emit sweet odours; it also contained an organ.[53] In the middle was the earthly stage, which was made as large as possible. Below was Hell, sometimes represented as the jaws of Hell by the opening and shutting of the mouth of an enormous dragon.[54] The poet's words were then literally true:

> " Within the stage's narrow bound,
>   The whole creation circles round ;
>   Each soul, with measured haste, is driven
>   Through this wide earth to hell or heaven."

Brunelleschi, who could arch the great cupola of the Florentine cathedral, did not consider the erection of the stage for a festival play a degradation of his art.

In Germany, less care was usually bestowed on the accessories. There Paradise was generally at one end of the stage, raised a few steps above the rest. In one Easter play, the devil had for his infernal habitation only a very large cask, in and out of which he could spring like a true hell-hound; while another large cask set on end served for the mountain of the Temptation.

If unity of place was thus preserved amid all changes, unity of time seems to have caused even less anxiety. The Divine Hero was born and laid in the manger in the morning; and in the evening He hung on the cross; while a mere wave of the hand could dispose of centuries or ages.

All the players, or at any rate all who were required for the half-day's performance, came on the stage at once, even the ass appeared according to his Scriptural pre-rogative.[55] Each actor was supposed to be invisible, till he received his cue and stood forth.[56] It occasionally happened that the action went on at the same time in different parts of the stage, in cases where there was no immediate personal manifestation—as, for instance, when a voice was heard from heaven or from hell. It was then possible to carry on the action in one place by dumb show only, while in another the words would be spoken.

On his first appearance in the play every actor had to state what he represented, or else some appointed person announced him to the audience. A similar herald often introduced the play by a prologue in the style of an oration, which he continued by a simple description of the action, whenever it was not trusted to proclaim itself.

Sometimes he appeared in the form of an angel, or of St. Augustine, the celebrated teacher of the Western Church, who unexpectedly, though perhaps not altogether undeservedly, had to act as stage manager.([57])   It was part of his work to admonish the spectators to silence : *Silete.* This was also the duty of the deacon in old churches before the reading of the Gospel.   In the theatres, judging by the manuscripts, the admonition was often repeated, and appears to have belonged to the part.   It was probably necessitated by the crowd of spectators, and the discomfort of the places where they had to sit or stand ; and even by the very warmth of their sympathy, as is still often the case in Italian theatres.([58])

At first in the churches the costume of the players was only the ordinary priest's gown, and for the sacred personages the officiating robes.   Even in the beginning of the twelfth century, we find that a learned Norman who had been summoned to England to fill the Rectorship of the Great School of the Abbey of Dunstable, when he caused his scholars to perform a miracle play of *St. Catherine,* borrowed the priestly vestments from the sacristan of St. Alban's for the dress of the players.   The women's parts, which had to be acted by men and boys, were the first to require a fancy dress.   In the popular festival plays, as far as we can discover, the sacred personages wore the Byzantine robe, Christ, as well as the Jewish High Priest, being sometimes attired as a bishop. For the crowd of subordinate players the ordinary costume of the Middle Ages was picturesque enough ; but as the people liked mummery, some would at their own cost provide a more fantastic attire.   As in hell the condemned souls were supposed to wear no clothes, this was indicated by close-fitting shirts.   Children might wear the garment of Eden.

The stage tricks which are occasionally revealed are of the simplest order.   In an Easter play at Donaueschingen, Judas was to be hanged in due form by Beelzebub—" The devil must take care of the fastening and sit behind him on the bar of the gallows." Judas was to carry concealed in his coat a black bird and the entrails of some animal, so that when the devil tore his coat the bird might fly away and the entrails fall out. Then both he and the devil slid down to hell on a slanted rope. Sometimes, however, more ingenious mechanism was invented, so that Aaron's Rod suddenly blossomed, or the fig-tree withered at the curse of Christ. Instead of the ladders which ascended from the infernal to the earthly stage and thence to heaven, ropes and pinions were brought into play. One scene at the execution of a martyr was particularly admired, in which the head made three jumps, and at each jump a stream of blood issued.

It was in France that a division first arose between *Mysteries* and *Moralities*. The subject of the *Mysterium* was derived chiefly from Holy Writ. The primary meaning of *secret*, inherent in the word, was suited to the original purport of these plays, the visible illustration of the Incarnation and Redemption, the Secrets of the Kingdom of God (Matt. xi. 13; Ephes. v. 32). With the mysteries of ancient Greece, during the celebration of which the legends of the old gods were presented in dramatic form, the word has also an incidental connection : just as with some reference to the mysteries of Paganism, the Greek Church gave the name of Mysteries to those ceremonies from which the Latin Church afterwards made a careful selection, and which by her were called Sacraments.([50])

The first *Moralities* were allegoric representations : Faith, Hope, and Charity appeared as personages, or Virtue and Vice—like the entities which Robespierre harangued in his debased Festival of the Champ de Mars. And though such personified ideas have no power over the hearts of men, a moral sentiment could derive an illustration from them, in combination with an imaginary tale or a popular legend. The Morality and Mystery were in some measure united in the representation of a parable from Holy Scripture, as in the parable of the *Wise and Foolish Virgins* and of the *Rich Man and Lazarus;* or we have in the mystery the appearance of single allegorical figures, as when the Virgin at the Birth of Christ was supported by Dame *Honestasse*, or Judas was led to death by *Desespérance*. A still more striking instance of their conjunction is in the once so favourite representation of a legal tribunal, when, as a prologue to the Passion of Christ, the case of sinful humanity is argued before the Throne of God, Justice being the pleader on one side and Mercy on the other. There these allegorical figures represent the two great ideas on which the Church founds her theory of salvation through the Redeemer's death. God the Son ends the dispute when He offers Himself to satisfy Justice by His Incarnation and Death, and thus to identify Mercy with Justice.[60]

The Morality had its principal development in the fifteenth century in Paris, when the corporation of legal associates, the *Clerks*, or *Kingdom of the Basoche*,[61] who had been accustomed to represent comic pieces on the erection of the May-pole in the courtyard of the Palais de Justice, were incited by the example of the *Confrèrie de la Passion* to undertake more serious pieces, while they were debarred from the Mysteries by the charter granted to the Confrèrie.

An English moral play, *Every-Man*,[62] is designed as an illustration of the lot of all human beings. God the Father complains of the degenerate state of humanity, summons Death, and warns every man of his approaching end. Every-Man in his terror has recourse to Relationship, to Conviviality, to Riches, but they all in turn forsake him. He then appeals to Good-works, who, after gently reproaching him for his long neglect of her, leads him to her sister Wisdom. Wisdom takes him to a holy man, Knowledge, who assigns him a penance. He inflicts this on himself upon the stage, and then goes aside to receive the Sacraments. On his return he is overcome by the weakness of Death—Strength, Beauty, Intellect, and the Five Senses take leave of him, only Good-works remains with him till his blessed end, when an angel descends from heaven and sings the requiem.

The drama of the Cavalier, who pledges the wife whom he loves to the devil,([63]) has not nearly so good a moral, but it is even more in keeping with mediæval sentiment. A nobleman has wasted his substance, and the devil promises to make him again rich, if he will give him his wife at the end of seven years. The nobleman is at first horrorstruck, but his need is pressing, and he signs the contract. As soon as Satan has pocketed the agreement, he demands, as a necessary sequence, that his debtor should deny God. The nobleman again shrinks with horror, but he yields to the demand. At last the devil insists on his denial of the Blessed Virgin. He absolutely refuses to commit so great a sin, and the devil is obliged to desist.

The seven years are past, and the creditor demands the fulfilment of the contract. When the nobleman with a heavy heart is taking his wife to the devil, they pass a church consecrated to the Virgin, and the wife asks to be allowed to go in for a few moments. While she kneels in prayer before the altar, the Virgin assumes her form, goes out, and is given to the devil, who immediately penetrates her disguise and reproaches the nobleman with having broken his plighted faith. He, however, honestly believes he has given his wife. The Virgin solves the puzzle, obliges the devil to relinquish the contract, and reunites the couple with a friendly admonition.

Between Mysteries and Moralities lay the plays derived from the legends of the Saints, which in England were specially distinguised as *Miracle Plays*,([64]) because they represented the miracles of the Saint as well as his martyrdom—Faith being thus glorified both by his conquests of the powers of nature and by his final submission to them.

The first play of this class which we find is a miracle play of *St. Stephen*, the first martyred witness of the Church, which from his place in the calendar might seem naturally to belong to the realm of the Christmas play, but which in the fifteenth century was expanded into a whole history of the Apostle.[65]

On the occasion of the visit of the Emperor Sigismund to England, A.D. 1416, the exploits of St. George were enacted before him at Windsor Castle. The patron saint of England typified the triumph of the Church over the Old Serpent or Dragon, and also the victory of Mind over Nature's brute force.

Again, between miracle plays and mysteries came the plays of the Virgin, when they no longer followed the Scriptural narrative, and exhibited the joys and sorrows of the Divine Mother during her lifetime; but depicted what had from time to time been accomplished for her worshippers by her whom the Middle Ages honoured as the Mother of Compassion, the Bride and Mother of God, the Deliverer of the World, whose tears were of equal avail with the blood of her Divine Son.[66]

There was, however, no very close adherence to these distinctive appellations. In France in the fifteenth century, the name *Mystère* became so prevalent that the few serious secular pieces which existed were similarly entitled. We hear of the Mystery of the *Countess Griseldis*, who, as a test of her love, bore every indignity, even the cruellest; and of the Mystery of *Robert the Devil*, the human opposite of the Son of God.[67]

In the past century only a cold and indifferent regard was paid to the half-obliterated traces of the miracle play; but owing to the warm interest of our own time in its inheritance from the Middle Ages, several old manuscripts have been discovered and made public. Many, no doubt, perished with the age which they gratified, and many remain amid the dust of old libraries. Some few of the names of the authors, priests, or troubadours have been discovered, but none are among the more celebrated poetic names of the Middle Ages. Almost all of these dramas were written on some special occasion, for some definite local purpose, and most of them, like national songs, are of quite unknown origin ; or perhaps we have the name of the place where they were performed. As the mediæval poets received neither payment nor percentage, the plays vere unhesitatingly rearranged to suit local tastes or exigencies, so that the form in which we possess a piece is not always any secure warrant of its origin. Many bear, independently of the dialect, a very clear local stamp. In a Mecklenburg Easter play the Holy Sepulchre is placed at Wismar, and the watchman on the tower sees something approaching across the Baltic.([68]) At Easter nearly every church had its own Holy Sepulchre, as at Christmas its manger.

The chronicles generally record the miracle plays only when they were disturbed by some catastrophe, such as might easily enough occur when so vast a crowd was assembled. In Bautzen in 1412, when a play of St. Dorothea was being acted in the Market Place, the roof of a house fell, owing to the weight of the people seated on it, and thirty-three persons were crushed to death. This drama appears to have been the one which we still possess in an old manuscript.([69]) It is in very short sentences, something like the descriptions under old engravings, and contains the received legend of the noble Roman maiden, who was loved and wooed by the Governor of Cæsarea, but as the affianced of Christ rejected him ; and after suffering the cruellest tortures, in which her fair frame was almost torn to pieces, still appeared fresh and blooming ; till at last her head was cut off.

In Florence in the spring of 1304, the Festival Company of one of the divisions of the town issued a proclamation that whoever wished to receive news of the other world might repair to the bridge *alla Carraja*, or to the banks of the Arno on each side of it. We see here something of

the same sentiment which in the same age produced
Dante's *Divina Commedia.* On boats on the stream
scaffolding was laid, fires were kindled, and all sorts of
tortures exhibited, to typify the *Inferno* in which the condemned souls appeared grievously tormented by the devils.
The bridge, which at that time was still of wood, tottered
beneath the press of spectators, then gave way, and a
great number of persons perished, either in the waves of
the Arno or in the infernal flames.[70]

The miracle play was very seriously regarded by the
actors, as well as by the spectators. It was the custom
before commencing, that the whole troupe kneeling on
the stage should sing the hymn *Veni Creator Spiritus,*
either in Latin or in the national version.

In such hymns of the Church, many of which originated at this time, the whole crowd would join; somewhat as in Weimar, when the play of the *Robbers* was
acted, the students innocently joined in the Song of the
Outlaws. The prologue [71] usually closed the piece with
pious counsel and an admonition to sing the *Te Deum.*
Easter plays would terminate with one of the popular hymns
—" Christ is risen," or " Christ, Thou art good and merciful."

At Eisenach, after Easter 1322, when the whole land
had been pacified, a play of the *Wise and Foolish Virgins*
was acted in the royal park before the Landgrave Frederic
of the Scarred Cheek. When the Foolish Virgins found no
mercy even on the intercession of Mary, the Landgrave
exclaimed—" What sort of thing is Christian faith, if
Christians cannot be pardoned even on the intercession
of the Mother of God and all the saints ! "—and from that
time the alienation of mind commenced, which darkened
the last years of the life of that heroic prince.[72]   The
circumstance long remained deeply engraven on the
memories of the Thuringian people, but the play itself
appeared to be lost, till a miracle play of the *Ten Virgins*
was discovered some years ago in the neighbouring town
of Mühlhausen, once a royal city, and published as be-

longing to that town.([73])   Later it was decided, with
every appearance of probability, that this must be the
Eisenach play.([74])   It is in German, but interspersed with
the Latin words of the parable and with Latin hymns and
chants.   Part of it is arranged to be sung by the choir
in antiphony, and part of it to be spoken by individual
actors.   It only resembles the early Provençal mysteries
in its elements, and is very much more richly illustrated.
At the commencement of the play, Christ, His Mother,
and the Angelic Choir on one side, and the Virgins on
the other side, chant parts of the Liturgy.   After that
Christ sends a messenger into the world, who introduces
the play by giving the Church's views of life.   He is
bidden to say to the good friends of Christ, who for His
sake are willing to suffer much sorrow, that an everlasting reward awaits them; they are to make ready for His
great hospitality—(*Wirthschaft*, the middle-high-German
word both for a marriage feast and an ordinary festival)
—when He will seat them by His side, and replace all
their sorrows by joy.

The moral of the parable, in its strict orthodox application, is certainly not illustrated in any special manner in
the action, but only in the speeches of the Virgins, which
are divided among the five voices on each side, without
further specification.   The Wise Virgins rejoice when
they are hated by men, they have forsaken the world and
loved Christ only; the hour of the decisive sentence, which
shall admit them to the great feast, is the hour of death,
and the burning lamps are the visible symbols of true
wisdom.   The Foolish Virgins do nothing so very wicked,
indeed they almost seem to be delineated with the same
sympathetic lenity which caused Wilhelm Schadow, in
his picture at Frankfort, to paint them as more beautiful than their wiser sisters.   All they wish, frivolous
children of this world, is to have pleasure in their
young lives, to dance and to amuse themselves, trusting in
God's compassion; and they scornfully term the Wise

Virgins who pray and fast, Church goers (*Tempeltreterinnen*).
One of them says—

> " For thirty years a life right brave
> We'll lead, then off our hair we'll shave,
> And hie into a cloister—
> If God His kingdom doth bestow,
> St. Peter 'll ne'er keep us out, I know."[75]

This sounds a little heretical, but afterwards, in the
self-accusation of the condemned, a special offence against
the Church is adduced—" that for so many years they have
refused to disclose their sins to a confessor." They dance
and feast, then they lie down. On awaking, their anguish
and regret commence, while they in vain seek oil for their
extinguished lamps. When the Bridegroom comes and
tells His Mother to place beside her the Virgins who have
been ready all the time, and to recompense them for their
weary waiting, those who are shut out cry imploringly—

> " Heavenly Father, Lord Almighty,
> By Thy bitter death we pray Thee,
> Thy great forgiveness let us taste,
> Through folly led our days to waste."

He rejects them, because the beautiful kingdom of heaven
must remain closed to all who have wasted their youthful
years and have not repented of their sins. They then
seek a merciful mediation—

> " Since God our suit hath now denied,
> We Mary pray, the gentle Maid,
> The Mother of Compassion,
> To pity our great agony,
> And for us, sinners poor, to pray
> Mercy from her loved Son."

She is willing to try, and she prays again and again
tenderly and earnestly—

> " Oh, my beloved Child,
> Am not I Thy Mother mild ?

Think only of the agony,
Which through Thy sad death pierced me,
When a sword went through my soul.
By the pangs I bore through Thee,
A boon I pray Thee grant Thou me,
Make these poor sinners whole."(76)

But Lucifer demands justice, and with both simplicity
and cleverness he urges against the Lord God, the Lord of
love, that he and his hosts, on account of these sinners,
whom by his counsel he has misled, are suffering more
torments than there are drops in the sea. Christ also
rejects His Mother's prayer; and with that calm, awful
severity with which it is fitting that the sentence of
eternal damnation should be pronounced against a sentient
being, and which reminds one of Michael Angelo's conception of Him in his picture of the Last Judgment, He
says—

"Justice shall have her right!
Let the damned pass out of sight,
Into the depths of hell,
With the devils to dwell!"

The identity of this play with that of Eisenach may be
called into question, because only the intercession of the
Blessed Virgin is offered, and not that of "all the Saints;"
indeed one of the lost souls says, "We are hated by all
the Saints." But the addition of the words may easily
have originated, either in the chronicle or even in the
speech of the excited Landgrave, from the common mode
of expression, and it has to some slight extent a foundation in the drama itself. When the Redeemer reminds
His Mother of the Scriptural sentence—" Heaven and
earth shall pass away, but My words shall not pass away "
—He adds, that when He has thus spoken the words of
condemnation, all the hosts of heaven may not save a
sinner. The closing scene, too, is very greatly calculated
to fill with anguish the imagination of a compassionate
man of simple faith. The women, who have sunk to the

ground in supplication, are chained by Satan, and dragged crying and lamenting across the stage, and then through the midst of the spectators, to hell.([77])   The first says—

> " Alas ! the woful way
>   That e'er I saw the day !
>   Woe to thee, mother, that I was born,
>   That thou slew'st me not at my birth forlorn,
>   Casting me forth unnamed to die,
>   Like a dog to perish utterly."([78])

One after another they describe the miseries of the eternally lost : how they are shut out from God's compassion ; how they cannot be aided by His sweet Mother; how for them Christ's deep wounds are vain ; and how even death cannot destroy them, though they are eternally dead. Their friends and kinsfolk need not trouble about them and be at any cost or give alms, as prayers and masses for the dead are wasted on them.   After each separate lamentation they sing in chorus—

> " Oh woe ! woe !
>   We shall see Christ nevermore."

Till at last the refrain dies in the abyss—

> " We have deserved God's anger sore,
>   And so are lost for evermore."

The mere tale of the parable as here given appears in irreconcilable opposition to Christian sentiment, and the contradiction is increased when we recollect the many different mediators recognised by the mediæval Church. Yet we cannot suspect the poet, even should he by chance have been a Dominican monk, of any intentional revolt against the worship of the Virgin.   On obvious Christian grounds, a man influenced by such an intention would not also have represented a repentant heart as excluded from the mercy of God and the benefit of the Saviour's wounds.([79])   It was the Biblical parable itself, in combination with the Church's interpretation of the two groups of

Virgins, as respective types of the contrasting portions and destinies of humanity, which made it necessary that the Foolish Virgins should on no account be saved. The truth of the parable as it was uttered by our Lord, with His solemn moral warning, contrasted with the parable of the Last Judgment which follows, cannot but offer in dramatic representation an aspect other than that which is observed in the original. It was in vain for the learned to try to persuade the Landgrave that the terrible state of eternal perdition " only commenced on the judgment-day and not sooner."[80] Dramatic necessity caused the Foolish Virgins to be exhibited as still alive ; and Christian hope confidently affirms no soul to be lost beyond recovery, which, with repentance and faith in God's compassion, flees for refuge to the cross of the Redeemer. To this cross the Church of the Middle Ages superadded the prayers of the saints, and the purifying fires of purgatory. It may perhaps have been some dim sense of the contradiction involved which induced the poet to depict in the plaints of the distressed Virgins their fate as so pitiable, and also to endeavour by these plaints to reach the moral end at which he aims. Thus, one of the lost souls says to the people—

> " Ye may remember, as we pass the abyss to enter in,
>   If ye yourselves would win God's grace, to keep yourselves from
>   sin."[81]

We have in the legend of Tannhäuser a specimen of the Church's more merciful sentence, which is confirmed by a miracle in spite even of the severe decision of a Pope—

> " Let never then a priest again
>   Dare bid a man despair,
>   But welcome penitence and pain,
>   God's grace if he would share."

And this mercy, which bids none despair who yet can weep and pray, we find illustrated also in the miracle plays, as in *Theophilus* and *Dame Jutta*. In the first it forms the preliminary basis of the dramatised legend; in the latter it is merely an addition to a subordinate incident. A Greek legend télls how Theophilus, the administrator of a bishopric in Cilicia, was at first greatly respected, but under a new bishop was unjustly calumniated and dismissed. In his despair he gives a bond to the devil, in exchange for a promise of restitution to his honours and office. The promise is immediately fulfilled, and Theophilus for a while rejoices in his renewed favour and reputation, but afterwards he is consumed by melancholy. In his repentance he appeals to the Mother of God, who obtains the deed of contract from Satan, and restores it to the purified penitent. Theophilus—Lover of God—became known to the West as early as the eighth century,([82]) and almost rivalled the Magdalen as a proverbial type of the merciful and miraculous power of Christianity, which could change even lost sinners into saints.([83]) Of the *Miracle de Theophile*, the author was Rutebeuf, a noted *Trouvère* of the thirteenth century.([84]) It begins with the complaint of the Viscount Theophilus, that after all his services the bishop allows him to die of hunger. "I cannot depend upon God, for no man can reach Him." He consults a magician, whom he tells that he must regain his office at any price. The magician promises that if, with clasped hands, he will deny God and the saints and swear to become his bondsman, he will reinstate him in his charge. Theophilus does so; and he also traces a manuscript with his own blood, as the devil complains that in default of such a written bond he is often cheated. Satan then promises to give him wealth and power, but in return Theophilus must always reject the prayers of the poor and must never fast. At first he rejoices in his earthly grandeur, but at the end of seven years he becomes suddenly repentant. Entering a chapel consecrated to Our Lady, he says, "I dare not turn to God, nor to His saints, nor to His sweet Mother; but since in her there is no harshness, I cry aloud to her for pity, *Reine sainte et belle*."

She begins by repulsing him, but at last she promises to seek the paper, and she asks Satan for it. He replies, "Give it back to you, I'd sooner be hanged." He cannot, however, resist her, and she returns it to Theophilus, on condition that he shall confess everything to the bishop, who is then to reveal his confession to the people. The bishop does so, assuring them that the story is as true as the gospel; and the play ends with an exhortation to sing the Te Deum. In the legend the closing scene is more graceful. Worn with sorrow and fasting, Theophilus falls asleep in his canonical stall, and dreams that the Madonna has laid on his knees the fatal paper. Waking he finds his dream a fact, he confesses all to the bishop and the assembled people, and so dies—the precursor of Faust, the harbinger not only of the old German or Gothic plays, but also of the dramas of Goethe.

Dame Jutta (*Frau Jutta*), which was composed in High-German verse about the year 1480, by a priest, Theodoric Schernbeck, and which appears to have been represented in Thuringia,[85] was long accounted the first original German tragedy. By Gottsched, who reintroduced·it to the German nation,[86] it was as such opposed to the mysteries, the boast of the Latin nations; and he affirmed that the first French tragedies were thirty or forty years later in date. He did not suspect that *Frau Jutta* is itself a mystery, and that its historical relationship is only intelligible if we regard it as the last German scion of the mediæval miracle play. It retains the triple division of the stage into heaven, earth, and hell; but it has dropped all Latin and liturgic components. It is throughout in keeping with the teaching of the Church except on one point, the delivery from hell, where it is not quite orthodox. The foundation of the drama is the legend which prevailed from the beginning of the thirteenth century, and which in Rome was long accepted as historical. A girl in masculine attire runs away with her lover, and studies at Paris or Athens, till she attains to great learning;

after which she is made a cardinal in Rome; and finally, in A.D. 855, she becomes Pope, under the title of John VIII. During the procession to take possession of the Chair of the Lateran, she is recognised as a woman in the fulfilment of the most undeniable function of her sex, and she is slain by the enraged populace, by whom she is henceforth termed Pope Joan.

The material of the legend, which is equally fitted for a great tragic or for a comic development,([87]) is, in its terrestrial portion, handled in this drama only in a dry, short, rather meaningless manner. We have the decision of the girl Jutta and her lover to leave England for Paris, in order to prosecute their studies; and there the period of tuition is dismissed without detail, till both are promoted to the degree of doctor. They then, as men of learning, receive an honourable welcome in Rome, and are appointed cardinals by Pope Basilius. Finally, after his death, we have the election and coronation of Dame Jutta, who, as the Holy Father, dispenses indulgent spiritual promises. The journeys to Paris and Rome are, for the imagination of the spectators, quite naturally accomplished by a few steps across the stage; and the period of study, judging by the marginal note, is thus disposed of, "Here some verses are to be sung." The real fully-developed interest of the piece, and that which renders it a mystery, lies in the attempt to personify the jurisdiction of the other world.

The play begins in hell, where Lucifer, with much amiability, calls together his "dear children of hell," who are various beings with the impish names familiar to us in German witches' sabbaths, &c., *i.e.*, Unversün, Fledderwisch, Astrot, Kreutzelein, and the devil's grandmother, Lillis. When they have danced, sung, and enjoyed themselves ([88]) in the cool May weather, Lucifer sends to the fair maid Jutta, who already thinks of repairing with a young clerk to the High School at Paris, a devil to confirm her in her intentions. The messenger accomplishes his errand in a very direct manner by promising her wisdom and great honour.

The infernal powers do not reappear till Pope Jutta tries to expel a devil from the possessed son of a senator. The devil—who indeed departs, because, as he says, it is the will of God—is Unversün. He threatens her, and she begins to tremble. From this point the remainder of the action is carried on almost entirely in the other world. The "Salvator" complains to his "liebe mutter zart" of the woman-pope, who sins against the sacred laws of the Church and of nature, and in His wrath He is ready to destroy her. Mary prays for her—

> " Since Thou didst choose me Thy mother glad,
>   Forsake not for aye this soul so sad."

Christ hearkens to her prayer, and sends the angel Gabriel to Pope Jutta with the sentence of death ; but he leaves it to her to decide whether she will bear for ever the pangs of hell, or submit in this life to worldly shame. She chooses rather to bear temporal disgrace, than to be forsaken for ever by God's mercy. As soon as Christ receives the message, He sends Death, who appears in person to the woman-pope, with the customary assertion of his power to level all things. In her sorrow she appeals to the Redeemer, and she utilises her learning by reminding Him of various sinners—

> " Adam broke Thy first command,
>   Yet he won mercy at Thy hand.
>   Peter is blessed in heaven by Thee,
>   Who three times straitly did deny Thee.
>   Thomas doubted of Thy word,
>   But Thou forgavest him, dear Lord.
>   Paul, too, did once Thy Christian folk
>   With persecutions sore provoke,
>   And yet Thy mercy bade him live,
>   And Thou didst all his sins forgive.
>   His soul to hell Theophilus gave,
>   But Thou wast gracious, Lord, to save.

The Magdalen's great sins forgiven,
Now happy days she spends in heaven.
Zacchæus who had been unjust,
Became Thy servant and Thy host.
Longinus pierced Thee through the side,
And Mary saw the bloody tide,
Yet in the very self-same day,
Thy mercy bade him live for aye.
Since these were all once men of sin,
Who yet Thy blessèd heaven did win,
Wash Thou away my sinful stain,
O God of mercy, by Thy pain !
Oh, leave me not, great Lord, I cry,
Thus sadly in my sin to die !"

Then, in a song of which the musical notes are given, she cries to the Blessed Virgin—

"O Mary, Mother pure,
    Who sinners comfortest,
    To thee I make my moan,
    A sinner with the rest.
    I weep so sore that bloody drops
    Mix with mine eyes' salt rain ;
    Oh pray for me thy lovèd Child,
    Let me not weep in vain !" [80]

Mary replies that she will do what she can with her beloved Son to induce Him to compassionate her. Death, however, will wait no longer; she is delivered in the streets of Rome, and the play ends as the legend relates.

With this temporal expiation one might naturally expect the drama to conclude, for the celestial conditions of pardon seem fulfilled by it. But this appears to be overlooked, and the devil Unversün carries off Pope Jutta's soul.[90] While on the central stage there figures a procession of the Roman clergy and people with banners and tapers, who endeavour to appease the wrath of Heaven —for showers of blood have fallen, and the earth has quaked at the unprecedented crime—and the action is continued in hell, where Pope Jutta's soul is dealt with.

She is at first mocked by the devils, who, as she is a learned man, appoint her choirmaster of hell. Bidden to deny God, she is yet, with odd devilish inconsistency, made to suffer all kinds of torments for her offence against God and His Church. Meanwhile in her repentance, to the disgust of the spirits of evil, she cries courageously and unceasingly to Mary, the celestial Maid, to obtain for her the grace of her dear Son; and she also appeals to the holy bishop, St. Nicholas. Both pray for her to the " Salvator," who is at first silent, but at length yielding to such worthy intercession on behalf of her wretched soul, He sends an angel to rescue her from the pangs of hell. The piece becomes, then, scarcely less mild and pitiful in its conclusion than the second part of Faust. St. Michael repels with his sword an imp who tries to retain Jutta, and the Saviour greets her—

> " To thee, loved child, I welcome give !
> With Me rejoicing thou shalt live,
> In this My heavenly home ! "

And so, while the chant of the earthly procession mingles with the hallelujahs of the heavenly hosts, the pangs of hell are exchanged for an apotheosis.[91]

If to the gazing Landgrave, who in earlier days had been known as the Joyous, the poetry of a miracle play once became so cruel a reality, the actors themselves also were not always entirely free from danger. We read in the Chronicles of Metz that in a Passion play the priest of St. Victor almost fainted, and was obliged to be removed from the cross before the proper time, and that Judas by inadvertence nearly hanged himself in fact. At Seure in Burgundy in a play which was acted to the glory of God, the Holy Virgin, and the great and famous St. Martin, the patron of the town, Satan, on his exit from the jaws of hell, burnt the back of his shins; and when the first alarm was over, he had to bear derision as well as pain. The chronicle of the play relates that since St. Martin himself had taken the thing in hand, the actors, who had before been rather nervous, continued the performance with the boldness of lions.([92])

It could not but happen that the representation of the majestic personages,([93]) and events of the Scripture narrative, should at times sadly miscarry in the hands of incompetent or occasionally even unworthy actors. The amusing stories which lingered in the memories of our fathers and grandfathers, with regard to the personifications which more than half a century ago were still common in Catholic churches on great festivals, easily allow us to believe that, in spite of all pious reverence, there would be found in the performance of the mysteries a large share of the same unintentionally humorous element. What it was possible to do voluntarily we learn from a story in *Eulenspiegel*, that mirror of the fun of the mediæval Low-German populace.([94]) Eulenspiegel had entered a priest's service as sacristan. The priest's one-eyed cook did not regard him with the same favour that her master did. At the service on Easter morning, the Resurrection had to be represented. The priest put the cook into the grave to act an angel, while he himself, with a banner in his hand, represented the Lord. Eulenspiegel, as manager of the performance, selected for the three Maries the three simplest rustics he could find, and instructed them in what they had to say. When the angel asked them, "Whom seek ye?—they replied, "We seek the priest's one-eyed hussy." The cook jumped out of the grave in a rage and beat the three Maries, who returned the blows; the priest threw away his banner and helped the cook; while the rogue Eulenspiegel made off in the midst of the general confusion.

Much that we find comic in the miracle plays is only a mode of expression to which we are unaccustomed, a mediæval naïveté, rusticity, or uncouthness. We certainly can scarcely help smiling when a saint is termed Monsignor—"Monsignor St. Paul"—or when an angel addresses as "Madame" the departed soul of Jesus—or when God the Father calls to Adam in Eden "Beaufrère—or when the Saviour on the cross says to John, "John, dear cousin mine!"—or he to the Virgin, "Mary, my dear Aunt!—or when our Lord is commended by Mary Magdalene as a "cask of all virtues."(95) Births are unhesitatingly made to take place on the stage, and at the saints', or at the highest of all births, the angels sing.(96) In one mystery, God the Father is represented as sleeping on His heavenly throne during the crucifixion, and as being afterwards roused by an angel with very sharp words.(97) In a favourite miracle play of *St. Barbara*, when she is suspended by the legs and burnt on each limb, she compares herself to a bit of roast meat, thoroughly done and just fit to be served.(98) The souls of the dying depart from their mouths in the form of small images, as we also see in contemporary pictures, and are received by angels or devils. As Judas denied the Lord, a very grimy soul is seen to leave his rent body as he falls. Seth refers to the first book of Moses, and then says the Lord's Prayer.(99) The learned Solomon rejoices the heart of the Queen of Sheba by the promise that the poet Æsop and the great prophet David will both remember her in the time to come; then he quarrels with one of his wives, and drinks a mug of beer.(100) Of the institution of the Lord's Supper, we find it said that Christ then sang the first mass.(101) Nero, as well as the French king, Clovis, is made to swear by Mahommed and then by St. Ignatius —a sort of pattern oath for the heathen of every age.

The exclusively ecclesiastical significance which we find attached to political events, arose from the usual mediæval mode of regarding the world. In the mystery of *St. Peter and St. Paul*, the insurrection against Nero is treated as the immediate sequel of the execution of the apostles, who manifest themselves to him, and assure him of their glorious life and his miserable death. After their appearance the devils carry him off, in order that he may be tormented and suffer the pangs of eternal death, without being able to perish.([102]) In the *Mystère de la Veugéance de Jésus Christ*, there is a nearer approach to the usual belief of Christendom. The destruction of Jerusalem is depicted from the narrative in Josephus, but it is regarded as a chastisement for the crucifixion of the Messiah.([103])

Sharply-defined contrasts were also dear to the mediæval spirit; and as the noble diction of the Church was gradually relinquished, and the representation fell into the hands of the populace, their devout enjoyment of the spectacle was sustained during the long summer day through by-play and cheery laughter; so that in these dramas we find prefigured, if but rudely and awkwardly, the humour of Shakespeare.

The hosts of hell (*la diablerie*) certainly appear as a Nemesis from the deep, awful and menacing, and also as emblematic of the powers of darkness in strife with the Son of God. But in wonderful satyr-like masquerade, in which neither horns, tail, nor hoofs were ever allowed to be wanting, the devil prosecuted on the stage his special business of fetching souls, often enough in ridiculous fashion, perhaps wheeling off his victim in a wheelbarrow. As in the mediæval legends also we often find any private sentiment of fear surmounted, and the devil boldly exhibited as marching off in the character of a poor, stupid, outwitted imp; so in the miracle plays his rôle is not unfrequently that of the comic personage; until, in the fifteenth century, he was able to abdicate in favour of the *Fool*, who thenceforward in the drama, as in the palace, opposed his witty foolishness to all assumption of wisdom or superiority. The Fool was also the embodiment of the homely good sense of the audience, in whose midst he was sometimes seated; or by his travesty of a scene he tempered its pathos, as in the miracle play of the giant St. Christopher. When the saint, who desires to serve the Lord of lords alone, has borne the infant Christ across the stream, and lies sleeping, exhausted by the weight of the Ruler of the World, the fool comes forward and takes his wife on his back, but instead of carrying her over the river, he drops her in the middle, greatly to the delight of everyone.([104])   In acting the part a certain amount of improvisation was anticipated, indeed in many pieces the places where the fool is to speak are merely denoted " stultus loquitur," without any words.   In a morality of the sixteenth century, he expresses his consciousness of his popularity ([105]) :

> " I will behave right fair and fine,
> That swear I by this pate of mine ;
> But if no fool were to appear,
> The place of people would be clear."

Even after farce and Carnival play had in the fifteenth century been separated from the *mystère* with which on festive occasions they were still placed in close conjunction,([106]) the special distinction of "tragedy" and "comedy" remained unknown to the Middle Ages.

In the mystery of the *Sacred Host*,([107]) after a circumstance which more than once has occurred through the painful encounter of Christian and Jewish superstition, namely, the martyrdom or wounding of the Sacred Host, a Jew, who has thus pierced it till the bloody drops have issued, is condemned to death for his attempted murder of the Lord.   He and his unhappy fellow-believers are exhibited only in a ridiculous light, with their jargon which passes for Hebrew, while the undoubted hero of the piece is the Holy Wafer, the suffering and yet invincible Christ. That a Jew should be burnt probably appeared as little painful to the Christian spectators, as did once to the Roman people the action of the Hermes, who after the gladiatorial games searched among the dead bodies to find if any fallen combatant were only feigning death from his wounds, in which case he despatched him with a hammer. In the mystery of *St. Stephen*,([108]) the Jews are made to throw their stones at his head with very jovial remarks.

The interval between Judas's betrayal of our Lord and his despair, is sometimes rather absurdly treated in a scene in which he haggles over the thirty pieces of silver, and protests against the bad coins with which Caiaphas tries to pay him.

The climax of the tragedy, the crucifixion, was closely followed by the ascension; after which the Holy Sepulchre was perhaps immediately connected with scenes in the lowest popular taste—such as the wrangling and fighting of the soldiers who were set to watch the grave ; or the discourse of the gardener (here a separate person from the risen Christ), who describes in scarcely equivocal terms the effects of his herbs ; or the chattering of the ointment seller, who first quarrels with his wife, and then like a true pedlar, all the while laughing in his sleeve, extols his wares to the women who come to the grave. He also clubs with a certain Master Rubin, a favourite figure in this by-play,[109] who boasts that he is both young and well bred, and that though he knows how to filch old women's purses, he has always escaped the rope's end; only once in Bavaria he was burnt on the shins, and would have been hanged if he had not escaped.[110]   Between all this resounds the plaint of the women—

> " He has gone,
> Who once to comfort us was born,
> The Holy Maiden's Son.
> Parted from us is Jesus Christ
> Of all the world the Saviour blest." [111]

Such an extraordinary mingling of burlesque with the most sacred subjects seems, at the Easter festival in particular, after the long dull Lenten fast, to have found a sort of popular authorisation in the Easter story, a tale containing all sorts of merry jests at the expense of the great apostles, the lesser saints or Satan, which the priest on Easter morning used to relate from the pulpit in order to excite Easter merriment.   This custom may have arisen from the habit found in children and common people of expressing, by bursts of hearty laughter, deep inward joy, which causes tears to more sensitive nerves.[112] The Church occasionally protested in the decrees of her councils, but the popular usage held its ground up to the time of the Reformation.[113] Even after that, in Latin countries, the Fools' and Asses' Festival was tolerated with but slight opposition. This festival seems to have originated in mere jest, and to have taken its place among Christmas amusements. On the Holy Innocents' Day [114] all the offices of the Church were conducted by boys, and from the pleasantry of the children's bishop was gradually derived a Bishop of Fools, who in churches which had separated from the Roman Communion became a Pope of Fools. In this travesty of sacred subjects, perhaps originally a burlesque of Paganism, when its memory still powerfully affected the minds of men, the whole clerical staff of a church appear to have acted as mere buffoons; while the younger deacons and sub-deacons on the subsequent Feast of St. Stephen, the first martyr and their colleague, seem to have considered themselves particularly licensed to indulge in all sorts of extraordinary harlequinade— indeed these feasts were a species of Christian Saturnalia, of which the spirit was in later times transferred to the carnival. The ass could show a threefold claim to be commemorated by the Church; *i.e.*, his discourse with the refractory prophet Balaam; his supposed services on the occasion of the flight of the Holy Family into Egypt; and lastly on account of the colt, the foal of an ass, on which our Lord entered Jerusalem on Palm Sunday. Young priests and acolytes solemnly led an ass, adorned with cope and mitre, to the front of the high altar, where an extraordinary service was sung, in which the chorus joined repeatedly with a sustained he-haw. The hierarchy could well enough admit a laugh at herself on such a day of merry enjoyment, the fool's cap and the long ears could not cleave to her, she was too powerful and too shrewd.[115]

With the same union of the comic and the terrible,

Dances of Death were represented in the churches during the excitement of that awful pestilence, the Black Death, which appeared at intervals throughout the fourteenth century. They seem to have been originally depicted in deprecation of it, and afterwards intended as memorials of it. As we see in the well-known pictures which remain to us, they showed how Death summoned, from business or pleasure, every rank, every sex, and every age, and carried them off for his terrible reel.[116]

Dances also occur in the mysteries, but, as far as we can remember, never in connection with sacred personages.[117] Side by side with solemn chants re-echo, though but seldom, the tones of mere secular popular songs; for instance, in the call-song from the tower to the warders who have fallen asleep at the grave, which is in the usual style—"Slumbering in your true-love's arms," or in the love songs of the Magdalen and her adorers.[118]

Mary Magdalene, who is identified by Catholic tradition not only with the woman who anointed the feet of Jesus, but also with the sister of Martha, is a favourite character in the Easter plays. She at first appears as a mere child of this world, without much harm in her, only over eager in her desire to enjoy her young life, adorning herself before her mirror, and objecting to her sister Martha, who reproaches her with conventual solemnity, that she would willingly act in the same manner if her lips were not cold with age—as it is, she may twirl her distaff and hob and nob with the devil. Thus the two sisters form contrasting pictures of the sex, which differ widely from the Scriptural portraits of Mary and Martha.[119] Later she is seen as a very free and easy dame, remarkably impartial in her favours.[120] For her sudden conversion but little motive is anywhere assigned. Sometimes it is effected simply by a sentence about death, and the subsequent judgment; or by the mere vicinity of Jesus, with whom she tries to amuse herself, till some one says that He is no lover for her, but a God who cleanseth from all sin. At other times she is converted by an angel, and in her sleep.([121])

In some of the mysteries a secular element is still more evidently an ingredient, either, in national or in romantic form. Of the first we find a specimen in the mystery of the *Baptism of Clovis*,([122]) which in its matter-of-fact straightforwardness still adheres to historic truth. Clotilde certainly preaches the Trinity to her husband in a most orthodox manner; but she admonishes him at the same time to demand her inheritance, and to avenge her on her uncle, the King of Burgundy, who has slain her father and mother. The supernatural motive power, by which the piece becomes the *Miracle de Notre Dame*, only appears when the Mother of God, in answer to prayer, descends and heals the dying son of Clovis, who has been baptized against his father's will. The play concludes with the baptism of Clovis, who repeats the Apostles' Creed, after which the priests strike up the Te Deum.

The romantic element predominates in the mystery of the *King of Hungary's Daughter*,([123]) borrowed in the thirteenth century from a romance of the Troubadours. The king has sworn, on the death of his dearly-loved wife, that he will never again be wedded except to a woman who exactly resembles her. The single such person to be found is her only daughter, the mother's image. As the people demand an heir, the Pope grants a dispensation for the marriage; but the daughter finds it too terrible, and against all reason; ([124]) so she makes her moan to the Madonna, and at last cuts off her own hand. The enraged King commands that the girl thus crippled should be burnt, but his agent only pretends to burn her, and in a boat without a sail she is carried to Scotland. There the King marries her, but again she has to be rescued with her child from the craft of her mother-in-law. Without a helm she is driven to Italy, where she is reunited to her husband. In Rome, on the Thursday before Easter, she meets her father, who repentant for seven years has mourned her—

her hand is also floated to the shore, and the Pope fixes it on again.   The play ends with a hymn of thanksgiving in the Papal chapel.

The miracle play was a natural product, as long as the Church, which almost alone possessed any intellectual culture, retained her empire over the minds of men, and could succeed in bringing home by visible portraiture the lofty truths of Christianity to a people strongly affected by their senses, and yet with a firm basis of simple faith, and as sincere a desire to be edified as amused by sacred themes.   Moreover, it was necessary that the Church, while she desired the continuance of her supreme influence, should satisfy every sentiment which could appear to wear the livery of her service, were it devotion or love of amusement.   These representations were great popular festivals, in which the people found much edification, and which all, both young and old, long enjoyed in antici- pation, and long remembered with delight.   As once be- fore in Greek tragedy, the plays had one advantage, the Christian populace was generally familiar with the plot, so that a few roughly-marked features were sufficient to cause each character to be recognised as an old acquaint- ance.   The people delighted in seeing these personages, whose words they had so often heard read in the churches, and whose images they had perhaps from their very child- hood devoutly contemplated in their sacred pictures, de- scend, as it were, from their frames, and stand before them as living beings in the semblance of their own compatriots.

The sacredness of the Biblical narrative, nevertheless, in a certain measure circumscribed, even in the mediæval Church, the free play of creative fancy: its best effort was only a dilution of the words of the Bible, a converse to the miracle of Cana.

The scenes, although not devoid of separate graceful or elevated passages, succeed one another with too epic a simplicity to allow of any dramatic intricacies, or any development of the subjective side of individual characters, in which the pathetic element of mental struggles could be introduced. The poverty, as well as the wealth of these plays, lies in the fact that they express simply the universal faith of their age, and bear no impress of any individual poetic mind.

A great drawback to the morality was the monotonous effect superinduced by the lack of all real characters, and therefore of every active human interest. In the lives of the saints a far wealthier domain lay open to dramatic fancy, but piety and popular necessity compelled adherence to the traditional legends. And miracles in eternal contrariety to nature, terrific tortures in painful accumulation visibly and materially represented, afforded no theme for a noble human treatment.

Protestantism wrested from Faith a large share of her working material. In its spirituality and earnest care for eternal salvation, it showed everywhere but little favour for any light play of fancy around solemn subjects. In the severe struggle with the Reformation even the Roman Church in her high places underwent some transformation, and she no longer retained her naïve credulity and child-like delight in the ancient plays. Paul III., in 1549, forbade the representations in the Colosseum. In Paris the Brotherhood of the Passion placed their arms, a shield emblazoned with the cross and other implements of the Passion, over the first modern stone theatre, which was of their own erection; but about the same time the Parliament forbade the performance of the mysteries, not so much because they had degenerated as because they had been left behind by the prevalent culture and tone of thought, and had thus become an incitement to the mockery of solemn subjects. Pieces commendable from a secular point of view might be exhibited.

When the human mind had begun to perceive the infinite depth of Christianity, and at the same time to explore its own recesses, and thus in the wealthy imagination of the Teutonic nations the basis had been laid for

D

an art and literature of their own—then there arose in the
fifteenth century from the grave, which the Church who
had closed it had also carefully protected, the immortal
spirit of classical antiquity, and a new Easter festival
commenced. The learned, and through their means all
educated persons, recognised with astonishment a lofty
secular culture, which like its predecessor had its root in
the ideal, and, while it gained strength from the justness
of its proportions, rested on wholly different grounds from
the former culture.

In consequence of the great discoveries and social
changes made in this century and the following, the life
of the people of the West assumed a new form, and confid-
ingly attached itself to its antique prototype ; so that the
rival strife of Christian and classic culture, which in the
early centuries had been all too hastily decided, now first
attained its full intensity.

At the same time, within the parchment and beneath
the marble memorials of antiquity, were discovered both
Greek dramas and Roman comedies. In the palace of the
Merchant-Prince on the Arno, the comedies of Terence
were acted with an accompaniment of flutes, as in our
own days the Antigone.

The new secular culture only smiled at the artless
naïveté of the miracle play with its simple effort to portray supernatural events. As men esteemed the divine
story too solemn to be made the plaything of dramatic
fancy, secular interests were now represented in the drama,
with the happy or tragic solution of their conflicting claims.
Thenceforward the stage, which has for its office to typify
the World, has been erected far apart from the Church.

LECTURE II.

POLEMIC PLAYS AND ECHOES OF THE MYSTERY.

THE Modern Drama, which exhibits real characters acting upon one another with fortunes determined by that action, arose when secular interests in their rich variety had become predominant, and men had discovered that these interests were once the subject of faithful artistic representation in Greece and Rome. Only in three or four of the great civilised nations, a branch of the drama, as a distinct species of literature, still clung to the ancient walls of the Church — some imagine not without the deleterious effect which has been ascribed to the race of creeping-plants.

Whatever may have been the disfavour of Protestantism, the miracle play proved of service to the Reformation at the period when every spiritual force was enlisted in the great struggle. Even in the golden age of the mystery, we hear of isolated attempts to use the drama as a polemic weapon against the Church, when her worldly corruption was contrasted with the reminiscences of Christianity as it once had been. Thus when in Provence the dark and menacing apparition of a heretical Church first manifested itself in opposition to the dominant Church, it engaged on its side many voices of the Provençal poets. In the beginning of the thirteenth century a drama by a troubadour, entitled *The Heresy of the Fathers,*[1] was acted at the country residence of the Marquis Boniface of Montferrat. It endeavoured to prove, in the straightforward style which distinguished the first controversy, then a controversy of Catholic with Catholic, that the heretics were more properly the true Church, and that the Fathers, the teachers of the early Church, were the originators of heresy. But the Roman Church was still powerful enough to destroy drama, heretics, and troubadours.

The *Procession of Reynard the Fox*, which King Philip the Fair caused to be exhibited in Paris as the last of the entertainments on the knighting of his sons, contains a comic representation in the style of *Reinecke Fuchs*, and in keeping with the form which that ancient legend of the animal world received at Clugny. It shows how the fox, in the guise of a priest, reads mass to the geese, and at length, having become Pope, devours them, goslings and all. Those were the days in which Philip, by an appeal to French patriotism, had succeeded in unseating the mediæval Pope; and finally had erected a Pope of his own, who, to obtain the dignity, betrayed the Papal See.

But the greater the moral decline of the sovereign Church became, the more innocent seemed a jest at her faults. In France the *farce* almost attained its full maturity beneath the sacred mantle of the *mystery*, and, as early as the beginning of the fifteenth century, a royal license was granted to young men of good family for the exhibition of *Soties* in Paris. When Louis XII. undertook to defend against a martial Pope the liberties of the Gallican Church, together with some Italian liberties of which he intended himself to assume the control, Gringore, Herald of the Court of Lorraine, composed as a *sotie* the *Chasse du Cerf des Cerfs* a satire on the *Servus Servorum*, the Servant of the Servants of God. A play by the same author, *The Prince and Mother of Fools*, was acted on Shrove Tuesday, 1511. In it the holy Mother Church appears adorned with the triple crown, and she acknowledges, with audacious frankness, that she has been guilty of the various tricks which were ascribed to her, not by the reformed only, but by many merely worldly-minded persons. But when the suspicion is roused that she cannot be the true Church, her priestly vestments are torn off, and the Mother of Fools is discovered beneath the disguise.([2])

About the same period we find a seraph introduced by Gil Vincente, a Portuguese poet, into a play intended to be acted in honour of the Virgin at an annual fair.([3]) The seraph offers the fear of God to the Pope and the lesser clergy. at so much a pound, and while the devil protests, Mercury cites the example of Holy Rome, who sells for gold the salvation of souls.

During the excitement of the Carnival when every one was obliged to submit to some jest, there seemed less danger in satirising the Papacy, and the most serious religious controversy was sometimes veiled in a Carnival play. In Berne on the Shrove Tuesday of the Nobles (*Herren-Fastnacht*), 1522,([4]) when the tide of spiritual strife was still wavering, the Swiss artist, Niclaus Manuel, arranged for the representation in the Kreuzgasse by some Bernese citizens of his play, *The Devourer of the Dead.*([5]) This drama was a kind of satirical morality, founded on the profit derived from the masses for the dead by the priesthood and all persons connected with the priesthood; so that even the pastor's maid expected a gown at least on behalf of the wealthy defunct just buried—

> " Which must be black, white, brown, or green,
> Beneath must a yellow hem be seen."

In the mere list of the actors the intention of the play is clearly manifested. We have Chancellor Surface, Abbot Neverenough, Dean Slaythepoor, Provost Moneybag, Vicar Fabler,([6]) Bishop Chrysostom Wolfjaw, Cardinal Haughty, and Pope Unchristian. With but little action each player proclaims his own character and his selfish aims, and between the speeches of the principal personages, members of the populace lament the deterioration of the Church. The Pope rejoices that in spite of all his knavish tricks he still has power in heaven and hell, and that he is therefore able to pluck the feathers of many fine birds, while to him belongs the sweat of the poor, and a thousand steeds are his to ride.   He is brought in borne aloft among his guards in the sumptuous style which is still customary on great festivals.   Then St. Peter and St. Paul enter, and the former, after regarding the press for some time *through his glasses*, inquires of a courtier—

> " Good priest, I would right fain be told
> What kind of man I now behold ;
> Whether a Pagan or Turk he be,
> Whom on men's shoulders aloft I see ?
> But if indeed he has lost his feet,
> To bear him thus it may well be meet. "

Courtier.

> " St. Peter ! what is it thou whom I see !
> And thou know'st not who this man may be ?
> Well truly a miracle that I call,
> But readily I will tell you all.
> Thou see'st the greatest of Christendom,
> For not alone is he Pope of Rome,
> But Naples he rules and Trinacria,
> And the island fair of Sardinia,
> With Corsica too, and Bivaria,
> O'er Spolet as duke and the Tuscan plains,
> And over great Venice with force he reigns.
> As a god's on earth is his regal state.
> But sooth, this to thee I need not relate,
> Since thou gav'st him thy regent on earth to be,
> With the mission the Holy Christ once gave thee."

St. Peter.

> " Of all this I knew not one single word !
> Of my great vicegerent I never heard.
> How should I ever a kingdom give,
> Who on earth had scarcely wherewith to live ?
> Whence hath he then these lands so wide,
> O'er which he reigns in power and pride ?

> I verily think I cannot recall
> That ever I was in Rome at all,
> And if indeed I ruled there in might,
> Why then my memory fails me quite." (7)

The Roman courtier remains convinced that such is the fact : all these things happened a long time ago, and Peter is so old he has forgotten.   At last a learned man comes forward, and in a sort of sermon announces the pure gospel of salvation by faith alone in God's mercy through Christ.

The same year, on the *Bauern-Fastnacht* or general Shrove Tuesday, another piece of Manuel's was represented, " showing the great difference between the Pope and our Saviour Christ."   On one side of the street, on a mean foal of an ass, " our dear Lord, the only Saviour of the world," rode crowned with thorns, and accompanied by His disciples, together with many blind, halt, and maimed. On the other side rode the Pope in rich armour, followed by a great train of warriors of all nations, and by his own Swiss Guards in the Papal uniform, with trumpets, trombones, drums, pipes, and cannon ;(8) " as if he were Emperor of Turkey."   The play forms a dramatic picture, similar to the illustrations representing on the one hand the lives spent in poverty and suffering by our Lord and the apostles, and on the other the evil and sumptuous lives of the Roman prelates, which with varying details are found in picture-books from the time of the Wickliffite and Hussite agitation.   Meanwhile the simple drama flows onward to a conclusion in the dialogue of two Swiss peasants, who, as they remark the contrast, assert their faith from that time in Christ's mercy alone, and express in rough terms what they would like to do with the Papal indulgences, even if their action were to cost them the loss of their poniards.(9)   The chroniclers of the Reformation in Switzerland mention that both these Carnival plays were represented with great effect, and that a large number of persons were influenced by them in choosing between Christian freedom and Papal bondage.(10)

A carnival play by Burkard Waldis, a monk in Riga, who afterwards became a Protestant pastor in Hesse, commences like a mystery with the hymn *Veni Creator Spiritus* (*Nu bitten wir den Heiliger Geist*), but set for only five voices. The prologue announces that the intention of the play is to treat in an entertaining manner of the Gospel story of the Prodigal Son, and that there will be no display of wanton merriment such as is usual in Rome, where in Carnival plays *senior poltron, madonna putana,* and *ribaldus* are introduced. The prodigal, whose sinful life in a hostelry with a sort of Doll Tearsheet furnishes some very secular scenes, on his repentant return home, is made, by a bold application of the parable, to typify the man of the Reformation, who, in accordance with the pure Gospel, is justified by faith alone; while the other son represents the Romish Church with her self-confidence and her dependence on her own good works. Dedekind, pastor of Neustadt on the Leine and of Lüneburg, illustrates with greater simplicity the Protestant theory of the Law and the Gospel, the Church of the Law and the Church of the Gospel. A knight, richly endowed with worldly goods, is anxious lest he should fail to obtain eternal salvation also. Moses instructs him in the law of God, but the knight, not having kept it entirely unbroken, is merely terrified at the thought of the judgment. Then St. Paul explains to him the gospel of salvation by faith alone in God's mercy through Christ; and clad in the spiritual armour of faith, the knight is able to defy all the attacks of Lucifer and his angels.[11]

It was more especially in England and in Scotland that the stage afforded a similar aid to the Reformation. In Germany the sacred dramas were acted chiefly by students. The memory of the martyr John Huss was revived by them; [12] while Luther was recalled to life [13] and celebrated as the man of God casting his stone against the Roman Goliath; and Tetzel's stall for the sale of indulgences adorned the first jubilee festival of the Reformation.(¹⁴)   A different kind of play was the *Pammachius*, originally dedicated to Luther, in which the characters all have a sort of representative or almost allegorical significance.   The very title-page exhibits the Papacy as grown worldly and pledged to Satan, and Christ is afterwards shown as rousing against it, by means of His truth and by the aid of the Apostle Paul, the *Gottlieb an der Elbe*.   It was apparently not intended for representation, as at the end of the fourth act the prologue announces that the reader is not to expect a fifth, since that will be performed on the Day of Judgment by Christ Himself.(¹⁵)

The earlier course of the German Reformation, as influenced by certain prominent personages, is pictured in a comedy said to have been acted in Paris before Francis I. in 1524.   The Pope is represented sitting on his throne surrounded by his great courtiers, and in the midst of the hall is seen a large brasier, such as in Italy still suffices to moderate the winter cold.   The coals are entirely covered with ashes.   Reuchlin comes forward, a venerable grey-headed old man, and admonishes his audience that if they do not abolish the secular splendour and the spiritual abuses of the Church they must all perish.   With a small stick he brushes aside some of the ashes, so that the fire commences to sparkle slightly. Then Erasmus appears, and counsels delay, and a quiet doctoring of the Church's wounds by external applications of plaister.   He does not touch the fire, and he is highly extolled by the cardinals as a future ally.   Upon this Ulrich von Hutten, clad in armour and martial both in·frame and temper, reviles the Pope as Antichrist and as the despoiler of all Christendom.   He scatters the ashes, and with a pair of bellows so agitates the flame that the whole assembly is paralysed with terror; but in the midst of his anger he suddenly falls dead, and the joy of the beholders conquers their fear.   At last some one enters in a fool's garment, that is to say, in the cowl of a monk. This is supposed to be Luther, who, like Isaac, is charged with a great load of wood. He says, " If the cause of Christ is depressed, by the help of God I will elevate it in spite of your opposition, for this fire which shines dimly I will so set ablaze that it shall illumine the whole world." This "marvellous monk" then throws the wood into the fire, which burns with great force, while he himself slips away. In this new and greater danger, the monks, who formerly subdued Huss at Constance, are incited by the promise of benefices and honours to make an attempt at extinguishing the flames, but they only throw spirit on them and then run away. At length the Holy Father, to whom power is given in heaven and earth, endeavours to check the conflagration. He pronounces a terrific curse both against it and against those who kindled it, but the fire is in no way affected by the anathema, while the Pope is so enraged that he gives up the ghost.

We have no original document of this play,([16]) and Francis I. had at that period already issued penal laws against the newfangled heretics. It is true that he never favoured the monks; that he had then considerable griev- ances against the Pope; that he invited Melancthon to Paris; that he took counsel with von Hutten; and that he frequently aided the German Protestants. There is thus no intrinsic reason for believing that the fire lighted by the "marvellous monk" may not have been figuratively kindled before him. Beza's *Sacrifice of Abraham* in which the devil comes forward in the dress of a monk, and rejoices in the amount of evil which from beneath a similar guise has been disseminated through the world, was certainly represented in his presence. In the same way a comedy was produced in 1558, before the King and Queen of Navarre at Rochelle; but this later piece appealed, doubtless, to a more sympathetic audience. It exhibited the abuses of the Papacy, and showed how help against these might be found in the Holy Scriptures.

A play which is said to have been performed before the

Emperor Charles V., in 1530, by unknown actors, is more exactly similar to the Parisian comedy, but it is in dumb show and more concise. Permission having been given for the representation of a piece after the early dinner, a masked player entered in a doctor's gown, with the name Reuchlin inscribed on his back. He was made to throw down a bundle of sticks, some straight and some crooked, and then to go out. A second person followed in the dress of a secular priest, who was supposed to be Erasmus. He arranges the sticks and tries to straighten the crooked ones, but when he finds how useless his efforts are, he shakes his head and retires. Then Martin Luther is introduced as a monk. He sets the crooked sticks on fire, and as soon as they are thoroughly kindled he too goes away. A person apparelled as an Emperor then appears, and with his sword thrusts amongst the sticks, but instead of extinguishing the flames he only excites them. At last the Pope enters. He throws up his hands, and tries to think of a means of quenching the fire. Finding two pails, one of water and one of oil, in his great anxiety he seizes the oil and throws it on the fire. In the confusion caused by the violence of the ensuing flames, it is said that the actors disappeared, and the search instituted by Charles proved unavailing.

The record which we have of this play is a century later in date.([17]) Although the Emperor about 1530 really took warning, yet to warn him in the style described would have been, to say the least, a dangerous attempt. Perhaps this allegory of the actual course of the Reformation was only derived from the French play, and the perilous representation before the Emperor was itself only an ingredient of the fiction.

Catholicism in its rejoinder seems seldomer to have employed the dramatic form, yet instances of such an employment are not wanting. We hear of a Latin comedy acted at Greenwich before Henry VIII., who was soon afterwards himself to become an apostate defender of the faith. In it Luther and his wife, Katherine von Bora, are brought to great disgrace, and the Reformation is exhibited as a tissue of lies, scepticism, and sedition.[18] The Massacre of St. Bartholomew was also celebrated in Madrid, by command of Philip II., in a festival play entitled *The Triumph of Faith.*

A scholastic comedy by Lennius, which indeed was never brought on the stage, is dedicated to Luther as the Archbishop of Wittenberg, the Prophet, Revolutionary Leader and Tyrant of Germany. It regards the Reformation from a well-known point of view, ascribing to it the design of procuring the marriage of priests and monks. The deities of Love and the goddess Venus knock at Luther's door, and Babylonian and Cyprian girls sing him a festal song. It is a coarse piece, without much wit or coherence.[19]

A Corpus-Christi drama which was acted in 1682 at Urdingen on the Lower Rhine,[20] on the borderland where Catholics and Protestants dwell in such close proximity, is more popular in style, though still entirely doctrinal and controversial. On behalf of the Catholic faith appear various allegorical personages ; on behalf of the Protestant chiefly one only, *Hæreticus.* An angel repeats the prologue, and mentions Christ's caution against false prophets—

> " Prophets such and unbelievers,
> Soul tempters and deceivers,
> Have both Luther and Calvin been,
> Whom in this world we late have seen—
> These apostate monks and preachers,
> Oh, accursed and lying creatures !
> Were never called nor sent in sooth,
> As all the world doth know is truth,
> By God ; but tempted by Asmodeus,
> By the flesh, by Cupid and Venus,
> By their own vices, sin, and shame,
> They have forsworn the priestly name."

Hæreticus, a simple blockhead who has his head full of

Luther and Calvin, has an argument with *Catholica* on the doctrine of the conversion of the Sacred Host into the body of the Son of God. Christ, he says, taught us to pray—

> "'Our Father, Thou who art
> In heaven!' How canst thou, Papist, say,
> 'In the Sacrament He is to-day'?"

A reply to this question is easily found in an appeal to the Divine omnipotence and omnipresence. When the Protestant side, begins to show signs of weakness, its *Spiritus familiaris*, the evil one, whispers—

> "What, are you so soon put in the wrong?
> You would to these godless Papists belong,
> Who so unnatural are and so bold,
> That their own Maker they'd eat, I am told!"

If the devil cannot prevail by means of the Holy Scriptures, he will try what he can do by the aid of the five senses only. But suddenly *Hæreticus* finds no more to say, and he and his followers are at once converted. While through the appearance of two condemned souls, who have lost their day of repentance, the importance of this conversion is made all the more apparent, *Catholica* affirms that no Pope ever forsook this gospel, and that there is no salvation out of the Roman pale—

> "Save those who in Noah's ark were found,
> Every living creature was wholly drowned!"

Hæreticus, who, as *Doctor Poeniters*, has now become an undoubtedly zealous Catholic, begins, by way of farewell, to make merry jests on himself, after the fashion of a charlatan. He announces that he is a master in every art, who when he tries doctoring makes short work with his patients. He is also an excellent musician, who thoroughly understands the proper method of beating time; though when he practises it, his wife does not seem much obliged to him. He then recommends himself to the prayers of the faithful, and the prologue concludes.

> " Thou little Rhenish Urdingen,
> Thou hast in thee of evil men
> A many. Turn to God with zest,
> Lest by thine enemies opprest
> Thou e'er become. Forsake not ever
> The faith thy Church did thee deliver—
> Our simple faults we pray you pardon,
> And peace and goodwill be your guerdon.
> And so in train we walk away,
> Wishing you all a kind good day."

The internal dissensions of the Reformed Church were also reproduced in dramatic form. After the German Reformation had finished its victorious course, and the Protestant party had become divided into Lutherans and Calvinists, even the theses of union suggested by Melanchthon were in the struggle with Calvin exposed on the stage to the hatred of the Lutheran populace. In the electorate of Saxony, when this attempt at union had been repressed with great violence, we find a piece entitled *The Calvinistic Outrider* ([21]) with the motto—

> " Right well hath Luther kept the field,
> God grant that Philip may not yield !
> The Calvinistic dragon brood,
> With much regard to-day are viewed,
> Once hardly worth a stiver."

The learned . poet Frischlin in his *Phasma*, of which both the name and the idea were derived from a comedy of Menander, had a short time before sharply censured the sects of the Rebaptizers and Sacramentarians, as the Baptists and Calvinists were then termed.([22]) The prologue announces that even as in the comedy a maiden appears to a youth in a dream, and inspires him with love, so the form shall here be represented in which the devil has shown himself to the sectaries. The piece commences with the apprehensions of a simple peasant, that, in this confusion of the sects, he shall not be able to find out what to believe ; and it closes with a manifestation of our Lord, who condemns everything which does not accord with Luther's pure doctrine.

During the miseries of the Thirty Years' religious war, Pope Calixtus, however little desirous he may really have been to obliterate the historical peculiarities of the differing Churches, yet found it expedient to admit a common basis of Christianity, sufficient unto salvation, in the faith of the first centuries. This admission caused much horror to the zealous watchmen of Zion resident at Wittenberg. When Dr. Deutschmann was appointed rector in 1676, the students represented in his honour the triumph of Wittenbergian Lutheranism, and Calixtus was made to appear as a dragon with horns and claws, vomiting fire.[23]

Amid such bitter passions the mediæval mystery, with its harmless merriment and simple delight in sacred themes, had become transformed to an angry polemic play. Its old form did not, however, at once entirely disappear even in Protestant lands; only no play of the kind any longer ranked among the principal interests of the day, it ceased to be considered a form of religious worship, it was no more a matter of great popular concern. Even as the "Holy Wise Men with their Star" did not disappear until after the beginning of this century, when prose and police regulations proved too much for them; and as Gregory the Great, gorgeously attired, but with his Papal rank long ago forgotten by the Protestant populace, still continued to lead the choristers to church on festivals,[24] and even after his disappearance was by his name still connected with German school feasts—so these plays were also shadows, many-hued but pale, cast by the mediæval Church.

We find the mystery reappearing as a pleasant amusement for children in the electoral castle at Berlin, where the children of the Elector and their playmates, in the year 1589, acted a little New-Year play, *The Birth of our Lord.*[25] The children were all from six to eight years old, with the exception of the infant Christ, the

Margrave Frederic, who was only one and a half, and the Madonna Elizabeth von Mansfield, "a wondrous fair maiden."[26]   Here, therefore, it is recorded that the female sex had its share in the action, though only in the midst of a family circle.

The scenery is very simply treated, and we have the marginal note—" A puppet angel descends with a rocket and two stars tied to a string, which alarms the shepherds." But a living cherub sings Luther's Christmas Hymn for Children.[27]   In the graceful representation of the shepherds and kings before the Royal Babe in the sacred manger, the doctrines of the early Church, and even of the Reformation, are interwoven with some cleverness. There is a specimen of this even in the introductory dialogue of one of the Three Kings with Joseph—

> " Who is the Royal Babe ? "
> " Immanuel."
> " What is His mission ? "
> " Peace and goodwill."
> " The Babe how may we reach ? "
> " 'Tis Faith alone can teach."
> " Why lies He there in low estate ? "
> " Yet might He owns as God All-great."
> " Why is He naked too and bare ? "
> " The sins of mankind are His care."
> " Why did He choose a manger poor ? "
> " God's word shall evermore endure."

In the Virgin's speech the loyalty of a subject of Brandenburg also finds expression—

> " A long, long way I come to you,
> Wearied I felt and none I knew—
> I'd gladly serve without rebuke,
> Augustus, our right noble duke.
> God ever loves obedience,
> Our rulers we should reverence,
> From God alone the right they gain
> By which o'er land and folk they reign."

A play which Schorus, a professor in Heidelberg,[28]

caused to be performed by his scholars, is, in all respects, a morality. Religion appears to the great men of the land and asks for shelter, but everywhere she finds closed doors. At last she appeals to the poor, and by them she is heartily welcomed. This play, although only represented to a private circle, attracted so much notice that the Emperor wrote to the Elector Palatine to say that he surely would not permit so great an offence to pass unpunished, for what would people think of the nobility if they allowed themselves to be depicted on the stage as scorners of religion? Schorus saved himself by flight into Switzerland, where he perhaps reflected on our Lord's parable of the Wedding Guests, and of those who were invited from the fields and hedges.

But many sacred dramas were exhibited on Protestant soil with happier results, and in Germany they were sometimes conducted by honourable citizens with a certain amount of popular participation. We find in old official ledgers that the magistrates would defray the expenses of a feast, or give a couple of tuns of beer to celebrate the occasion. The clerical register of Breslau complains in 1582—"the actors of the comedy got as drunk as beasts."

In the learned schools of Germany especially the enjoyment of dramatic exhibitions never entirely faded; [29] it seemed to blend with their lingering mediæval customs. Both in the sixteenth century, and after the cessation of the war in the seventeenth century, we find this delight in the drama pervading almost the whole town, penetrating to the council-room and the market, and all but making its way into the church. The prototypes of the scholastic dramas are, however, to be sought, long before the mysteries, in Athens and Ancient Rome. When on the introduction of this form of spectacle it became necessary to induce the boys to pluck up courage to speak before the people, and especially to speak Latin before them, [30] originals were not sought in the old ecclesiastical tongue, but, as far as possible, in the

E

language of Terence; and the old Roman comedies were
sometimes themselves exhibited, as is still occasionally
the case in English schools. In the provinces of Protestant Germany, in which Christian faith assumed an
especially austere form, there was long some hesitation
on account of the little attention paid to propriety by
classic writers. Yet in 1580 the school regulations in
Lower Saxony instituted the performance of the comedies
of Terence and Plautus. The reflection, however, could
not be avoided that, notwithstanding many good speeches,
the vice and craft displayed in these comedies rendered
them rather a questionable means of instruction for the
young. Consequently a Christian Terence ([31]) was created,
as at an earlier date by Hrosvitha, and Biblical and
Protestant dramas again became current, this time in such
Latin as was taught in the schools. But as mothers and
sisters wished to be able to participate in some measure
in the annual school feasts, these plays were alternated
with German pieces. Sometimes the same drama was
represented, first in Latin and then in German; or an
attempt was made to suit every taste, and as is the case
in Frischlin's *Phasma*, each speech was given first in good,
concise Latin, and then in bad, prolix German.

The greater number of these pieces were rather adapted,
than composed, by ministers and teachers of schools. The
words of the Bible, only increased in bulk by paraphrase,
seemed indeed especially to correspond to Protestant sentiment. The themes of the printed pieces which have been
handed down to us, " to be read with pleasure and profit,"
are derived principally from the Old Testament. We have
dramas founded on the *Call of Abraham; Lot and the
Destruction of Sodom*, with some pyrotechnic display ; the
Prophet Jonah ; Daniel in the Lions' Den ; the wise *Solomon,*
the brave *Judith*, and the upright *Tobias.* The greater
number of these subjects are variously arranged, so as to
form mirrors of virtue or vice for the delectation of youth,
although some few, such as the chaste *Joseph*,([32]) or the

pious *Susanna*, afforded reasons for the introduction of
very mundane scenes. In a Scriptural drama on this
latter theme, by Rebhun, a verse from the chorus might
lead us to expect as much—

> " O Venus, mighty is the power
>   Which o'er us thou dost wield !
> All human souls before thee cower,
>   And young and old we yield.
> Thy blind child, with his piercing dart,
> Hath quickly transfixed every heart,
>   And our defeat is sealed."[33]

Susanna was nevertheless an especially favourite subject, and it is the comedy which is especially recorded to
have been exhibited in church. People sustained themselves with the belief that its foundation was sufficiently
Scriptural; and the Weimar students never doubted that
their performance would be agreeable to God and to all
spectators.

The eccentric and comic element of the mystery is
subdued in these dramas, and the devil, who indeed in
the Lutheran cosmogony is a most powerful and solemn
personage, has vanished together with the fool. In a
decree of Duke Albert of Prussia, a patron of scholastic
comedies, we find it forbidden in advance to bring on the
stage devils, fools, or other abominable masks.[34]

In themes borrowed from the New Testament, the scholastic drama preferred to confine itself to simple morality,
or to subjects which offer also some secular side, as do many
of our Lord's parables. For example, the parable of the
Prodigal Son is exhibited to those who are in danger of
becoming truant scholars, and thus being reduced to a
dinner of husks ; or we find " a wedding play of Cana in
Galilee, performed in honour of the holy estate of matrimony ordained by God." Yet early Protestantism based
its scheme of salvation on the secrets and the deep things
of the divine revelation. It may, however, have been for
that very reason that it feared to give a lighter tone to the

sublimely sorrowful or joyous events of the Scripture narrative by presenting them as mere spectacles.

The *Passion of Christ* by Hugo Grotius, though very decidedly a school drama, was not intended for representation, but was a cold, learned tragedy, classical in its form, and containing scarcely any action, the story being retailed in oratorical monologues, or by some person appointed for the purpose.[35]

The solemn event of the Easter festival was at one time the most readily attempted in the form of a dramatic scene. Thus in Weimar the students gave a representation in Latin of the *Condemnation of the Saviour*, in which distinct parts were assigned to the players. Their performance was rendered the more edifying by the introduction of the *Pietas*, or by the aid of German verses sung at intervals by the chorus. In Arnstadt the actors were contented with an indictment of Peter for his injury of Malchus, and the trial ended with the acquittal of the accused by the Roman governor.[36]

One Christmas play was, however, derived entirely from popular custom, and was not properly a school drama; although acted almost exclusively by students, and at first under the direction of members of the university bodies, who derived some profit from it. We speak of the Procession of Christ (*die heilige Christ-Fahrt*), with angels and disciples, at Christmas. This procession is certainly a remnant of mediæval customs, and apparently descends even from the days of Paganism; for the singular fact of the appearance at this time of year, of an adult Christ, instead of the Divine Babe, is easily explained, if we suppose that the God of the new religion was made to replace Odin in his wanderings on the Yule feast, while the old heathen god was allowed to accompany him as Knecht Ruprecht.[37] In its mode of representation, this Christmas play much resembled the old Carnival plays, for the night wandering procession called at different houses and made sport with the children of the house. On one such occasion Ruprecht first enters :[38]

> " Good day, good Sirs, good day ! the wicked man you see !
> All children here would make a single meal for me."

He threatens the naughty children and encourages the others to be hopeful, for the holy Christ is outside with his angels. A chair is immediately placed, and the Christ enters during the singing of the following verses :—

> "Oh, all men, ope your doors to-day,
> For Christ the Lord doth pass this way !
> Let each who can assistance bring,
> For Christ the doors wide open fling.
>
> Come in, oh, holy Babe ! for, see,
> The doors stand wide to welcome Thee ;
> Come in, and let us, children weak,
> Be blest by Thee, Redeemer meek.
>
> Sit down, O Saviour, with us stay !
> One word of mercy speak, we pray,
> That when the children hear Thy voice,
> They too may bless Thee and rejoice."[39]

The Christ seats himself on the chair and says that he has quitted his heavenly home, because, through his indefatigable servant Rupert, great complaints have reached him, to the effect that the world is in a bad way, for children will no longer obey their parents, and therefore he has come himself to see if so much evil really exists. Then Rupert commences his suit : the children will neither pray nor sing, and will not learn anything at school ; the best thing that can be done is that he should put them into his sack and carry them off. "If it be so," says the Saviour, "well let it be; into the sack with them." Rupert makes pretence to catch them, and the children, if they did not understand a jest, must have shrieked rather loudly. On this the Archangel Michael proposes that the Lord should be patient, and listen to some one on the other side. Peter, being called on, reminds our Lord that children, as he well knows, are often rebellious, and he proposes that Christ should himself examine them. The gentle Saviour does so; and being readily satisfied, he

orders his servant Rupert to fetch little gifts from his
chariot. Lastly, Gabriel admonishes the children to behave
better in the next year, as another time they shall not be
let off so easily. The visitors then proceed on their way
during the farewell hymn—

> "Pass on, O mighty, holy Christ,
>   To dwell within Thy kingdom blest;
> Pass on where thousand cherubs wait
>   Around the sceptre of Thy state.
>
> May God preserve this household all,
>   And may no evil here befall!
> And may God keep you, children sweet,
>   And for His heaven make you meet."[40]

A great variety of figures was associated with this procession, Moses, David, Isaiah, shepherds, a special *Exami-
nator*, &c. Joseph and Mary seldom appear, for Protestantism had at one stroke definitely separated itself from
the gracious Mother of God. A comic personage comes
on the scene, already familiar from Luther's "Table Talk,"
Hans Pfriem the Philistine, who in all God's works sees
something to find fault with, something that he himself
could have done better. In the continuation of the fable
he is only admitted to Paradise on one condition, that
he should censure nothing. After having for some time
contemplated in silent astonishment the supernatural be-
haviour which he there beholds, he can no longer withhold
his blame, and it becomes necessary to turn him out. But
every saint who is despatched to him with the command
to depart, he reproaches with some of the shortcomings of
his earthly career—if these have not caused the forfeiture
of Paradise, why should he, Hans Pfriem, be deprived of
it on account of one or two harmless words? At last the
innocents of Bethlehem are sent. As he can find no fault
in them, he takes them for a walk, and shaking a tree from
which splendid apples fall, he gives them nuts, ginger-
breads, and almonds. The children forget their commis-

sion, and Hans Pfriem must even be allowed to stay where he likes. The universal fault-finder thus becomes the children's friend, and as he has also the part of the driver assigned to him, it is his especial business to represent Christ's real or imaginary chariot with the aid of the apples and nuts which he produces.

We chiefly meet with this Procession of Christ in Thuringia during the sixteenth and seventeenth centuries.[41] An original document dated 1645, belonging to Weimar, affirms the necessity of a reform on account of "noise and wantonness" (*Geschreis und Ueppigkeit*).[42] Only certain students chosen by the clergy were to accompany the procession, and they were to assume the appearance of saints not of evil spirits. Also they were to enter or to attend at the houses of gentlefolk and citizens by request only, and in order to promote the fear of God among the children. All persons not regularly appointed, the watch was to carry off. In the following year, however, twenty-eight families in the small town desired to have the performance as usual, in return for a small honorarium. In the voluntary participation of the multitude in this saintly masquerade, we may see traces or a renewal both of the old German December festivity, and of the December merriment of old Rome transplanted centuries before into Christian Rome.

In the beginning of the eighteenth century, a great number of the clergy objected to this partly heathen, partly Christian, abuse of Christmas as being contrary to the First, Second, Third, and Fifth commandments, and because the streets, on an evening which ought to be one of holy rest and reflection, were filled with knavery and rude noise, jugglery and mummery.[43] From that time there was a sudden cessation of the play on account of prohibitory laws : a vestige of it only remained in a much simplified, informal game for children among themselves on St. Andrew's Eve.

The Biblical dramas still continued to be acted in the

schools, but always in alternation with secular pieces. Christian Weise, Rector of Zittau,(44) whose insipid plays were common at least throughout Saxony, introduced at his annual school festival, a Scriptural drama on the first day, and a historical play on the second day, while on the third day he gave a piece entirely of his own invention. This last was occasionally followed by some buffoonery. Later, the sacred drama was entirely set aside in obedience to the sentiment of the larger body of the clergy. The University of Arnstadt, long one of the chief theatres of the Scriptural play, in 1705 was satisfied with the production of a piece entitled *The wisdom of the magistrature as shown in its regulations for beer-brewing,*(45) an operetta of which the music, for aught we know, may have been composed by Sebastian Bach, then organist of Arnstadt. The secular scholastic comedy existed, however, far into the eighteenth century; and here and there in our own time it has been revived in noble form through the reproduction of the Antigone.

At one time an emulous zeal for the school drama was kept alive by the Scriptural plays at the Jesuit colleges, though the latter always maintained an unrivalled supremacy in splendour of representation. These pieces, which were composed in the colleges, were in Latin, and a programme in the vulgar tongue, with a complete advertisement of the contents of each scene, insured that they should be intelligible to the audience, of which in Vienna the Imperial Court not unfrequently formed a part; (46) while the list of the youthful actors was adorned by the names of some of the first families of the Empire.(47) The Jesuit playwrights made bold encroachments on Paganism, sometimes for a definite object, but not always with happy results. Thus, in Hindostan, the play in which St. George was seen destroying the Hindoo gods, made it impossible for the Order of Jesus any longer to adapt its mission to the national feeling. Sometimes heathen subjects were employed merely for purposes of ornament or amusement. For instance, the drama of *Abraham's Sacrifice* is interspersed with a by-play representing the delivery of Andromeda to the sea-monster, and her rescue by the winged Perseus with the Gorgon's head. There is not the least attempt to trace any typical relation to the main theme, which indeed could be but farfetched.([48]) All was for the greater glory of God—*Alles zu grösserer Ehre Gottes.* ([49]) The stage machinery was ingenious, and for the poesy of the drama there was no demand. These Jesuit plays seem to have resembled the Jesuit churches : to the learning, ingenuity, and industry of this order, the consecrating flame of genius has ever been denied.

Splendour in the accessories of the stage had nevertheless been introduced into Germany and the Netherlands, as early as the beginning of the seventeenth century, by the so-called English actors. In the printed list of their pieces, we find, besides secular plays, some few sacred dramas ; ([50]) and such dramas by the travelling actors, both of this and the following century, were occasionally performed in alternation with their stock pieces (*Haupt und Staats Actionen*).([51]) Meanwhile, through this new formation of actors into a separate class, the rupture between the Church and the Theatre became more complete. In the marionette theatres a sort of home was still retained by Biblical subjects, not without some unconscious relation to the old mysteries. In the early operas, indeed, the musical purpose and the display of the religious drama seemed rather to revive ; but the growth of the musical element soon became so overwhelming that it ceased to be of any moment whether the text were profane or sacred.

When in the middle of the eighteenth century, German dramatic poetry, on the eve of bidding a long farewell to the Church, adapted itself to a sentimental and stilted form of Christianity, the great master of the reigning school, the poet of the *Messiah*, composed also Biblical dramas—the *Death of Adam, Solomon, David.* He did not lack imitators. Zacharias Werner attempted a revival of the religious drama on his own account, and in the language of poetry he preached Christ's blood and wounds not without occasional flashes of genius and real artistic inspiration. In the *Sons of Thales*, published in 1803, he availed himself of the tragic overthrow of the Templars to inculcate by means of their sacrifice, which he employed with some art for his purpose, a kind of secret bond of Christian freemasonry, as the regenerate form of Christianity destined to renovate the world. This writer, whose genius was at once sensuous and spiritual, when he undertook to bring Luther on the stage, represented him not as the Reformer, strong in faith and mighty in deed, but as a kind of night-wandering saint ; and the tinge of mysticism which was certainly discoverable in Luther and his followers, he exaggerated to a caricature.([52]) It was hardly only after his apostasy that it became advisable for him to atone for the *Consecration of Strength* (*Die Weihe der Kraft*), by a pitiful *Consecration of Weakness*. The German nation remained indifferent to these unnatural and supernatural compositions.

But in lonely mountain valleys amid the Eastern Alpine chain, of which the population is exclusively Romanist, the mediæval mystery—as Paganism once under similar circumstances—long subsisted in its *naïveté* and simple piety. The first evidence of a drama in the Tyrol is found in the tradition that Duke Frederic of the Empty Pockets, when, as the ally of the friend of a guilty Pope, he wandered hither and thither, despised and proscribed, caused a play to be acted in Landeck, representing the miseries of an outlawed prince. Through the sympathy manifested by the populace, he discovered that from them aid might be obtained against his faithless nobility. This performance and acceptance of a secular piece, even if it were acted by travelling companies, which in every kind were to be met with during the Council of Constance, are still explicable only on the supposition that the miracle play was already established in those regions. No pieces which have reached us are of earlier date than the latter half of the fifteenth century, and they do not differ in any material point from the dramas then generally acted throughout German territory; they are only more concise and freer from pageantry.[53] They are all derived from the Biblical narrative, and the popular scenes introduced are very uncouth. The gardener recommends his herbs for exceedingly dubious purposes, and treats the Mother of God with particular incivility. Peter appears as a comic personage, but of this we indeed elsewhere find some trace. The disciples at Emmaus act a regular tavern scene: after fighting the host and hostess, they eat up all the remaining Easter eggs, and drink all that is left of the wine. Finally, Peter proposes—

> " Now let us sing, the Risen Christ proclaiming ;
> The Jews thus shaming ! "

The *rôle* of the scorner does not seem to have been entirely unrepresented, for the prologue to the Sterzing Passion play contains the admonition—

> " Therefore be grieved for God to-day,
> Jest not, nor idle scorn display :
> For many a rough, rude man is seen,
> Who if he merely chance, I ween,
> A small trip in a verse to hear,
> At once is ready with a sneer,
> And scorn would cast on all.
> But this we sure may sinful call,
> Since all to honour Jesus blest,
> Is in humility addressed,
> That so through this our simple play,
> They who will listen patiently
> May to a pious frame be brought,
> Which in these words is truly sought.
> Therefore to grieve for God be fain,
> Weep for His martyrdom and pain,
> And join with heartfelt sympathy
> In the heavy woe of Mary :

> For grieving sore the Holy Maid
> Doth weep her Son to death betrayed ;
> So let us form with tender art
> His sepulchre within our heart."

In some communities the performance of one of these peasant plays seems to have been a kind of statedly recurrent festival, or else they were acted during the winter by travelling country folk, who thus earned their morsel of bread and meat. The mode of representation was always of the simplest. It may have been in a peasant play of this sort that the dialogue occurred in which God the Father was made to ask Adam, " Adam, where art thou ? but I know very well." To which Adam replied, " Well, if Thou knowest, why then dost Thou ask ? "

From 1791 the spiritual and temporal authorities of the Tyrol began to throw every kind of hindrance in the way of these plays, and here and there we find the interposition of the civil arm.(54) The fanaticism of the so-called Enlightenment (*Aufklärung*) remarked on the animosity shown in taking the sacred person as the subject of the play, whereby, in the Passion plays, the Christ was, as it were, crucified a second time. The non-attendance at the church services caused by the Sunday representations, and the drinking bouts which followed, furnished more serious objections. But the populace remained tenaciously attached to its customary amusement, and as late as 1816 the Bishop of Brixen besought the magnates to enforce " obedience to the most illustrious prohibition."(55) From that time the primitive play disappeared from those regions, and it was only reproduced in a tentative manner in 1848 and 1849, when every man followed his own will.

The official body of Botzen, in a memorandum on the abolition of the peasant drama, pronounced that—"only a population which on the one hand is enthusiastically attached to its ancestral religion, and on the other hand possesses but rudely sensuous and material conceptions of this religion—only such a population can entertain a

decided partiality for these curious religious plays.'
Under such conditions, a Scriptural drama has continued to
exist up to our own day in the village of Oberammergau
in the Bavarian Highlands.([56])   This Passion play is of
comparatively recent date.   In 1633, during a severe
disease of the flax, in which it became absolutely useless
on the spindle, the Oberammergau peasants made a vow
to God that they would every ten years publicly represent
the cruel sorrows of His beloved Son.   This circumstance
reminds us how the Romans, in a similar time of distress,
obtained the first players from Etruria.   On both occasions
the plague disappeared.   The Benedictines of the neighbouring convent of Ettal, who very likely may have suggested
the design, also lent their aid in its execution.   The first
fulfilment of the vow took place in the following year, and
it continued to be suitably accomplished at the end of
every decade, until, at the time of the Bavarian reforms
under Montgelas,([57]) the representations were prohibited.
A deputation of peasants was authoritatively informed in
Munich that they might cause their pastor to preach to
them the Passion of Christ, which would be far better than
if the Lord God were paraded on a stage.   They objected to
this, that every beautiful and impressive story becomes more
effective when the listener beholds its tangible representation;
and that their exhibition of the Passion had always proved
a salutary means of impressing the joys and sorrows of
the Redeemer more deeply both on themselves and on the
spectators from the surrounding neighbourhood, and had
worked for the sanctification of their lives.   Their remon-
strances appeared useless, until at length they obtained a
hearing from the good King Max, perhaps through the influence of his art-loving successor; and the play was permitted on the condition of its being rearranged to suit modern
ideas.   In 1811 it was once more performed in the church-
yard, and as through the modern enthusiasm for archæology
it begun to attract a great concourse of strangers, the
last three representations [preceding 1858], in 1830, 1840,

and 1850, have been held on the village meadow, and no longer only for the good of the souls of the inhabitants.

At any rate, the invitations for 1840 in the public prints were fairly laudatory, and seemed composed in anticipation of a large attendance. The union of the beauties of art and nature was set forth, and it was announced that the whole village would become a hotel. The prices of the seats, especially of the better places, were also fixed at no low figure.([58]) The same piece was, in 1850, repeated on twelve different days between May and September. These were generally Sundays, on which day the mass was finished very early in the morning, and on the stroke of 8 A.M., two small cannons proclaimed the commencement of the play.

In the last two dramatic years [preceding 1858] from five to six thousand spectators were present at every performance, and the actors numbered from three to four hundred, and included infants and octogenarians. Many of the younger members of the troupe were barefooted, not merely on account of the dramatic costume. All were home-born inhabitants of Ammergau, with one exception, which was remarked upon—that of the Ass on which our Lord was represented as entering Jerusalem.

The seats of the audience, which are surrounded by a wall of planks, rise gradually in a semicircle beneath the open sky, and consist chiefly of wooden forms without backs, but in the outer circle there are a few boxes of more pretensions. The stage was formerly intended only for the year of representation, and resembled that of an ordinary German summer theatre; but in 1840 there stood on it towards the back a smaller scaffolding, fitted with a curtain, for the purpose of representing a play within a play, as in Hamlet. On each side of this central stage passed a street of Jerusalem, down each of which there was a long vista. Immediately in front, to right and left, stood two houses with balconies. Above the central stage a pelican was represented feeding her young ones with her own blood, and below this there was a picture of the Crucifixion, in which again there was a small picture of the Fall of Man. An angel leaning against. the cross was seen wiping out this with a sponge, supposed to be dipped in the blood of the Redeemer. For the performances of 1850 the central stage was built with a view to permanence, and was lower, and the two small houses with balconies stood close beside it. Then on each side, through a large arch, the spectator looked into a street which was bordered by architectural side-scenes. A front stage was thus enclosed of perhaps eighty feet wide by sixteen deep. Six different spaces for the performance may thus be said to have been secured—for the balcony on the right hand represented the High Priest's House, on the left the Judgment Hall of Pilate; while the space in front served both for the chorus and the exhibition of scenes in which the multitude were engaged; and the central stage, which was alone capable of being concealed by a curtain, no longer served as formerly for the representation only of tableaux from the Old Testament, but for such parts of the Passion play as needed some change of scenery. The curtain was then employed, either to bring the action to a sudden close, or to conceal the shifting of the scene. Over the centre of the smaller stage was a colossal picture of Faith, Hope, and Charity, of the ordinary conventional type. The other decorations were in the usual style of provincial house-painting, and chiefly in bright green and rose pink. Behind the stage rose the Hochgebirge, a less magnificent background than Etna and the sea furnished to the ancient rock-hewn theatre of Taormina, but charming enough with its sloping pine-girt meadows. The weather sometimes very severely tested the endurance of the audience by days of rain, or in autumn even by snowstorms; during which the players continued their performance, unmindful of the stage wardrobe, under the shelter of their red cotton umbrellas, while to the spectators a similar shelter was denied by those who sat behind them

on account of the obstruction of the view. People seemed
rather pleased, especially when once an approaching
thunderstorm formed an accompaniment to the Crucifixion.

We have not been able to obtain the old piece which
was entirely in verse. The one which has been acted
since 1811 is by the Pastor Weise, formerly a Benedictine
of the convent of Ettal, who was still living in 1840.
It is, as might have been expected, entirely on the basis
of the old drama; but the devil has been sacrificed.
Formerly, seated on his infernal throne, surrounded by
his hosts with Sin and Death, he opened the play by his
defiance of the Nazarene, and he retained throughout a
considerable part; but he has been surrendered to the
progress of that enlightenment which even the Bavarian
Highlands have not been able to escape. The comic
personage has also entirely disappeared. The tone of the
later piece is sufficiently modern, and in some places
reminds one of Klopstock; but the sentences from the Bible,
of which it is largely composed, show a tendency to return
to that simplicity which suits the people, while the other
speeches introduced are verbose and trivial. Peter denies
the Lord in rather cavalier fashion—" On my honour, I do
not know this man." Only the pieces appointed to be sung
are rhythmic or rhymed, and for these, which are chanted
by the chorus, a special text-book is sold.[59] The musical
composition, the work of Dedler the schoolmaster of the
day, is a mixture of old and new; and although not
deficient in a certain cleverness of adaptation, it is rather
feebly melancholy and drily old-fashioned. The orchestra,
which is composed of musicians of the village, is also not
sufficiently manned to be effective in the open air throughout so large a space.

The chorus exercises almost its old office of forming a
link between the gazing crowd and the action by its pious
poetic reflections, and it is especially employed to announce and explain the Old Testament tableaux. Always

composed of seven persons, who by the populace are named the Guardian Spirits, it stands on each side of the front stage, and gradually retreats into the two streets, or, in the later performances, into the side scenery; while the curtain of the central stage rises and reveals an Old Testament scene in dumb show. These Old Testament types or symbols, which introduce each act of the evangelical relation, are in accordance with old tradition, and generally display in their selection a certain amount of reflection, and even at times some boldness—for instance, Samson and Delilah are given as the Old Testament type of the Betrayal by Judas. Any scene which bears the slightest reference or resemblance to events of the Gospel history, and thus links the ancient with the primeval, and affords an opportunity for introducing the rich variety of Old Testament life into the evangelical narrative, is used to show how the whole sacred story points to the Redeemer. The first tableau gives both the cause and the prototype of what follows. Adam and Eve appear, whom the cherub with the flaming sword is seen expelling from Paradise. Behind them a real tree with rosy apples recalls their guilt; while to the right Abraham, on Mount Moriah, is shown on the point of slaying his son. The curtain then falls while the chorus sings—

> " Gott, Erbarmer ! Sünder zu begnaden,
>   Die verachtet schändlich dein Gebot,
>   Gibst du, von dem Fluche zu entladen
>   Deinen Eingebornen in den Tod."

> " God most merciful ! In pity to sinners
>   Who have shamefully despised Thy command
>   Thou dost give, from the curse to deliver them,
>   Thy only Son to death."

The curtain again rises. Against a misty background is seen a lofty cross, and in front of it four figures in prayer.[60] The chorus also kneels and sings sentences in adoration of the Divine Mystery of Redemption. It is only after the curtain has again descended on the central

F

stage that the Gospel story commences with the Hosannas of the entry into Jerusalem—and we have the beginning of the tragedy which in very deed embraces the sublimest contrasts which have ever been seen on earth.

The catastrophe is brought about in a rather common-place practical style through the anger of the Jewish usurers at their expulsion from the Temple, during which the doves of the dealers merrily fly away; and by means of Judas, who is equally influenced by his vexation at the waste of the ointment, and by his anxiety about his future maintenance.

About mid-day the Judgment Scene is reached, when the whole company hasten to obtain refreshments in the village, the spectators intermingled with the actors in the varied costumes of the Old and New Testament—until at one o'clock the cannon again sound a summons. If, however, the afternoon threaten to be wet, the drama is acted in one sitting of eight hours long. Such a performance is rendered possible by the food which has been brought, by the neighbourhood of more than one sausage-booth, and by the beer-jugs which good friends pass to one another across the benches.

The scourging is heard behind the scene, and the raised curtain shows only the *Ecce Homo* still bound to his pillar of suffering among his torturers. In the same manner the fastening of the nails resounds behind the curtain, and the unveiling of the central stage reveals the crucified thieves, while the cross with the Redeemer is in the act of being raised from the ground. The wound of the lance is rendered by means of a bladder with the necessary fluid, but in the clear daylight the darkness over the land can only be suggested by some tumult and a few cannon shots. In the removal from the cross there is some truth to nature, as the body is partially stiffened by the unnatural tension, which has lasted about a quarter of an hour. Two white-robed angels with white woollen gloves push aside the stone of the sepulchre, the Risen Christ appears with a nimbus of goldleaf, while the watchers are dispersed by a discharge of cannon.

Since the historical termination through the Ascension cannot be attempted on account of the absence of the requisite machinery, the compiler has been emboldened to go a little beyond the Scripture story. The triumphant Christ appears in the background with the faithful kneeling in groups to the right and left, while prostrate on the ground lie the Jewish priests and the buyers and sellers of the Temple, in order, probably, that they may not be privileged to behold the Risen Saviour.

The parts, which are very suitably assigned with regard to age, sex, and character, are also by no means ill played. The employment of almost the entire village in artistic woodcarving, partly for ecclesiastical purposes, has given a certain artistic tinge to the population, and the delight of the actors in their work and their conscientious painstaking have supplied the other elements of success. The peasant on whom in 1840 devolved the great responsibility of representing the Redeemer was a carver of crucifixes, such as in those regions is termed a *Herrgottsschnitzler*. The performer also of 1850, though possessing a weak voice of a chanting monotone and rather mournful in cadence, was yet in his appearance not unworthy to represent the divine purpose and suffering. The scene of the institution of the Sacrament after the Last Supper, when, in imitation of the ritual of the Church, the Saviour moves round and lays the bread on the lips of each, and then in the same manner offers to each the cup, was of impressive solemnity. This scene has for its Old Testament prototype the descent of the manna on the Israelites, who are exhibited in very skilful grouping. In the foreground children are recumbent, behind them others sit or stand, then we have young girls and women, while the tallest men are in the background head over head. Many of the characters are hereditary in families. The Judas of 1850 had inherited from his father his *rôle*

and his red beard. His suicide displays an advance
upon the old-fashioned mysteries. On the central stage is
represented a wood of growing trees. Judas throws off
his mantle, unlooses his girdle, selects the tree on which
he intends to hang himself, in wild haste breaks off the
weak lower branches, and then throwing his girdle over
a bough, he loops it round his neck, and the curtain
falls.

The costumes of the players, especially of the principal
personages, are as suitable as those in which they are
depicted in old German altar-pieces, and the preservation
of the angular type gives us the sense of their having
descended from the pictures of the early German school.
The members of the chorus alone are plumed and fancifully
decked in a sort of operatic attire without any distinction
of sex. During the Crucifixion they, however, are black-
robed. In 1840 the musicians wore black frockcoats
and white waistcoats, but, in consequence perhaps of a
cry of horror from some historical and political journals,
they appeared in 1850 in the uniform of the Landwehr
sharpshooters. The tableaux were often clumsily grouped,
and in the bright daylight had no artistic effect on the
central stage, which received the least light. The dialect
was fairly evenly balanced between Bavarian and Swabian,
with a considerable addition of High-German, not always
of the happiest order.

Awkward and droll *contretemps* were not entirely
absent at the last performance (1850), but one characteristic of the true mystery remained intact. "All play
with spirit, unaffectedly and impressively, because each
honestly believes that in Jerusalem everything took
place exactly as it is now taking place in Oberammergau." Simple country folk see *The Passion* repeated
with delight and edification, while children watch it with
joyful excitement and heartfelt emotion. And even one
so familiar with the stage as Edward Devrient was
astonished by the unanimity of action shown by the mass

of players in the popular scenes; and from the profound religious impression produced upon him, he considered that by this play the vexed question of the admittance upon the stage of sacred subjects should be for ever settled.([61])

We understand that there has been a performance of a Passion play even more lately than at Oberammergau at Liesing in Carinthia, where, after a very long interval, an old drama was again acted in the Passion Week of 1852 on the village green by fifty-six persons.([62]) This play commences in hell where Pluto reigns, "the ruler and god of the Stygian realm," who hopes to seduce all the children of men. Astarot leads in the lost sheep attached to a chain. It has a black mantle thrown over it, and a very fine hat on its head, and "comes in quite proudly," boasting of its gallant life, which it will continue to lead without troubling itself about heaven and hell.

We have here a very common figure in the old mysteries, the lost sheep as the type of fallen humanity, the counter-type of the Scriptural image of the Good Shepherd, the first form in which Christ was portrayed by Christian art. The lost sheep is also sometimes represented as a shepherdess, to whom the Good Shepherd offers his love, while she gives herself up to a merry life with the huntsman, who is the devil in this guise. At last she is touched by the faithfulness of the Shepherd, and her heart and soul are delivered. In this allegory we have the material for a refined and tender pastoral.([63]) Sometimes the lost sheep is individualised as the Magdalen, herself a type of sinful, repentant, redeemed humanity.

In the Liesing miracle play, the lost sheep, which falls asleep in hell, is merely awakened by the Good Shepherd. It then immediately recognises the devil in his true character, and throws itself in remorse at the feet of the Shepherd, who leads it away, singing—

" Come belovèd lamb of mine,
And I will lead thee to the place,

> Where thee to save from misery,
> Thy God a bitter death doth face.
> Yea there may'st thou behold again,
> How the good God for thee was slain.
> In Isaac the mere type we see
> Of that which God Himself should be."

The parable of the Shepherd thus forms an introduction to the Passion, just as in an old play representing Paradise belonging to Upper Styria, it was made to serve as a conclusion by being brought in immediately after Adam's death.

Weinhold, Professor at the University of Gratz, who with painstaking affection has collected the lingering vestiges of the peasant play found in his native mountain land, regards these latest efforts at a revival as only the last flashes of a neglected sacred lamp.[64]   But to the Oberammergau mystery, which is entirely founded on the historical narrative, and which has steadfastly resisted a time of trial, a fresh breath of actual life seems to have been imparted.   To the traveller it may almost possess the interest of an antediluvian curiosity; and when it is played again many will no doubt seize their travelling staff with intent to behold it.   The railway line is also now carried right up to the shore of Lake Starnberg, behind which rise the Bavarian Alps.

SINCE Professor Hase's lectures were written, several accounts of the Oberammergau play have been published.   Two of these, *Das Passions-Spiel in Oberammergau*, München, 1860, by Clarus, and *Das Oberammergauer Passions-Spiel*, Eichstadt and Stuttgart, 1870, by Schöberl, have furnished some of the materials for the following note.   Schöberl's book of the play will be familiar to most of the visitors to Oberammergau in 1871.

The Passion play, as Professor Hase has said, was established in 1634 in fulfilment of a vow.   This vow seems to have been made during an epidemic which raged amongst the inhabitants of the valley in the preceding year.   Until 1674, the play was repeated every ten years; but in 1680 it was given again, and it has since been acted at the end of each decade counted from the beginning of the century, except during the interval mentioned by Dr. Hase.

The oldest text preserved dates from 1662. The action then began with the Supper in Bethany. The meeting of the Risen Christ with Thomas and the rest of the disciples immediately preceded the closing scene, in which Christ appeared in the sky, a great book with seven seals borne before Him, and the twenty-four elders prostrate around Him. These last gradually rose while the Genius of the Passion explained the meaning of the Apocalypse. The Genius of the Passion, the *Plausus*, the Epilogue, and the Chorus sang a song in conclusion. The play was introduced by an *Argumentator*, and contained the scene of the Descent into Hell. After 1680, Satan came prominently forward tempting the people to irreverence and impiety.

Father Rosner, from the Benedictine convent of Ettal (1740–1750), composed a new text in rhyme. The Guardian Spirit (*Schutzgeist*) with his six companions, and the typical scenes from the Old Testament which were explained by him, were now introduced. The Guardian Spirit and his companions, as at present, constituted the chorus, which was not increased in number, as will be seen by Dr. Hase's narrative, until after the performances of 1850. In 1770 the first scene was laid in hell, where Lucifer consults with Death and Sin on the means of destroying the disturber of his kingdom. Many other allegorical figures, Covetousness, Envy, Despair, &c., had parts assigned to them by Rosner. The Descent into Hell was still retained.

The last version of the play and its composition have already been described, for no material change has been made since 1850. The scenes, exclusive of the last and of the opening scene, are now seventeen in number, and are all introduced by one, two, or three Old Testament types, with the exception of the Crucifixion, which has no tableau preceding it. The parts of Satan and the allegorical personages have disappeared, and the Descent into Hell has been omitted. The short prologue by which the action is now introduced is ascribed to Alliani, who was also one of the Roman Catholic translators of the Bible.

The whole play in its present form has been carefully adapted to the requirements of modern taste and religious feeling. Not only has the part of Satan been omitted with all those characters which were invented or developed to suit the popular fancy, but there is hardly any reference to Catholic legend or to the Apocrypha. Of the former there is one touch in the display of the handkerchief of St. Veronica, first found in the old Donaueschingen Passion play ; and the parting of Tobias and his parents forms a tableau before the third scene in which Christ bids farewell to His Mother at Bethany. But the Book of Tobit has always been popular: it was a favourite with Luther, and in his preface to it he even recommends it for use in dramatic representation. The play is strictly Scriptural in the Protestant sense of the word. The Virgin Mother is not brought too prominently forward, nor is there any reference to her worship. There are no scenes borrowed from the Apocryphal Gospels. We may indeed regret the omission of an episode, so characteristic of the earlier mysteries, as the Descent into Hell. Such a scene would have formed an appropriate transition from the entombment to the manifestation of the Risen Christ, although it might have detracted from the Scriptural character of the rest of the play. The chorus has been judiciously used. Its functions may be compared with the part performed by Augustine, or by the prophets in the early spectacles. But it was a learned addition to the Oberammergau play, and has been borrowed, not from the old mysteries, but from the Greek drama.

The place of representation was originally the church or church-yard, probably the latter. In 1830 the play was transferred to the Passions-Platz, the meadow in which the great theatre described by Professor Hase stands. It is announced that the theatre is now being rebuilt and enlarged.

The peasants who sustain the character have all been carefully, and to some extent technically, trained. In former times a performance, called the *School of the Cross (Kreuz-Schule)*, was held some two years before each representation of the play. On these occasions Old Testament scenes were dramatically rendered, and others from the New Testament were depicted in tableaux, the present relation of these scenes in the Passion play being thus reversed. The last performance of this kind took place in 1825. For several years past the performers selected for the Passion play have, during the intervening years, acted in the village school-house various dramas of a secular character, and have thus fitted themselves for their more important task. Joseph Mair, the Christus of 1870, was a leading actor in these plays. The total number of those engaged in the Passion play is said to be no less than 450–500.

The parts are assigned with great judgment. A performer often sustains the same character more than once : sometimes he is transferred to another *rôle.* Tobias Flunger, who played the chief part in 1850, and who is praised by Professor Hase, and, as the reader of *Quits* will recollect, by the accomplished authoress of that work, appeared as Pilate in 1860 and 1870. The parts of Judas, St. Peter, Caiaphas, Annas, Pilate, Herod, Barabbas, and Mary Magdalene were acted by the same persons in 1860 and in 1870, and also in 1871, as the French and German war interrupted the play of 1870 after the first performances. It was resumed on the corresponding Sunday of 1871, and those players, the Christus among them, who had been called to the war the year before, were all spared to resume their parts in the following year.

Professor Hase's remarks on the character of Judas may be supplemented by an extract from an interesting article which appeared in " Macmillan's Magazine " for October 1860 :—" The particular mode in which the character of Judas is conceived is peculiar, and must be stated at length. He is conspicuous among the apostles, not only from the well-known red beard and yellow robe (as of envy) with which he always appears, but from his prominent position, always pressing forward, even beyond Peter himself, the restless, moving, active, busy personage of the whole group. The scene of the breaking of the box of precious ointment is worked to the utmost. The silent profusion of the Magdalene and the eager economy of Judas are contrasted from the two sides of the stage in startling opposition. From this moment a monomania, a fixed idea of replacing the three hundred pence, takes possession of his mind. He shakes his empty money-bag. He recurs to the subject with a persistency bordering, and apparently meant to border, on the ludicrous. The thirty pieces of silver are represented as an equivalent for the loss. He is filled with nervous apprehensions as to the destitution of himself and his companions, if their Master should imperil Himself at Jerusalem. In this state he is left alone to his own thoughts, and in a scene, perhaps too elaborately drawn out, he rushes to and fro between the distractions of his worse and his better nature ; until the balance is turned by the deputation from the chief priests suddenly entering, playing on his delusion, getting round him, and entrapping him into the fatal compact. The absorbing passion is brought out forcibly once more, when, with a greediness of the actual coin truly Oriental, and (if not suggested by some traveller or learned prompter) wonderfully resembling the Oriental reality, he counts over the silver pieces in the presence of the high priests. But the compunctions of conscience are never wholly repressed. The deadness of the grasp with which he takes the hands of his accomplices is very expressive. The shuffling agitation during the Last Supper ; the outbreak of remorse before the Sanhedrim ; the frenzy into which he is goaded by their calm indifference ; the fury with which he offers back their money to each, and with which he finally flings the bag behind him and rushes out ; all have the effect of exhibiting in strong relief the return of a better mind recovering from a dreadful illusion. With all this is mingled some of the ludicrousness, as well as the horrors of insanity." This conception of Judas is, according to Wilkens, at least in part traditional, as he is commonly represented, in the older dramas, to have been impelled to the betrayal by what he considered the unjustifiable waste of the ointment. In 1860 and in 1870–71, the character was sustained by a woodcarver named Lechner.

The popularity of the Oberammergau play has led to the revival of similar observances in other parts of the Tyrol. A performance of the same kind has been attempted at Brixlegg and also at Botzen, but with no great measure of success. A survival, although only two hundred and fifty years old, may be regarded with interest and veneration, but anywhere in Northern Europe it is too late to revive such plays after their disuse. The motives of such attempts are more than questionable. Many visitors to Oberammergau must have felt serious doubts whether even there influences are not at work which will inevitably lead to the degradation of what has been, and is, a simple and touching act of faith. But the effect of such a performance must depend on the spirit in which it is approached, and there does not seem to be any reason why in this case the play should not long survive. The peasants of Oberammergau are little affected by the movement around them, and they are endowed with singularly fine qualities. Professor Hase has very justly characterised them. They have an absolute belief that they can reproduce the historical events of the life and passion of Christ. But they are not dreamy ascetics. They enjoy life without affectation, and, like the players of the Middle Ages, they take a hearty pleasure in their own performance. To the strangers who flock to witness it, they give a welcome which leaves no suspicion of mercenary feelings. Such a suspicion would do them injustice. The devotion they bestow on the play has caused its popularity, and is independent of it. Those who come among them should possess something of their spirit. The lover of antiquity will find much to interest him, although a great part of what he sees is modern rather than ancient. But the whole scene appeals to something more than the love of antiquity. Ancient faith seems at home in that pure air under the shadow of the peaceful hills. Few who have surrendered themselves to the impressions which are borne in on them will not feel as if they had been transplanted to another epoch, and had recovered something of the freshness and simplicity of an earlier age.

REVIVAL OF THE SACRED DRAMA IN SPAIN.

IN Spain, where the story of the bloody and protracted strife with the infidel remained impressed on the popular memory, and every sacred building seemed to record the triumphs of a believing ancestry, mediæval sentiment long preserved its vitality, even amid the dungeons of the Inquisition and in the schools of the Jesuits. Thus, when in the seventeenth century the richly-gifted Spanish nation, by way of relaxation from its historic deeds in three continents, applied itself to the creation of works of artistic genius and to the enjoyment of them, the flower of the national poetry was once more displayed in the religious drama.([1]) Perhaps it was the imposition of fetters on learning that directly caused the then unbroken spirit of the nation to devote itself to art, to which some license was allowed, both from custom and on account of the partiality of the populace.

An immediate offspring of the mysteries during the fifteenth century, or by their form more properly of the moralities, had been the *Autos*—acts, sacred deeds. Thus we find *Autos al nascimiento*, or Christmas plays, which are generally simple scenes of pastoral life, associated with the manger of Bethlehem. It was this kind of pastoral which Encina, at the end of this century, produced in the palace of the Duke of Alva, under the title of *Shepherd Plays*. Gil Vincente([2]) was also author of a few Spanish autos, in which some secular scene introduces the "Sacra-

ment" of the Divine Birth. For instance, the shepherdess
Cassandra repulses the wooing of the shepherd Solomon
with the assertion that she will never marry. Her three
aunts endeavour to cure her folly by every argument for
matrimony that the female heart can supply, after which
Solomon's uncles point out to her the holiness of the
married state, the institution of God Himself. All their
efforts prove equally vain, and she at length confesses
that she remains a maiden because she has heard that the
Lord shall be a maiden's son. Both aunts and uncles
blame her presumption, and the curtain rises displaying the
Virgin and the infant Christ in the stable of Bethlehem.
Four angels sing a hymn, and the personages of the introductory piece offer their adoration.(³)

The place of the old Easter play was especially supplied
by the *Autos sacramentales*,(⁴) or spectacles in honour of
the Feast of Corpus Christi. In the more modern Roman
Church, this festival of the perpetual mystic change
through the priestly formula of the earthly element into
the body of the Son of God, has by its splendour cast into
the shade the Feast of the Resurrection.

In Madrid festive dances accompanied the procession
of the Corpus Christi through the streets, and in its train
were borne a stuffed giant and a monstrous snake, symbols
of Paganism and of the subject forces of nature. Before
the royal palace a scaffolding was erected on wheels, surrounded on three sides by small gaily-coloured houses
brought thither for the occasion, which served as dressing-
rooms for the actors; or, accordingly as they were required,
they were opened to widen or change the scene. In the
country the arrangements were probably more simple, for
Cervantes relates how Don Quixote met an open waggon
driven by a hideous devil. In it sat Death with the face
of a man, and at his feet Cupid with bow and quiver.
Next to him was an angel with great painted wings, while
behind stood the Emperor with a tinsel crown, and a man
in armour. These were all actors of the company of the

Evil Angel, who, it being the octave of Corpus Christi, had in the morning acted the *Auto* of the *Court of Death*.([5]) Wishing to repeat the same piece in a neighbouring spot, they were travelling in the costume of their parts.

In Madrid also, the whole theatre proceeded on successive days to exhibit the same play, by appointment, before different palaces. The performance was always in the afternoon, but tapers were kindled round the stage in honour of the Sacrament. The players were ordinary actors, the regular theatres being closed during the festival season.

The *Autos* were much shorter, not only than most mysteries, but than the usual dramas of the period.([6]) In the Corpus Christi play almost everything was allegoric— divine attributes, spiritual forces, virtues, vices, sin, death, the Church, heresy, Judaism, Islamism, idolatry, continents, provinces, nature, the seasons, light and darkness—all appear as conscious personalities acting in accordance with their main principle. Here and there we find some few historical characters both from this world and the other, but as far as possible these too are clothed in a veil of allegory. For instance, the Creator is seen as a painter painting his own portrait, which the devil mars; or Christ is the Good Shepherd, the Bridegroom, the Divine Orpheus. Characters from the Greek mythology are unhesitatingly associated with Christian personages, or perhaps are introduced in their later allegorical significance as mediums for Christian ideas. Thus in Calderon's *Auto* of *Psyche*,([7]) the World is the parent of three daughters: Idolatry, who is wedded to Paganism; the Synagogue, married to Judaism; and Psyche. She is in her typical character Faith, and without the knowledge of the rest she marries Amor or Love, the type of Christ. As soon as her marriage becomes known, the World banishes her to a desert island. Love transforms this to a paradise till Psyche, led astray by her relatives, desires to forestall eternity and to see instead of believing. On

this Love departs, leaving only a dismal wilderness.   At
length, after sorrow and repentance, Love becomes reconciled to Faith, Christ is reunited to the soul.

Lope de Vega with his intellectual vivacity and truth
to nature, and Calderon with his delicately sensitive and
boldly soaring genius, both composed numerous *Autos
sacramentales.* These plays possess a charm which is at
once ethereal and attractive to the senses ; and, according
to our German criticism, they oscillate between depth of
meaning and unreality, between the lofty and the commonplace.   But Calderon, like a second Pygmalion, threw
his arms around this phantom world of abstract ideas, till
he felt within it a living heart ; and these allegorical
figures, descending from amid the incense fumes, seem
like actual persons to appeal to our human sympathy.
We have here, in most singular blending, enthusiastic
piety, efflorescent poetry, and scholastic subtlety, to which
is added the popular intermixture of the comic with the
sublime.

The theme is usually derived from some Scripture narrative, for instance, from the history of the Creation and
the Fall of Man ; but Adam and Eve do not move in
Paradise—they represent, as it were, the general idea of
human nature.   Or we have Belshazzar's Feast, in which
Thought, that is to say, Thought in the abstract, is assigned
the comic *rôle.*   And in the elevation of the Brazen Serpent, in the parable of the Prodigal Son, and in all parables, we have rather the history of the human soul in its
earthly career, or the story of the Church from Paradise
to the Judgment, while the Cross of Salvation, re-erected
in eternity far beyond this dim world of dreams, remains
victorious in the end, and the miraculous Sacrament is
thereby glorified.[8]

For other festivals than the Corpus Christi, such pieces
were only composed on special occasions.   Thus Lope de
Vega wrote a festival play for the University of Salamanca, when that university celebrated the Immaculate

Conception, the dogma, then so greatly disputed, of the birth of the Virgin without taint or germ of sin.([9])   In it appear Contemplation, Doubt, Sin, King David, Jeremiah, Spain and some other countries, the University of Salamanca, students, shepherds, huntsmen, and musicians. Fame calls on all the nations of the earth to celebrate the Immaculate Conception; Germany argues with Sin, and Contemplation with Doubt; and Ethiopians and Indians come forward and sing national hymns in praise of the divine Maiden.   Meanwhile students and the *Graciosos*([10]) make questionable jests on the object of the festival; but at last all unite to adore the miracle of divine mercy.

Poets received from some of the great towns commissions for *Autos sacramentales*, and the Spanish populace seem to have contemplated these imaginative dramas and their ideal pangs, with the same enthusiastic interest with which they watched the bull-fights or the *Autos da fé*. These *Acts of Faith* (*actus fidei*), in which miserable wretches were burnt in terrible earnest as sacrifices to the idols of the State Church, were considered preludes to the Last Judgment, which human beings thought themselves well entitled to anticipate.   Both Catholic *autos* came to an end at about the same period.   Calderon in his lifetime may have observed both the rise and decline of the *Autos sacramentales ;* and over his recent grave the national poetry and the sacred drama suddenly perished. When Louis XIV. affirmed, " The Pyrenees have ceased to exist," the Spanish nation, amid the influx of French taste, quickly forgot or grew ashamed of the beauties of its own national poetry.

Beyond the Pyrenees the aristocratic instinct has always maintained a powerful sway, side by side with the religion which proclaims the equality of all the children of God. The decline of the national element is thus indicated by a play produced in Madrid on the Corpus Christi of 1679. The Knights of St. James being assembled, the Saviour enters and asks for admittance into their order.   Some of the knights are ready to welcome Him, but the elders among them advance the argument that it would not be fitting to receive into their illustrious fraternity a man of low origin, whose father was a carpenter. The Saviour awaits their decision with impatience. At first they reject Him entirely, and afterwards, undeterred even by His royal ancestry as recorded by St. Matthew and St. Luke, and by His far higher lineage as given by St. John, they have recourse to the expedient of creating for Him a separate order, the Portuguese Order of Christ.([11])

From the sixteenth century, a dramatic art and literature on a genuine national basis had been developed from the union of the mediæval mystery with the newly-acquired knowledge of the antique theatre. In the bright products of its genius the Spanish nation could behold both its examples and its portrait, as well as the various traditions of its past. Side by side with the delights of bold adventure, with the glorification of the national empire, with the bloodthirsty punctiliousness of conventional honour—the ethics of which became an intricate arithmetical puzzle—and with love's fiery passion, behind which lurks murder, we find also the most fervid Catholic devotion and the fanaticism of the Inquisition depicted in the dramas, which, on account of the predominant religious motive, were termed *divine*, in contradistinction to the so-called human dramas.([12]) Like the latter they were, however, exhibited in the ordinary theatres, for in Spain a separate class of actors had already grown up out of the never wholly extinguished mummeries of the strolling players.

The most nearly allied to the mysteries and *autos* were the *Lives of the Saints*,([13]) which were acted on their festivals, and which were dramatised legends of the heroes of the Church. These, too, by their prodigies were in correspondence with the popular love of the miraculous; all improbabilities were covered by faith, and all impossibilities became possible. There was scarcely a poet who did not make the attempt to bring his patron saint on the stage.

Lope de Vega in his sacred dramas has represented every shade of the religious peculiarities of his compatriots : unlimited credulity, dreamy mysticism, ecstasies of sympathy in superhuman joys and sorrows, and child-like simplicity of faith, united with a keen subtlety on points of faith, and with a gloomy rage for religious persecution. His *Human Seraph* ([14]) exhibits in a fanciful manner the lives of St. Francis of Assisi, and of such of his contemporaries as shared his enthusiasm, with the ecstasies and *Stigmata* of the former. In the life of the *Cardinal of Bethlehem*,([15]) St. Jerome, as he himself has related, is scourged by angels while a very young man, on account of his study of the heathen classics, and in the third act he dies, aged ninety-nine, and the Archangel Michael announces to the devil the foundation of the Order of St. Jerome. Satan, though foaming with rage, is obliged to promise never to enter a house in which there is a portrait of the saint. Between whiles appear saints of various periods, the Three Kings, a Lion and an Ass, and Rome and Spain as allegorical figures. Armed and masked priests wander about in Rome on midnight adventures, and Julian the Apostate is stabbed with a lance by St. Mercury, who descends from heaven for the purpose. The scene varies between Rome, Constantinople, Persia, Jerusalem, and Bethlehem.

The life of *St. Julian* is converted into a sort of tragedy of fate.([16]) Julian has in hunting slain a stag, which at its death has exclaimed, " It is but a small thing that thou hast slain me, for thou shalt one day destroy thy parents." Julian, deeply distressed by these words, leaves home, preferring rather never again to see his father and mother, whose only son he is. In Ferrara he marries the niece of the duke, whom he has rescued from robbers. A brother of the duke had wooed her, and as, although repulsed, he still pursues his suit,

G

Julian challenges him to single combat. Learning, however, that at the very hour fixed for the combat, which is to take place at night, his rival means to carry off his wife, instead of repairing to the place appointed he goes to his chamber. In the dim light he sees two persons, a man and a woman, asleep on the bed; and in his blind jealousy he stabs them both. His wife comes in and he asks, "Who are those sleeping on thy bed?" She answers, "Thy parents, they surprised me just now by their sudden arrival, and as I had no bed prepared for them, I gave them mine." Julian thus beholds the fulfilment of the prediction. His rival now entering to carry out his intention, the maddened Julian slays him also; then, accompanied by his wife, he flees to Rome to obtain absolution from the Pope. In obedience to the counsel of the Holy Father, the husband and wife found an hospital in Calabria, where they themselves wait on the sick poor. The devil causes himself to be carried into this hospital in the form of a paralytic, in order that he may persuade Julian that his sins can find no pardon, since his parents died without absolution. To give confirmation to his story, he reveals them surrounded by the flames of hell. Julian's faith is shaken; but the Saviour appears and promises to deliver the murdered pair from purgatory. Their glorified souls are seen floating to heaven, and the saintly penitent joyfully resolves to pass the remainder of his life in devotion and works of charity.

A denunciation of the sacred drama by Cervantes is especially applicable to these Lives of the Saints. "The sacred dramas too—how are they made to abound with false and incomprehensible events, frequently confounding the miracles of one saint with those of another, indeed they are often introduced into plays on profane subjects merely to please the people. Thus is our national taste degraded in the opinion of cultivated nations, who, judging by the extravagance and absurdity of our productions, con-

ceive us to be in a state of ignorance and barbarism."([17])
The justification of these plays lay, however, in the
general passion for the supernatural, and in the very
essence of the legends themselves. It was boasted that
these exhibitions were as powerful to awaken religious
sentiment as the most eloquent sermons, and instances
are recorded of persons who went straight from the
theatre to assume the habit of the monastery of the saint
represented. Some noted actors also closed their career
in a monastery.

In those religious dramas of Lope de Vega, in which
he invented the subjects as well as the treatment, he
has equally illustrated the doctrines of the Church in
their eternal truth and in their abuses. In the *Complete
Atonement*,([18]) Leonido is seen as a young rake at Palermo,
throwing himself with delight into every youthful vice.
When he is reminded of the Eternal Judge, he replies,
" Oh, Christ has taken our sins on Himself, so I can sin
at my ease." He beats his old father and endeavours to
injure his sister, but as he is on the point of killing her
husband, he is taken prisoner by Moors from Tunis. He
has not, however, the slightest objection to abjuring the
Christian faith, and in Tunis he attains to great dignity.
When after a while his father and sister are also taken
prisoners and brought thither, he ill-treats his sister and
goes so far as to order his father's eyes to be put out.
But finally his arrogance rouses numerous adversaries, and
he even quarrels with the King, with whom he engages in
battle. Being defeated, he escapes into the wilderness,
where he meets a shepherd lad chanting holy hymns, the
Good Shepherd in search of the lost sheep. After touching Leonido's heart by very impressive words, the shepherd
says, " Thou didst trust to my promise that I would take
on me thy guilt; behold how I have kept it, see what
I have suffered for thee ! " Leonido opens the pouch
which the lad offers him, and he finds in it the crown of
thorns, the nails, and the spear. After examining them,

he looks up, and sees, instead of the shepherd lad, Christ on the cross, while he hears a voice saying, "Thus have I answered for thee, but now the time has come when thou must bear thine own guilt." The sinner falls to the ground, and when he recovers himself he is no longer the same. He flings from him turban and caftan, and clothing himself in the hair shirt of a penitent, he beseeches God's mercy in remorseful prayer, and passionately desires to atone for the grievous sins of his evil life. When his pursuers approach he gives himself into their hands, and openly confessing that he has returned to the Christian faith, he welcomes the death with which they threaten him. Being brought back to Tunis, he beseeches with repentant tears forgiveness from his father and his sister. In the closing scene he is exhibited dying gladly on a cross with a crown of thorns on his head, while his father, whose sight has been restored by a miracle, watches with mingled joy and grief the martyrdom of his lost but redeemed son.

In the comedy of the *Innocent Child*,[19] an attempt is made to justify the bitter hatred of the Jews, which was a characteristic of Spanish Christianity, by means of a well-known melancholy legend, which is developed into a most poetic picture of infant martyrdom. In the beginning of the play, Queen Isabella is commanded by St. Dominic in a vision to purify Spain from the enemies of the faith. We have next the commencement of the persecution of the Jews, and the measures adopted for their complete dispersion. In their assemblies they devise plans for revenging themselves. A Jew promises to concoct a charm which shall bring destruction on their Christian enemies, but for it he needs the heart of a Christian child of extraordinary piety. Many undertake to seek such a child and to find the means of stealing him. It is now the Feast of the Ascension, and Juannico, a boy of angelic beauty and goodness, comes out with his mother to watch the great procession. As the banner is

borne past, on which the glorified Virgin is painted surrounded by angels, the child exclaims, " Oh, would that
I were one of the angels around the beautiful Virgin ! "
In adoration he follows the picture, is lost in the crowd
and stolen by the Jews. The frightened mother perceives
her son's departure, and after vainly seeking him she goes
in despair into a church, where, according to the Spanish
custom, she gets a blind man to repeat a prayer for the
lost child. He has hardly ended it, when a voice is heard
from the recesses of the church, " Thou who hast lost be
comforted, for that thou hast lost on earth thou shalt find
in heaven." The Jews resolve to slay the child by the
same cruel means by which they once slew Christ. Amid
their feasting and songs of triumph, we have the scourging, the coronation with thorns, and the crucifixion of the
boy, who bears all with heavenly patience and resignation ;
till at last his soul is borne by angels to heaven.

Even transmutation of 'spiritual plays into secular
seems occasionally to have taken place. Don Juan is said
to have originally belonged to the religious drama as the
Atheist struck-down,[20] and we encounter his figure on
the stage in this its early form in a play by Tirso de
Molina,[21] a contemporary of Lope de Vega, belonging to
the same social grade as his brother poet. The character
of the audacious sinner is drawn by Tirso in effective
outline; but in the terrible scene of the invitation of the
marble guest, there is an involuntary touch of the comic.
We thus have here a case which is entirely without
parallel: the solemn earnestness of the dramatic theme
finds suitable expression for the first time in the melody
of the opera, in which we seem, as it were, to feel the cold
shudder of eternal death penetrating the pride of earthly
passion. In another drama on the same subject, Don
Juan, like the modern Faust, is saved, but only through
a life of penitence in a cloister.

Calderon, the very breath of whose existence was
religion, even amid the alluring drama of life, which in a

hundred shapes he has reproduced on the stage—sometimes in plays full of finesse ;([22]) at other times, like a true
Spanish patriot, in heroic or historical pieces—seems in
his later days to have more and more considered himself
a kind of secular priest of the only saving religion.([23])
He, too, has therefore in some of his dramas represented
the religious sentiment of his nation ; and, with the wise
discretion of genius, he has introduced an imaginative
variety of poetic situations, such as are likely enough to
occur when the development of this religious sentiment
in a man is brought into contact with the actual historical
circumstances of a people.   Calderon's verse, in its manifold changes, becomes the material expression of his
passing mood.   In his earlier days it is often, after the
fashion of his day (*stilo culto*), inclined to be meretricious
and theatrical ; but we have amid the tumult of the action
frequent wafts of Oriental poetry—" Stars, the eternal
flowers of heaven ; flowers, the perishable stars of earth."
Also, it must be confessed, we have lyric flights and
romantic narrative where the nature of the action and the
hurry of passion demand a crisis.   A characteristic story is
told.   When on one occasion several poets were assembled
in the palace of Philip IV., a great patron of art, the King
resolved on the improvisation of a drama representing the
Creation.   He gave to Calderon the *rôle* of Adam, while
he himself retained that of the Creator.   Calderon in a
long poetic speech described the charms of Paradise.
Perceiving some signs of impatience in the royal actor, he
asked what was the matter.   " What is the matter ! "
exclaimed His Majesty, " I repent of having created such
a loquacious Adam."

A youthful work of Calderon's, the *Purgatory of St.
Patrick*,([24]) is founded on a legend which became very
popular in Spain.   This legend is not entirely in accordance with Catholic doctrine, although invented in illustration of it.   St. Patrick, the Apostle of Ireland, finding
that the rude populace would not believe unless he showed

them some visible proof of the other world which he described, was enabled to discover in a cave the entrance to purgatory. Through this entrance living persons, whose souls were heavily oppressed by sin, could descend to purge themselves by cruel sufferings; and if when they entered they were in a fit state of preparation, they could, on an appeal to the name of Christ, return to the light of day— but many were never more seen on earth. The piece opens with a shipwreck, from which St. Patrick and his friend, Ludovico Ennio, are rescued by swimming to the coast of Ireland, where dwells Egerio, the heathen King, surrounded by his court. Patrick relates the legendary story of his boyhood, which, together with his gift of working miracles, has convinced him that he is the chosen instrument for the conversion of Ireland; but Ludovico, although a Christian, boldly tells the tale of a very sinful youth. This infamous narrative is quite in accordance with the King's taste, but in his life at the court Ludovico heaps crime upon crime. He seduces the King's daughter, Polonia, and engages in a mortal quarrel with the commander of the army, Filippo. Being condemned to death, he is saved by Polonia. They escape together, but Ludovico, who is now weary of her, regards her as a hindrance to his flight, and murdering her in a wood, he goes on his way into the wide world. St. Patrick, on whose God she has called in her dying moments, restores to life the slain girl. The King is greatly astonished, and he now demands a sight of the fires of hell with which St. Patrick threatens sinners. Patrick conducts him to the cave which looks into purgatory, and the King, in spite of all warning, steps in unprepared, and disappears in the infernal depths. The effect of this incident is the conversion of the court and of the whole country.

Patrick, having completed his work, is now dead. When he and Ludovico separated for the last time, they both, the saint and the sinner, promised that in life or in death they would seek one another. After long wandering, Ludovico now returns to wreak his vengeance on Filippo. While he is lying in wait by night, a masked knight appears and challenges him. He begins the combat, but his strokes only fall on the empty air; and the knight, revealing himself as a skeleton, the emblem of the human soul sunk in deadly sin, exclaims, "Behold thyself! I am Ludovico Ennio." Ludovico falls to the ground and asks, "By what atonement may the crimes of my life be expiated?" An answer comes in music from heaven, "By the fires of purgatory." In his search for these he approaches the neighbourhood of the cave, where he meets Polonia, who has embraced the hermit life, and she shows him the way. He descends; and after some days he returns purified, a changed man. In a long speech he relates what he has seen and himself experienced of the terrors of the under-world; but these fantastic torments in their visible show are to be only patterns for the sufferings of a life of prolonged penance. To such a life from that time forward he intends to devote himself in order to reach the heavenly goal, of which he has already had a distant glimpse when St. Patrick came to meet him accompanied by angels and saints singing the praises of God.

In the *Marvellous Magician*, Calderon has shown a far fuller comprehension both of the depths of the human heart and of Christianity.([25]) This play, a second precursor of the redeemed Faust, is founded on a legend which is in itself highly imaginative. Cyprian, a celebrated philosopher of Antioch, is first excited to discontent with Paganism by a sentence in Pliny,([26]) and in anxious uncertainty he seeks the true God. In order to divert him from the pathway to salvation, the demon appears in the form of a cavalier, and attempts to soothe his doubts of the old gods; but Cyprian points out how entirely their deeds are in opposition to the very idea of divinity. Being beaten in argument, the devil then resolves to seduce him by earthly passion, and he chooses Justina, the daughter of a martyred Christian matron, to be at once his instrument and his victim. Two young men, inflamed with unrequited love for the maiden, bespeak the aid of Cyprian, who promises to help them; but in his wooing for either lover he is himself seized with a mad passion for the lovely Christian. She has sworn to become the bride of Christ, and can only love him in death; so rejected and hopeless he rushes to a lonely spot on the sea-shore, where he cries amid the storm—

> " So beautiful she was—and I,
> Between my love and jealousy,
> Am so convulsed with hope and fear,
> Unworthy as it may appear,
> So bitter is the life I live,
> That hear me, Hell! I now would give
> To thy most detested spirit
> My soul, for ever to inherit;
> To suffer punishment and pine,
> So this woman may be mine.
> Hear'st thou, Hell'! Dost thou reject it?
> My soul is offered."
> —*G. H. Lewes.*

A voice is heard in the distance: "I accept it." The elements rage around, even as the tempest within his soul. A ship is shattered and a man escapes to the shore, who is the Spirit of Evil in another guise. In dim poetic imagery he relates the tale of his revolt from God, and states that he is now seeking a man—

> " Of a word,
> Which he spake and which I heard,
> Fulfilment to demand."

The speaker is, of course, found. The demon then boasts of his power over nature, and he shows before the eyes of the philosopher that he can move mountains, for a mountain travels across the stage. Cyprian conducts to his home this potent magician, who promises to instruct him in a magic art by which he shall be enabled to attract

to himself the object of his passion, but a bond is required—

> " Which, as an assurance, thy hand
>   Must write with thy blood."

Albeit shuddering at his own frenzy, Cyprian writes it at
once on a linen cloth with a dagger dipped in blood from
his arm—

> " I, the great Cyprian,
>   My immortal soul do resign
>   To him who will teach me an art,
>   Whereby to me I may bring
>   Justina, my mistress cold."

The period of instruction lasts a whole year, during
which Cyprian continues shut up in a cave. He then
comes forth in triumph, armed with the words which are
to enthral his ladylove. But the demon is well aware of
one fact—

> " My mighty power may not hold
>   Man's will in subjugating fold ;
>   And so I weave to do him harm
>   Such joys, of such enchanting charm,
>   That in their toils he fain would be,
>   And thus not forced but led is he."

He has already succeeded in destroying Justina's good
name, by entering her house in various disguises, and by
letting himself down from her balcony by a ladder of
ropes. She has become aware only of the results of his
machinations, and she is deeply distressed at a loss which
she finds so unmerited and so inexplicable. The Evil One
now calls his familiar spirits to float around her and
admonish her of the bright joys of mutual love. She
hears the voices, which in their gentle tenderness penetrate her heart and fill her at once with felicity and
anguish. She listens also to the song of the nightingale,
as she calls her spouse, and she is filled with a longing
to see Cyprian, of whose fate she only knows that, great

as he is, he has disappeared in apparent desperation on her account. She greatly fears that if she knew where to find him, she would go to him. But she resists the alluring fancy, not as in the legend with the sign of the cross, but by asserting the freedom of the will.(27) The demon then himself appears before her, as it were her thought in visible shape, the Will of the Wisp of her mad fancy—

> "Since thou hast the thought permitted,
>   Half the sin is almost done ;
> Wilt thou, since 'tis thus committed,
>   Linger ere the joy be won ?"
>
> —*G. H. Lewes.*

He endeavours to lead her to her lover, to happiness in his arms, indeed he has already seized her by the hand to draw her on, he will compel her to be happy. She, however, exclaims—

> "Could we call the will then free
> If to force it e'er should yield ?"

But she is actually in his toils, and he asks, "Who may aid thee ?" She answers—

> "My succour is from God alone !"

The demon is overcome and disappears. Then first she lifts the prayer—

> "My cause, O Lord, is truly Thine !
> Rise for Thine own defence and mine !"

The Evil Spirit, in order to fulfil his pledge to Cyprian, contrives that Justina shall apparently approach on the utterance of the charm, but in reality he has only had power to send an image of her. Her lover pursues the phantom, and tearing off its veil he sees a corpse, which, as it vanishes, addresses him—

> "Even thus, O Cyprian,
> Doth fade all earthly splendour !"

and Cyprian sees that in his eager strife for mortal happiness he has only encountered death. The demon now confesses that Justina is protected by One greater than himself; and he at length allows the admission to be wrested from him that this mightier One is Christ. In Him through all that He has done to save Justina from dishonour, Cyprian recognises the one true God, omniscient, omnipotent, and the one Chief Good. He supposes that he is loosed from his bond, as the demon has not fulfilled his share of the covenant; but the latter argues that he only promised to give him a charm to bring his ladylove. When Cyprian is about to appeal to the God of the Christians, he says—

> " Too late ! Too late !
> On Him thou canst not call ;
> Thou, who my bond-slave art,
> May not worship Him as thy Lord."

Cyprian endeavours to regain the contract at the point of the sword, but he has to deal with an adversary whom no sword can touch, and who now stands confessed—

> " That thy senses may perish
> In yet more utter despair,
> Learn that he whom thou hast obeyed
> Is Satan ! "

Thus in this play, as is ever actually the case, the human soul in dim terror yields itself to evil, and it is only by degrees that this evil is revealed in its full infernal shape and power. The crisis now approaches, Cyprian in despair turns his sword upon himself, and is about to become his own executioner, when he reflects—

> " He, who
> From thy grasp didst save Justina,
> Can He not also rescue me ? "

The All-powerful and All-merciful can loose that which is bound. Satan endeavours to check his appeal, and to kill him; and while they wrestle in terrible combat, Cyprian in direst need exclaims—

> " Great God of the Christians, hearken
> How in my anguish I cry unto Thee ! "

and Satan disappears. The philosopher obtains baptism from a hermit; and, eagerly desirous of martyrdom, that by his blood the blood-written contract may be effaced, he makes his confession of Christianity and is led to death. On his way to the place of execution he meets Justina, who had already been condemned for her Christianity. She soothes his terrors with regard to the remission of his pact with the Evil One.

CYPRIAN.

> " Alas ! for immense
> Is my guilt ! "

JUSTINA.

> " More immense
> Is His mercy ! "

CYPRIAN.

> " Will He
> Have mercy even on me ? "

JUSTINA.

> " He hath."

CYPRIAN.

> " How ? When to Satan himself
> I did pledge my soul as the price
> Of thy loveliness ? "

JUSTINA.

> " More
> Than the stars in heaven's circuit,
> Than the sparks in every flame,
> Than the sand in the wide seas,
> Than the birds throughout the air,
> Than the dust in every sunbeam,
> Are the sins He can forgive."

Now, according to her promise, she is ready to love him in death. Thus united, they go to offer their lives for the Everlasting Truth. The thunder rolls, the curtain at the back of the stage rises, the bodies of the headless martyrs are displayed, and Satan, during his exit on the back of a snake, proclaims their purity and his own defeat.[28]

In two of Calderon's most celebrated dramas, the two principal tendencies of Spanish Catholicism are depicted in sharp contrast. In the *Devotion to the Cross*,[29] the devout piety of the principal personages is from their very birth directed to an outward image; and while they place entire confidence in this, which is indeed a symbol of the divine love, they yet show an unbridled readiness in yielding to every passion; and after the most odious deeds, they continue to find a protective divinity in the sign of the cross. We encounter similar instances in many of the lives of brigandage recorded in Southern Europe: the man plunges ever deeper and deeper into crime, while the Church's visible signs affect him with undiminished, or perhaps even with increased, power. We see in this the influence of the residue of his better nature, which is thus partly sustained, and yet at the same time eluded. The hero of the drama, in consequence of his father's suspicion of his innocent mother, is born in a wilderness at the foot of an ancient cross with the mark of it on his breast. He becomes a captain of robbers, owing to a duel in which he has slain his own brother without being aware of the relationship; and he breaks into a convent in order to ravish the girl he has formerly loved. Yet in spite of his crimes he reverentially places a cross on the grave of the man he has slain, and kneels in worship before the holy sign whenever he meets with it. Even after death he obtains the fulfilment of his provident desire, and his dead body is reanimated in order that he may insure his eternal salvation by confession to the priest who has promised him absolution in his last hour. His ladylove, who is in fact as well as in her character and fortunes, without his suspecting it, his twin sister, escapes from the cloister to follow her lover, who has drawn back in religious terror on beholding the cross on her breast. She has secretly assassinated with her own hands many persons who have shown her kindness; and yet when her father in his vengeance is about to slay her, she clings to the cross at the foot of which she was born and is raised with it to heaven. The Christian lesson intended to be conveyed is the boundless mercy of God, but this is obtained entirely by the external sign, and there is only an occasional interposition of any inward or moral force. In its lofty poetic talent this drama is a consummate glorification of the element of Paganism, or rather of fetishism, which is to be found in the Roman Church; and it is unintentionally the parody of the thousand marvellous legends of the power of the Cross—

> " On Heaven's throne of such avail
> 'Tis held to adore the Cross."

The drama we have mentioned as contrasting with this, the *Steadfast Prince*, which illustrates the triumph of the spirit over every material circumstance, is founded on a historical fact.[30] We have in it a picture of the perfect Christian heroism with which the Infant of Portugal, who was taken captive by the Moors, endured a terrible captivity; and, more patient than Job, died as it were on the ash-heap, because he would not purchase his freedom by the sacrifice of a Christian town, a rampart against Islam. His is the heroism not of action, but of endurance; but it is to this very martyrdom of endurance that the Church from the early ages has lent the halo of sanctity. He is a sacrifice at once for the honour and to the greatness of Portugal; and while this union of religion and patriotism appeals to our modern sentiment, it may besides seem especially to become the son of a king. The composition of the play is also full of poetic beauty, especially when we allow for the unexciting uniformity of the theme, from

which an ambiguous relief is sought in the vague account
of the passion of the Moorish Princess, and for the re-
dundance of the style of the period, which is particularly
visible in this work of Calderon's youth. The plan is very
artistically arranged. In the opening scenes at the court .
of the Moorish King, the importance of Ceuta becomes
evident, the Christian town which the King has resolved
to win at any price. Then Prince Ferdinand, Grand Master
of the Order of Christ, as a conqueror in Africa, is given
opportunity fully to exhibit his chivalrous magnanimity.
Afterwards when the King of the Moors endeavours to
break the spirit of his captive in order that he may agree
to pay the price of his freedom, the other Christian slaves
try, as well as they are able, to show respect for the son
of their King. Enfeebled by the dark dungeon, by work
and starvation, covered with sores and almost too abject
in condition for a really artistic picture—forgetful of his
princely rank, he humbly beseeches his torturer to allow
him for one day longer the petty gift of life. Yet with
all this his Christian steadfastness never fails, and he dies
in the assurance—

> "God will protect my cause,
>   Since His I have striven to guard"

—and in the hope that his rescued bones shall one day
rest beneath the shelter of a Christian Church. He is
thus finally victorious over every earthly surrounding,
when the King of Portugal, his nephew, comes with his
army to deliver him by the sword. The glorified spirit of
the Prince, in the mantle of his Order and bearing a torch,
marches at the head of the Christian army during its
night attack. It gains the battle, and the beautiful
daughter of the Moorish King is captured among the spoil.
She is offered in exchange for Ferdinand, but he already
lies in his coffin. The King of Portugal, however, considers the dead body a sufficient ransom for the young
beauty; and the dream by which she has long been

terrified, that she should be the price of a corpse, is thus fulfilled. The King receives the Prince's remains with the greeting—

> " Thou sainted prince and martyr,
>   A noble and holy temple
>   I will consecrate, fitting monument
>   Of this thy sacred body."

The *Virgin of the Sanctuary*([31]) has its foundation in the same principle as the *Adoration of the Cross*, but it is superior in moral tone. It was composed in celebration of a miraculous image in the Cathedral of Toledo, and was designed for representation in that city, a sacred city of Spain. It is derived entirely from local tradition and popular legends, and from Spanish memorials of the sufferings of the Moorish conquest, and of the final victory of Christendom. When on the capitulation of Toledo, its sacred treasures were preserved by being taken to the Asturian mountains, the ancient image appeared to be unwilling to forsake the people in their need. The bishop, in the act of carrying it off, is impelled by an irresistible force to replace it on the altar. When the infidels enter the town, some pious Spaniards drop it into a deep well. After Spain has once more become a Christian country, and only a dim legend of the sacred image lingers, it reveals itself by its miraculous brightness, and before the eyes of the searchers rises by its own power from the depths, and is borne in triumph into the cathedral. The ceremony closes with the chant of the choir, *Salve Regina!* The story extends over several centuries, for the Spanish drama was as little incommoded as the old mystery by a century or two more or less. Beside these plays Voltaire's scoff sinks into insignificance, when he derides a Chinese tragedy, in the first act of which a peasant is born who dies in the fifth. But the image of the Virgin is here itself the unity around which each religious and patriotic sentiment gather. As in the *Adoration of the Cross*,

H

we have certainly only the external sign; but it is one which is entirely in keeping with the popular faith on which this drama was based; and in it a believing people beheld an illustration of the compassionate care of the Virgin, which itself has its root in the gracious manifestation of her Divine Son.

In the *Sybil of the Orient*,([32]) the Queen of Sheba, who adores the tree of mingled palm, cypress, and cedar, which should one day form the tree of the cross,([33]) typifies the earnest anticipation of the nations of ancient heathendom; while in prophetic verse the building of Solomon's is made to represent the formation of the Christian Church.

The aurora which is displayed above the Temple of the Sun in Peru,([34]) celebrates the rise of the Sun of Christianity in the New World. The existing worship of the Sun, even in its bloody savagery, is made to appear as a dim presentiment of the Sun of Righteousness; and the discovery of America is associated with its original and noblest intention—the opening of a new world for the reception of the cross of salvation. The Catholic worship of the Virgin is in this play also symbolised by a miraculous image of the Madonna. The converted Peruvian hero, who during a night when the little Christian army was surrounded by a conflagration, has with it been a witness of the protective manifestation of the Holy Mother, has ever since been under the influence of an eager desire to give outward shape to the form which has been so deeply impressed upon his spirit. But some of the Christians oppose his wish, and his unskilful hand cannot accomplish it. At last he carries his rude picture, veiled, into the desolate church, and in earnest prayer he appeals to the original. After he has gone, two angels descend from heaven with paintbrush and palette, and finish the picture with ethereal tints, singing the while sweet childlike hymns. When the service has commenced, the veil is withdrawn, and the Virgin Mother and the infant Christ are beheld in unexpected loveliness; while chants of praise rise from the assembled people. One might fancy this an allegory of the creation of a Madonna of Raphael.

In the *Great Prince of Fez* ([35]) Islam is recognised as a pathway to Christianity. The victorious Moorish Prince, in his nightly study of the Koran in his tent, muses deeply on the passage which relates how Mary and her Child are alone exempt from original sin, the common curse of mankind.([36]) His devout longing, and a vow which he has made for the deliverance of his noble-minded wife and his child, cause him to undertake a pilgrimage to Mecca. Being taken prisoner at sea by Knights of Malta, in his indulgent captivity among the Christians he comes across a Life of Loyola; and when he reaches the passage where the holy Ignatius defends the virginity of Mary against a follower of Islam, he thinks of the words of the Koran. That which he has read takes shape as a vision; he sees the disputants and hears them speak. From that time he is a Christian; and in order to remain one, he leaves wife and child and kingdom to fare as they may. Muley Mohammed is now Don Balthasar Loyola, and he desires to preach the Gospel as a comrade of the Company of Jesus. When he vows the pilgrimage to Mecca his evil angel triumphs, but his good angel replies, " In every religion true piety can become a stepping-stone to salvation." A wicked Christian and a wicked Mohammedan join in a plan of assassination. The poet's moral is conveyed through his characters: it is as difficult for a bad Christian to become a good one, as for a Moor to become a Christian; and the proverb holds good: A devout Mohammedan will make a pious Christian.

But for the Christianity which has seceded from the Church, Calderon's genius has no greeting save that of bitter enmity. The great Spanish poets generally pay but little heed to the heresy of the Reformation; Spain had in their day nothing to fear from that quarter, having already burnt her own Protestant children.

Lope de Vega's *Corona Tragica* merely celebrates in fiery hatred of all Protestantism the downfall of the attractive Queen whose death on the scaffold, though not caused by Protestantism, closely followed in its wake. Pope Urban VII., a patron of modern poetry, to whom the poet dedicated his *Tragic Crown*, rewarded him with the diploma of doctor and the cross of the Maltese Order.

Calderon attacked the Reformation exactly where its supernatural origin was most open to question, and its victory most humiliating to Spain. His drama of the *Schism of England* ([37]) corresponds on one point with Shakespeare's *Henry the Eighth*. The intention of the English poet was to celebrate the birth of Queen Elizabeth, Calderon's to throw contempt on it; and history is evidently more favourable to the injustice of the Spaniard than to the delicate flattery of the Englishman.([38]) The one point on which they correspond is in their beautiful and also historically just delineation of the unhappy Queen Catherine; but Calderon calumniates with the hatred of fanaticism the not less unhappy mother of England's greatest Queen. ([39]) The opening of the play is significant. Henry sits asleep in his cabinet, and before him lies a paper at which he has been working, part of his book against Luther, the "Assertion of the Seven Sacraments," from which he received from the Pope for himself and for his successors the title of *Defensor Fidei*. He dreams, and writes and speaks in his dream. Close to him stands the visionary form of Anne Boleyn whom he has never seen, and with her left hand she effaces what he has written with his right. Cardinal Wolsey, the King's potent favourite, enters bringing a letter from the Pope and a new pamphlet of Luther's. The King takes both, with the intention of laying the Holy Father's letter reverently on his forehead, and of casting the heretic composition beneath his feet; but in the excitement produced by the recollection of the vision, he exchanges the papers.

Anne Boleyn enters the service of Queen Catherine with a great appearance of humility, but with haughty heart detesting her servitude. She has an amorous conversation with the French Ambassador, whose willing lady-love she already is. When the King sees her among his wife's attendants, he at once recognises the image of his dream. Her glances ensnare him more completely; she dances for his amusement and falls, as if by accident, at his feet. The Cardinal is exasperated at the Emperor's having barred his advance to the Papal throne, and he determines to avenge himself on the Queen, the aunt of the Emperor, who has detected his arrogant ambition beneath his garb of humility. He applies to her a prediction that a woman shall bring him disaster. With joy he reads the hearts both of the King and Anne : finding in the former intoxicating passion; in Anne's, sinful ambition. He quickly comes to an understanding with her, and she swears to consider his interest in every way if he will aid her advance to the throne ; and she imprecates on herself death from the hand of the executioner, if she should ever forget to be grateful. The King wooes her love, but she repulses him with the semblance of the warmest, though most carefully-repressed, passion. The Cardinal now says, "Thy marriage with Catherine is void, she was once thy brother's wife." The King's good sense opposes this veto, but his unbridled passion leads him to agree to it. In a solemn session of the Parliament he pronounces the nullity of his long union with Catherine —if any one does not agree with the premises on which this conclusion is based, his head shall immediately be cut off. The Queen appeals to her husband solely in words of resignation, and in submissive prayers that he will not imperil his soul. He turns from her, the Cardinal treats her with contempt, and Anne, whose mediation the unfortunate Queen desires, draws back with ill-concealed delight. In the third act Henry and Anne are married. As the Pope would not confirm the dissolution of his first marriage, the King has separated from the Catholic Church, and has enriched himself with the spoil of the monasteries and the property of the Church. He shows his beloved wife a letter of empty consolation to the divorced Catherine, but Anne induces him to let her read it over, and strews it with poison before he affixes the seal. Wolsey requests her aid in his efforts to obtain the Chancellorship, but she has already promised the post to her father. In his rage the Cardinal threatens to hurl her back into the nothingness from which he raised her; but she complains to the King of the audacious pride of the priest, and by flattering speeches coaxes him to avenge her. He banishes Wolsey with ignominy from the court, and confiscates all his wealth. A woman has thus brought him disaster. The rightful Queen, in quiet sadness, is walking in the meadow of her little country house when the Cardinal comes, hungry and a fugitive, and beseeches an alms. Catherine has drawn her veil in order not to shame him, and she gives him her last jewels. Servants of the King approach, and he thinking they have come to seize him, flees and falls over the side of a rock. The servants bring the poisoned letter, which Catherine receives with respect, as sent by her master and lord.

The French Ambassador has now returned to London, and has met again his former love as Queen. He is determined to have an interview with her, and to restore the pledge of her faithless affection. She has contrived the absence of all her ladies, and she swears that she still loves him alone, and that she has never cared for Henry, but only for his crown. The King, whose evil conscience renders him suspicious, has been listening, and he causes her to be arrested by her own father and issues the order for her execution. He now wishes to take back his divorced wife; but Mary, his daughter and hers, enters in mourning, and announces that her mother, in pious esignation, has fallen asleep in God. The King bows his head in conscious guilt. He then causes Mary to be proclaimed his heiress, and places her on the throne before the assembled Parliament, while at her feet lies the corpse of Anne Boleyn. As a true daughter of the sole Church of salvation, Mary asserts her inability to concur in the new religious liberty and the plunder of the property of the Church. The King advises her to postpone her protest to a more favourable season. The . people swear allegiance, and a captain closes the play with the words—

> " And here endeth now the drama
> Of the learned bungler Henry,
> And the death of Anna Boleyn."

—a conclusion which is certainly rather less effective than that of Shakespeare's drama, which at the baptism of Anne Boleyn's child, Cranmer closes with a prophecy of that child's future greatness. ,

On the universal Catholic and Christian principles of the weakness of humanity and the mercy of God, Calderon has erected with care two other religious ideas. While fully recognising the forces of temptation within us and without, he asserts the victorious force of the moral will, if honestly exercised. Thus in the *Marvellous Magician* we have Justina's victory over the Spirit of Evil ; and in *Life is a Dream* we find—

> " For the fates the most unfriendly,
> The passions hardest to subdue,
> The stars whose sheen is balefullest,
> Have only might to guide the will,
> And may not force it."

The poet's second ruling idea is the inexhaustible capacity of pardon reserved in the mercy of God for every truly penitent heart. He seems, as it were, to enlarge on the comforting words in which St. John illustrates the fulness of the divine love—" If our heart condemn us, God is greater than our heart." We have seen the working of

this thought also in the *Marvellous Magician ;* and in the
Devotion to the Cross we read—

> " I hold
> Great confidence in God's compassion.
> The many stars in heaven that shine,
> The clustering sand-grains heaped in seas,
> The dust in spreading sunbeams floating,
> Not all united reach the number,
> Nay are not nigh to the vast mass,
> Of sins which God can pardon."

But amidst all the intensity of religious feeling (or in
some cases of theological sentiment) which is visible in
these dramas, we find also scattered jests and comic scenes
in which the principal part is played by the *Gracioso*, a
sort of rather more sharp-witted cousin of the German
Hanswurst and of the English clown, and by the wife of
the Gracioso ; or else by the common people, to whom as a
rule a merely secondary *rôle* is assigned in the main action
of the Spanish drama.   These scenes the reader, according
to his individual disposition and inclination, may regard
as an interruption to the religious solemnity of the piece ;
or by the very absurdity of the contrast, as a foil to it : but
no one can suspect the poet himself of any definite purpose, or any covert irony.   The comic element is merely
an inheritance from the mystery, and a concession to the
feeling of the mass of the people, who were determined to
have their fun out of the festival.([40])   As the aim was but
to please these, the wit of the jests was often poor enough.

The *Devotion to the Cross* is, as it were, introduced by
the jump of a donkey, which thereby falls into a ditch.
The peasant and his wife having in vain tried to drag him
out by the ears and tail, the wife goes to fetch assistance,
exclaiming, " Oh, you darling donkey ! " — while the
peasant harangues his beast—

> " Oh, dear donkey, my light and blessing !
> In the village highly honoured
> Wast thou amongst donkeys ;

For thou hast ever discreetly
Avoided treading in evil ways
With people of low condition.
Thy fall was truly from no love
Of gadding—for thou would'st rather
Stand in thy stall in all comfort
Than out of it wander forth.
In sooth I could take my oath,
No other donkey has seen thee stand
Lovingly at the open window,
Protesting with melodious vow.
Certes 'twas no naughty tongue
Which brought thee to this trouble ;
For 'twas not thine to raise thy voice,
In harsh rudeness and unchecked.
I have seen oft at thy feeding time
Thou didst remember thy poor brothers,
And gave them that thou needed'st not,
Pitying the poor beasts."

This same peasant, in order to secure himself from the
hero of the play, of whose veneration for the cross he is
aware, has bound all the wood he is fetching from the
forest in regular crosses, of which he places the largest in
front of him, and goes on his way a moving cross. In
the *Steadfast Prince*, Brito, a soldier of the Christian army,
in his cowardice plays the common trick, and escapes
death in the battle by pretending to be dead. But when
he is imprisoned with the Prince, he is his faithful attendant, and it is he who advises Ferdinand to beg an alms
from the Moors to satisfy his hunger. He is to enlist
their sympathy by beseeching it—

"For the sake of the holy great toe
Of the Prophet Mahomet."

Occasionally, certainly, the poet has infused a deeper
meaning into these comic scenes and figures. They then
represent commonplace reality as opposed to the ideal ; and
the judgment of the homely common sense which takes
care of its own interests, in contrast to the enthusiasm
which sacrifices itself for an abstract idea—the jest is the

reflex of the earnestness, the Gracioso the caricature of the hero—the frightened soldier is made the ludicrous reverse of the fearless self-sacrifice of the Prince, and even the peasant with his cross becomes a quaint foil to the devotion to the Cross.

In the *Marvellous Magician,* a cold dropping shower of ridicule falls almost too profusely amid the most pathetic scenes in the prosaic comments of the two servants of Cyprian, and of Livia, the servant of Justina; and Livia through an agreement, which she most conscientiously observes, to love each of the servants in turn during his day, is made the ironical counter-picture of the purity of her mistress.   One of the servants, in order to discover whether she does not often trick him on his day, is ready also to devote himself to the devil.   He pulls out a grimy pockethandkerchief: " One who often weeps cannot carry a cleaner one "—and undertakes to strike himself on the nose, in order to write on the cloth like his master—

> " Why should it not serve just as well,
> Whether from nose or arm it fell ? "

Finally, when Cyprian and Justina are being led to execution, the other servant exclaims—

> " With what content they pass
> To death ! "

> LIVIA.
>
> " Much more contentedly, I think,
> We three remain alive."

And indeed, amidst all the emotion and sympathy of the audience, by far the larger number would be struck by this expression of the actual fact of their lurking consciousness.

On the other hand, in many of Calderon's numerous secular dramas, the attentive listener becomes aware of a religious keynote.   Thus in the well-known drama of *Life is a Dream,*[41] we have not only a picture of the dreamy mist in which the past seems often to lie behind us, and with which even the present is sometimes clothed ; but a most easily interpreted allegory of the evanescence of all human life, with the lofty moral lesson of this evanescence. All which is finite is as it were set aside, to display the Eternal as the sole Reality. Thus the sentiment merely, and not the sublime moral of the piece, is expressed in the closing sentence, which in some bitter hour has probably been present to each of us, either on the lips or in the heart only ([42])—

> " I have learnt
> That human joy is transient as a dream."
>   —*G. H. Lewes.*

LECTURE IV.

OCCASIONAL TRACES OF THE RELIGIOUS DRAMA IN THE FRENCH CLASSICAL TRAGEDY.

DURING the century of the Renaissance the French Drama passed almost without a stepping-stone from the Mystery to the Classical Tragedy. It is true that Desmazures, in his triple drama of *David*, the combatant, the conqueror, and the fugitive, illustrated, particularly in the chorus, some Calvinistic doctrines; and also that during the whole of the sixteenth century, *Tragédies saintes*, on Old Testament subjects, continued to be exhibited—as, for instance, Jean de la Taille's *Madness of Saul*, and Garnier's *Jewesses*.[1] But these plays followed antique models, even if their tone was that of Seneca rather than of the Greek tragedians. And in the following century when Cardinal Richelieu swayed Church, State, and Theatre, that form of the drama became supreme, which, in complete divorce both from the Church and from Christianity, was subjected to the strict laws of the supposed Aristotelian unities of place and time. In the pursuit of an artistic ideal this new drama caused the conflict of the passions, on which the respective destinies of the actors were rightly made to depend, to be expressed by them in words, while the action itself was supposed to take place almost entirely behind the scene. The comic element was entirely eliminated.

Corneille first naturalised this imitation of the antique tragedy by his gift of elevated sentiment and by his

French rhetoric. And as he had already made a happy incursion into the region of Spanish romance, with its subtle scholastic treatment of the strife between passion and the dictates of honour,(²) he in like manner ventured, in the midst of his various historical and antique subjects, to bring on the stage, in his *Polyeucte,*(³) the heroic period of Christian martyrdom. He does not seem to have been influenced by any reminiscences of the national *Mystère,* which Boileau was the first to refer to with conscious superiority,(⁴) but he derived encouragement from his acquaintance with a few other Christian-classic dramas of his own time.(⁵) His model continued to be the antique, and he seems to have bestowed more anxious care on the maintenance of the French pseudo-classic unities of time and place, than on the preservation of any unity of action which should be in accordance with nature.

St. Polyeuctus appears to have been first introduced to the French nation on the stage. According to the legend from which Corneille derived his drama,(⁶) Polyeuctus the Armenian, being instructed by a friend in the Christian religion, suddenly receives the gift of the Holy Spirit, and tearing to pieces the Edict of Persecution of the Emperor Decius, he casts down the images of the gods. His father-in-law Felix, who has been sent to Armenia to enforce the edict, seeks by means of his daughter Paulina to attract him back to his old deities; but Polyeuctus regards her tears as temptations of the Evil One, and dying a martyr, receives the Baptism of Blood.

Corneille, however, did not venture to develop this fertile theme entirely on its own basis, but added to it a more mundane complication—a woman divided in sentiment between her newly-married husband and her lost and successfully resisted lover. Paulina has obediently repulsed Severus, whose rank did not satisfy her father, and who has sought and found death in a battle with the Persians in which by his heroism he has saved the Emperor Decius. Paulina's father, the Roman Governor of

Armenia, gives her in marriage to Polyeuctus, a scion of the royal house of Armenia; and she is induced by her sense of duty to yield to the wooing of her bridegroom the love that she would willingly have bestowed on another—

"Je donnai par devoir à son affection
Tout ce que l'autre avait par inclination."

The action commences with her intense anxiety about his fate in consequence of a dream she has had. In it she has beheld her former lover, not as a phantom from the tomb, but in fierce anger, and resplendent on a triumphal car, and he has assured her that she shall that very day weep the husband she has preferred to him. In instantaneous fulfilment of the threat, she has seen a crowd of Christians fling Polyeuctus at the feet of his rival, and her own father draw his dagger against him. Even in her dream she became so blinded by terror, that she could only perceive her husband's streaming blood, and knew not who had been his slayer. All had united to cause his death.

The legend too relates a dream, which is the means of converting Polyeuctus. Christ appears to him, and instead of his sullied clothing, bestows on him a white and shining robe; and a winged steed that he may be enabled to follow Him. The poet, who was not bold enough to attempt to picture the mysterious process by which the Holy Spirit obtains a hold on the human heart, has replaced this dream by that of Paulina, which although in no way necessary to the plot yet, like Chriemhild's dream,([7]) fills us from the first with a foreboding of the final catastrophe. It stands at the opening of the play as a prophetic sentence, which emanating from the unfathomable recesses of the spirit, is at once misinterpreted by the intellect; for Paulina fears that the Christians, against whom she shares all the customary Roman prejudices, menace the life of her husband, in revenge for her father's persecution of them.

The accomplishment of the dream commences with the intelligence that Severus, who has been wonderfully saved from amid the dead, and by the favour of the Emperor raised to the highest honours, is now approaching the Armenian town in order to offer there a great sacrifice to the gods in acknowledgment of new victories. He comes to share his happiness with his loved Paulina, whom he supposes still free and faithful. All the feelings which have been subdued and entombed in her heart, revive at this news; but Felix, apprehensive of the anger of the powerful favourite, insists that she shall see him and appease him. An agitated scene ensues, which commences with Paulina's assertion to Severus of her love for her husband, but she is unable to withhold the confession of her earlier sentiment; and it ends with a mutual renunciation.

The interpolated domestic drama may here be said to have come to an end. Corneille has retained from the legend one effective stroke: Polyeuctus makes his confession as a Christian while disturbing the great sacrificial ceremony by his bold speech and action. Another more spiritual feature the poet has relinquished—the elevation above mere ceremonial, nay above the very Sacrament of Salvation itself; for Polyeuctus, before he is actually baptized, becomes a martyr, receiving thus the Baptism of Blood.[8] In the tragedy, on the contrary, his baptism is rather thrown into especial relief, for in order to receive it he quits Paulina, while she, wholly unsuspicious of his design, endeavours to prevent his departure.

Such arbitrary self-assertion on the part of Christians, combined with the mutilation of heathen sanctuaries, certainly occurred during the heroic age of the Church, though discountenanced both by her more enlightened teachers and by her laws. But Polyeuctus's action is made to bear the semblance of mere fanaticism, and hardly appeals to any healthy human sympathy. Instead of with quiet courage regarding his confession as a solemn duty and necessity, he sets himself to disturb the old form of worship, which but yesterday was his own; and then seeks death from the civil arm, without for a moment reflecting on the bonds of affection by which he is encircled. Paulina, though horrorstruck at his secession to Christianity, yet gives up all to save him, led by her duteous love, which would still continue to guide her even though to her too he had proved faithless—

> " Je l'aimai par devoir, ce devoir dure encore.
>   Je l'aimerai encor quand il m'aurait trahie."

He coldly repulses her; his one longing is for the glory of the other world; he will not have her even follow him in death, unless she shall first renounce her errors—

PAULINE.

> " Je te suivrai partout, et mourrai si tu meurs."

POLYEUCTE.

> " Ne suivez point mes pas, ou quittez vos erreurs."

Yielding to Paulina's persuasions, Severus exerts all his influence over the prefect to save his at once favoured and unfortunate rival, even though he should remain a Christian. Felix cannot conceal his satisfaction that his now burdensome son-in-law should thus rush upon destruction, and afford him the opportunity of at once gratifying and appeasing the man who has become the Emperor's favourite. Influenced by his daughter, he too, however seeks to deliver Polyeuctus, but on the condition that he should deny his Christian belief, if but for a short time while Severus is present. In his short-sighted prudence, he imagines that Severus is only endeavouring to induce him to spare a Christian criminal, in order that he may ruin him by denouncing him to the Emperor. So Polyeuctus goes to execution, and Paulina sees him die. She returns from the place of execution a Christian; God Himself has enlightened her through the death of her husband; her cruel father may now finish his work and slay a second victim. But Felix, who has just received the maledictions of Severus for his deluded, ambitious cunning, at once is ready to become a Christian also, and to die with his daughter.

It is true that such sudden conversions actually took place, so quickly grew the harvest from the blood of the martyrs. In Paulina's lofty temperament, in spite of the numerous attractions which held her to life and to the fulfilment of her brightest hopes,—perhaps even in consequence of these attractions,—such a change is not inconceivable: she too is, as it were, baptized with the blood of Polyeuctus. But the repetition of a sort of diluted miracle in the conversion of her father, with his low order of mind, is not supernatural, it is unnatural, and we remain cold to any impression from it. Even if we admit that such marvels really occurred, they can be of no service to the true poet. Corneille has to a certain extent retained his poetic judgment; with refined self-control, he has not continued to heap sacrifice upon sacrifice. Severus, who is no stranger to the virtues of the Christians, though he does not proclaim liberty of belief as his gospel, which would have been as little appreciated in France under Richelieu as under Louis XIV., yet asserts the injustice and futility of persecution: he will risk the Emperor's favour to put an end to these horrors. A prospect of freedom is thus unfolded such as really opened before Christianity after more than half a century of human sacrifices; and the action closes with the reverent resolve to bury the body of the martyr with fitting solemnity.

The Hôtel Rambouillet, in which the *beaux esprits* of the day sat in judgment on their peers, condemned this tragedy, as did also Richelieu himself, who desired to be supreme in art as in other matters. It found acceptance, nevertheless, with the French nation, who were affected partly by the heroism which Corneille successfully portrayed even in the unusual form of a Christian martyr,

I

but still more by the noble fidelity of Paulina, in spite of her divided heart. People remarked at the same time that it would not be particularly desirable to have either a wife or a ladylove who should exactly resemble her.

In the German arrangement of *Polyeuctus*, composed by Cormarten, and acted in Leipsic in 1669 by a company of students,([9]) the influence, both of the modern opera and the old mystery, combined to produce a rougher and more popular version. Scenes which Corneille has merely related are brought on the stage, and even Paulina's dream receives the visible form which Goethe gives to the dream of Egmont. The idols are destroyed, and the Christians impaled, crucified, and burnt in the sight of the audience. Polyeuctus's spirit, headless like St. Dionysius, effects the conversion of Felix, and heaven and hell open their gates.([10])

Racine in his *Phèdre* imitated the form and matter of the Greek tragedy with as great success as was perhaps attainable by a Frenchman, whose Greek heroine was to be addressed as *Madame*, and whose heroes wore powder, court-suits, and rapiers. But after the publication of this his latest secular piece, the recollection of his pious childhood spent under the care of the evangelical hermits of Port Royal, caused him to break with the drama as a fleshly, sinful occupation, and to renounce all the pursuits and fame of his maturity; ([11]) till Madame de Maintenon, who together with her royal husband had become devout after a self-invented fashion, induced him a few years later to write a Biblical drama for the use of her great institution for the education of young girls, Saint-Cyr. This was the origin of his *Esther*, which was composed entirely on the basis of the Scriptural Book of Esther. According to the poet, God Himself in His Word had prepared the scenes of this drama, which was destined to exhibit devotion to God and abstraction from the world even in the midst of the world.

The prologue is repeated by Piety, and its secondary object is to eulogise a decided lover of frivolous plays,

Louis XIV., on account of the political attitude he had at that period adopted. It commends him as one who, steadfastly grounded in faith alone, had undertaken the defence of the things of God against the perfidious selfishness and blind envy which had allied itself with baleful heresy. To imitate the Greek chorus, the hymns to the Greek gods and the laudation of antique virtue are replaced by the praises of God in the poetic phraseology of the Old Testament, and by encomiums on purity and humility. The history on which the drama is founded is but doubtfully authentic and canonical. The dramatic composition, which is in harmonious verse and only lightly marked with any features of Jewish nationality, is innocent and colourless enough to be suitable for young girls educated in a convent. The parts were gracefully performed by gentle girls, and the choruses were very sweetly sung; but the great temporary success of the piece was procured by two extraneous causes: it was considered a great privilege to be invited by Madame de Maintenon to the representations at Saint-Cyr; and the courtiers, perfectly astonished to find that anything religious could be interesting, were determined to recognise Louis XIV. in Ahasuerus, the dismissed Madame de Montespan in the proud Vashti, Madame de Maintenon in Esther, and in Haman the Minister of War, Louvois, whom many would by no means reluctantly have seen elevated on a gallows fifty cubits high.([12])

Incited by the success of *Esther*, Racine two years later completed, for the same institution of young girls, a second Old Testament drama, *Athalie*. Even in the original history, which is found in the Second Books of the Kings and of the Chronicles, this subject suggests a tragedy. Athaliah, the daughter of King Ahab of Israel and the terrible Jezebel who was thrown down from her palace window and devoured by dogs, was married to the King of Judah, and after his death and the death of her son, she destroyed all the children of the latter, her own grandchildren. She then rules without rival over the kingdom of Judah; and following the example of her mother, she erects a temple of Baal side by side with the worship of Jehovah. The young child Joash has been saved from the massacre of the seed of the house of David, and he is secretly brought up by the High Priest in the Temple of Jerusalem. After six years the priests conspire with some of the leaders of the army, the child Joash is anointed in the Temple and presented to the people as their king, and in the popular outbreak which follows Athaliah is overcome and slain.

Racine has diffused over his entire theme the consecration at once of religion and genius. The sense of the Old Testament narrative is expressed in the contrast between the idol-worship of Baal under a bloodstained Queen, full of bitter hatred to the house of David into which she has married, and the worship of the One Almighty God, which is united with allegiance to an innocent child, king by a hereditary divine right. The royal child being regarded as the last scion of the house of David, on whose head rests the sublimest of all prophecies, stands as secure under God's protection as was once the son of Abraham beneath the uplifted sacrificial knife; and a vista is opened for beholding Him who should one day be born to the house of David for a blessing unto all the nations of the earth. The High Priest, in accordance with the Jewish belief that at certain moments it was not he who spoke but God who spoke through him, describes what he sees amid the darkness of the ages, the wondrous blossom from the Root of Jesse, the destruction of the Holy City, and a new and more beautiful Jerusalem. The chorus of young Levite maidens, in solos alternating with full chant, during the intervals of the acts, gives expression in elevated psalmodic verse to the religious sentiment and reflections of the piece. Athaliah, already shaken and vexed in her strife with the One God by the vision of her mother, has also dreamt of a child who draws a dagger against her, and she recognises this child in the boy who is serving at the altar.   The royal child, ignorant as yet of his birth, answers her crafty questions so frankly and innocently that she finds herself unexpectedly affected by a sentiment in which one may perhaps trace the unconscious feeling of the grandparent.   This feeling causes her to defer the sacrifice of the child of her dream ; until at length, when her suspicions are roused as to the designs of the priests, she demands his surrender, and thus hurries on the catastrophe by which she perishes.

As the poet has made the boy of tender years a half-grown lad, his *rôle* would have formed a particularly graceful one for a young maiden ; but *Athalie* was never performed at Saint-Cyr.   People said Madame de Maintenon had begun to be doubtful of the good effect on young girls of a theatrical exhibition.   But the real reason lay far deeper, in the constitution of the tragedy itself, and in its very excellences.   The scene is certainly laid in the Temple of Mount Zion, the composition is inspired by religious devotion, and the Jewish colouring is raised to a purely human and Christian tone, as when the Levite maidens sing—

> " Il nous donne ses lois, il se donne lui-même :
>   Pour tant de biens, il commande qu'on l'aime."

But with all this the story, like many another in the Old Testament, is a political history, the tale of a revolution : an absolute Queen is slain in a popular riot by the priestly body in the name of their God.   In much more recent years a Mecklenburg theologian, perhaps in other respects of a slightly fanatic turn, managed to get himself into his first difficulties by deducing from this history the question whether it was not permitted by the Word of God to conspire against the ruling power, in order to reinstate the legitimate dynasty (in this case the Bourbons).   The drama is also not deficient in speeches expressive of that spirit of independence, which is sustained by a firm religious conviction in the presence of the greatest earthly power, not in priests only but also in the meanest of the populace. For instance, the High Priest replies—

"Je crains Dieu—et n'ai point d'autre crainte."

Another political bearing in this drama might have tended to recommend it to Catholic France, which at that time regarded King James II. as having lost the throne of Great Britain for the sake of a mass. The usurper Queen, Athaliah, was interpreted to represent Mary the daughter of James who, with her husband William III., had ascended the throne of her father; while the boy King, Joash, signified her brother the Prince of Wales, who, robbed of his inheritance, was to be restored by the might of Catholicism, or at any rate by the might of Heaven. The subsequent history did not accord with this interpretation; if the poet himself had it in view, we do not know.

But in any case *Athalie* was not the kind of drama suitable for exhibition by white-robed girls before an absolute king.

It was also received with indifference by the nation generally. The fashionable circles were of opinion that a Scriptural play written for young girls could not fail to be dull. Racine was mortified; and it was not until after his death, which took place in 1699, perhaps hurried by vexations other than the denial of a royal glance, that France at length recognised in *Athalie* the greatest work of her greatest tragedian.

But it was reserved for a comedian to expose to everlasting scorn the abuse of religion for self-interested ends. In 1664, before Louis XIV. had affected a pious character and begun to persecute piety, the performance of the *Tartuffe* was rendered possible in Versailles, because in the struggle between the two Catholic parties, the Jesuits and the Jansenists, each party readily set itself to recognise in the arch-hypocrite the traits of the other side. Molière could not indeed dare to clothe his hero in the cowl of a priest; but a priest declared the author of the *Tartuffe*, even as it stood, to be deserving of the stake. In those days, however, as in all others in which valuable earthly rewards await an outward show of pious zeal, originals of Tartuffe were not wanting outside the clerical body. When the President of the Parliament of Paris suddenly interdicted the advertised performance, Molière was able to take a cutting revenge by announcing to the assembled audience, " Messieurs, nous allions vous donner le *Tartuffe*, mais Monsieur le prèmier Président ne veut pas qu'on le joue."

Voltaire, during the first decade of his brilliant career, seems rather to have hated the Church, in whose principles he had been educated by the Jesuits, than Christianity itself ; indeed to this latter, which he never understood, he bore at no time a consistent hatred. His *Zaire*, written in 1732, was even ranked with *Polyeucte*, and in Paris it went by the name of the Christian Tragedy. Its claims to this title are dubious. He himself states in the introduction that since the world has complained that his plays lack the motive power of love, he has written *Zaire*, a drama full of the tenderest affection. He also affirms that he completed it in twenty-two days, and the readiness of the style, together with the absence of depth and the abounding improbabilities, induce us readily to believe this. Christianity is here only of importance in so far as the difference of religion interposes the most effectual obstacle to the union of the lovers. For, according to the observant poet, "A man is fairly sure of success when he appeals to the passions of men rather than to their reason. A love story is demanded, even by the best of Christians; and I am quite persuaded that the great Corneille judged rightly when he was not satisfied with merely causing his neophytes to break the statues of Jupiter. The human race is now so degenerate that perhaps even the noble spirit of Polyeuctus would have attracted little sympathy, and the Christian verses which he declaims would have been received with disapprobation, if it had not been for the affection of his wife for the Pagan whom she prefers, and who deserves her love far better than her pious husband." The scene of the drama is the same which Lessing afterwards selected for *Nathan*, Jerusalem during the time of the Crusades. Zaire has been from her infancy brought up as a slave in the harem of the Sultan, who now passionately loves her; and his love being fully reciprocated, he is on the point of marrying the maiden and making her his only wife. She becomes aware that she is a Christian by birth, a child of Lusignan and of the royal race of Jerusalem, but that immediately before baptism she had been captured by the Saracens. Her aged father, who has been delivered from a long captivity by her intercession while she was yet unconscious of the relationship, together with her knightly brother, importune her to return to the religion of her fathers in exactly the same words which might have been used by a zealous missionary in the Holy City, where our Lord met death for our sakes, and where the crusaders were seeking to avenge Him; where also it had now become her duty to deliver Him, as it were, and to restore the Holy City to Him—

"Délivrer ton Dieu même et lui rendre ces murs."

But she has already made use of the strongest argument which is suggested by experience against the idea of a single creed in which salvation is to be found—

"Les soins qu'on prend de notre enfance
Forment nos sentiments, nos mœurs, notre croyance.
J'eusse été près du Gange esclave des faux dieux,
Chrétienne dans Paris, musulmane en ces lieux.
L'instruction fait tout ; et la main de nos pères
Grave en nos faibles cœurs ces premiers caractères."

She nevertheless allows herself to be persuaded into a promise to receive secret baptism, and she is slain by her adored lover the Sultan, who misinterprets her secret intercourse with the Christians and believes her brother to be his rival.

In this so-called Christian tragedy, which depicts neither the beautiful sincerity of love nor yet faith in its solemn earnestness, Christianity appears simply as an obstructive force; not even as the rock on which love is shipwrecked, for it is shipwrecked through an accident, by a mistake.

On the other hand, we have the *Alzire*, published in 1736, which has been called "nothing less than a dramatic treatise against the Catholic Church!"(13) The historical background of the story is the rule of the Spaniards in Peru, immediately after the conquest. Of their greed and cruelty, the speeches of the subject race present a far from exaggerated description. No one will anticipate from Voltaire any portraiture of an actual nationality, and his Peruvians are merely Frenchmen, oppressed and worshipping other gods. Montezuma, the only remaining native King, has proffered a heartfelt submission to his conquerors and has embraced their creed. He has also betrothed his daughter Alzire to the haughty Gusman, the Governor of Peru. She too has abjured her ancient gods, but with a wavering mind; and, in obedience to her father's desire, she comes to the bridal altar to reconcile by her marriage America and Spain. Gusman loves her, but he has some reason for jealousy, if only of the dead. She makes no secret of the fact that the memory of Zamore, the other native King to whom she had been betrothed, still lives in her heart. On the day of the marriage, we have the same contretemps as in *Polyeucte :* the lover who fell in battle, and who for years has been believed to be dead, has now assembled an army and he forces his way to his beloved. With more frankness than Paulina, inspired by the passionate feelings of a child of nature, she responds to him with the assurance of her love and her despair. He is, however, overcome and imprisoned. She contrives sceretly to deliver him, but she refuses to follow him, as she is the wife of another—

> " J'ai promis ; il suffit : il n'importe a quel Dieu."

Zamore then attacks Gusman who is unprepared, and deals him a mortal blow. By the Spanish Council of State he is condemned to death, together with Alzire, who is held to be the sharer of his guilt; but Gusman, as the representative of the royal power, avails himself of his dying moments to bestow on his murderer life, freedom, and happiness. In this act he shall perceive the contrast of the gods whom they serve—

> " Des dieux que nous servons, connais la différence :
>   Les tiens t'ont commandé la meurtre et la vengeance ;
>   Et le mien, quand ton bras vient de m'assassiner,
>   M'ordonne de te plaindre et de te pardonner." (14)

To his aged father, who has from the beginning illustrated the lenity of Christianity in his dealings with the conquered nation, he recommends with his last breath Zamore and Alzire as his children.

It seems to me that, in spite of much in this drama which is unnatural, the cause of Christianity has been but little more effectively pleaded by many missionaries than by this atheist poet.

In his *Mahomet* Voltaire has pictured the horrors of fanaticism.(15)   The prophet causes a terrible assassination and parricide to be perpetrated in the name of God by a young enthusiast whose only desire is to love. The poet may very possibly have intended, in the cold egotism of Mohammed, who uses religion only as a tool, to symbolise the character of the founder of each of the three great religions by which, as he considered, the world has been deceived ; and there were some among the French public who, recognising this as his aim, made use of the pretext that his drama was likely to conduce to fanatical murders, in order to enforce its withdrawal from the Parisian stage.

This was effected after the third representation; but as Voltaire had skilfully selected as the representative of his idea the false teacher to whom theologians had affixed the name of the Eastern Antichrist, he was able to dedicate his tragedy to the learned Pope Benedict XIV., and thus to present this work against the founder of a false and barbaric sect to the chief of the true religion, this satire on the cruelty and errors of a false prophet to the follower and vicegerent of the God of verity and compassion. The Pope expressed his gratitude in a scholarly criticism which was accompanied by the apostolic blessing for his dear son Voltaire.([16]) The poet has characterised his play more justly in a letter to his royal friend at Potsdam: "Mahomet n'est ici autre chose que Tartuffe les armes à la main." He at the same time refers to various instances of fanatical deeds to which incitement had been found in the bosom of his own Church: to Kain Diaz, the Spaniard, who killed his brother, as the only way of severing him from the party of Luther; to the cruel persecutions of the Huguenots; to Clement and Ravaillac, the regicides. One admirer of Voltaire is convinced that if *Mahomet* had been composed at the date of the religious wars, it would have saved the lives of Henri III. and Henri IV. We have a proof, however, that its historical injustice to the founder of Islam had less power to influence the France of its own day, and yet that this influence might have been very seasonable. *Mahomet* was again acted in Paris in 1751, and was enthusiastically received; but more than ten years later we hear of the judicial murder of Jean Calas. In a treatise, at once more just and not less eloquent, Voltaire was then enabled to accomplish the higher aim of his drama.([17])

Goethe did not disdain to translate *Mahomet* for the Weimar theatre. But in his youth he himself for a long time cherished the idea of a drama on the same subject, at once far nobler in design and far truer to the historical

fact.   Mohammed's was to have been a real inspiration;
but as the laws of tragedy condemn divinity in its contact with this common world, to manifest itself in its forms
and to work with its instruments, the prophet was to have
degenerated into an ordinary conqueror; until, in his closing days, he should once more awake to his mission, and
save from the ruins of his work whatever was left to be
saved.   The poet's conception was never realised, and
Mohammed's Song, written in 1773, alone remains to us
as an indication of what he had imagined.

LECTURE V.

HANS SACHS AND LESSING'S "NATHAN."

THE shoemaker of Nuremburg and the librarian of Wolfenbüttel stand each on a frontier line in German literature, they at once belong to a departing past and inaugurate a new period. Both mastered the varied historical traditions of earlier ages : Lessing by thorough and accurate research; Hans Sachs as a man of the people, who in his love of knowledge reads whatever he comes across in his native tongue—though he has turned his gains to a far richer poetical use than the ordinary reader. Among the manifold creations of their genius, both poets included the religious drama, and both wrote as genuine Protestants. Hans Sachs greeted with quiet joy the springtide of the Nightingale of Wittenberg; but he seems to have felt no embarrassment in transporting his Lutheran belief into the very midst of his mediæval material with only a pious sentiment of the most general kind—or possibly with no object at all but that of gratifying his naïve delight in describing and composing. Lessing, on the other hand, illustrates Protestantism in a new shape. To him also, but with no touch of naïveté, the poetic form is only the machinery of his thought, and his drama of *Nathan the Wise*, without becoming a tragedy, is used as a vehicle for the expression of deep earnestness and a severe moral struggle.

Hans Sachs has employed in his plays a great deal of the same Scriptural material which we find in the old

mysteries, and he has especially chosen Old Testament subjects.(1)   Like the composers of the mysteries, he attempts
no subjective development of character, but simply causes
his personages to translate into action, or more often into
dialogue only, the event which he wishes to represent;
sometimes they merely relate it.   He has preserved the
approximation—shall we rather say the union?—of the
sacred and the facetious.   But, in addition, the worthy
master-singer has converted the fresh spring of his verse
to a certain extent to the even flow of the antique drama;
and borrowing portions of his material from ancient or
modern secular history, tradition, or poetry, he unhesitatingly places Christianity and heathendom in close
juxtaposition.   Next to God the Father and God the Son,
appear Jupiter and Apollo; at the Last Judgment the
bark of Charon, bearing the departed souls; with the
Judgment of Solomon the Choice of Paris.   His plays are
moulded on the life of the great free-towns, but they
contain much of simple human sentiment.

His comedy of *Eve's Unlike Children* and our Lord's
discourses to them, is thus introduced by the usual herald
of the mysteries—

> " A comedy and tale of delight,
>   Of which the original did indite
>   In Latin Philip Melanchthon."

This previous authorship is not to be too literally accepted.
Melanchthon merely refers to a graceful story found in
an existing poem,(2) and Hans Sachs has taken this as the
basis of his play.

The piece, which is in five acts, commences with Eve's
sad reminiscences of the conduct by which she lost beauteous Eden; she can now never be happy again.   Among
her troubles, next after God's anger and the curse of
eternal death, she reckons the subjection to her husband
which is now her due.   When Adam returns from digging
and hewing, he comforts her affectionately—

" My Eve, so deeply do not grieve !
Though such sore trouble we must see,
Though punished aye our Fall shall be,
Through many crosses and sad fears,
While dwelling in this vale of tears ;
Yet from the death which lasteth ever,
To save us, and through grace deliver,
The woman's blest Seed shall be born.
God hates us not, nor holds in scorn ;
For Gabriel tidings now hath given
The Lord to-morrow comes from heaven,
By us to hold high festival,
And this hath sent us to foretell.
He would see how our house we sway,
And teach our children to obey ;
If they have learnt their creed to tell,
And honour God and serve Him well."

Eve proposes to get ready the children, and to put on their best clothes ; she will also sweep the whole house, strew it with fresh grass, and adorn it everywhere with green boughs.

In Adam's inquiry for his son Cain, the darker side of this primeval family life becomes visible. Eve's reply, in which she complains of his running wild in the streets, suggests the idea of a home in a populous village rather than on the lone Asian plains. The good Abel, who has returned from feeding the sheep, goes to call him, and the brothers have an argument in which Abel expresses a fear that if Cain goes on in that way he will become a murderer, and Cain asserts that if he does he will certainly murder Abel. His answers to his father are scarcely more respectful.

In the beginning of the third act Adam asks if everything is now ready, and Eve assures him that all has been in order since the prayer-time of yester-eve. The children are assembled in two sets of six, five with Cain and five with Abel, and Adam instructs them how to receive the Lord aright; but he is shocked to see an expression of anything but welcome in the bearing of Cain and his set.

When the Lord enters with two angels, Adam receives Him with thankfulness and humility, and Eve with shame and repentance.   He, however, comforts her—

> " My daughter, be at peace this day,
>   For all thy sins are cleansed away !
>   Since grace and peace in Me ye find
>   Faithful I am, enduring, kind,
>   A Father to the poor who grieve,
>   Ye comfortless I will not leave ;
>   But in My name blest aid to give
>   The woman's promised Seed shall live,
>   Who you from evil shall deliver,
>   And back to hell shall tread for ever
>   The snake.   But till His face is seen,
>   In the long years beyond, between,
>   With a belief right firm and bold
>   To My Word ye shall closely hold.
>   Let no man rob you of your stay,
>   And it shall be your help for aye."

The good God then begins to examine Abel and the other well-behaved children on the principal points of Dr. Luther's Catechism.   But first—in answer to the question, " Do you know how to pray ? "—they repeat with clasped hands an exceedingly Protestant paraphrase of the Lord's Prayer—

ABEL.

> " O Father ! Thou in heaven who art,
>   We Thee beseech with reverent heart,
>   That first of all things on our head
>   Thou would'st Thine heavenly Spirit shed ;
>   That thus enlightened with love's flame,
>   We evermore may praise Thy name,
>   And Thee beseech in all our need
>   And sorrow.   Never may we plead
>   For any lower creature's care,
>   And thus Thy sacred name forswear."

SETH.

> " And, Heavenly Father, Thee we pray
>   To Thy bright home make straight our way ;

Through the blest word which Thou hast given,
For ever guide our steps to heaven ;
Its light upon our pathway shed,
That by it each we may be led."

JARED.

" Thy will on earth be done alone,
As by the angels round the throne !
And that we live but for this will,
We pray Thee crush our nature's ill ;
Through tribulation, day by day,
Teach Thou our souls to strive alway,
Till flesh and blood be conquered quite
And bend and bow before Thy might,
And e'en our reason too may yield,
And Thy will only rest revealed." ·

The others continue in the same strain till the Amen
is reached. When they have properly replied as to the
meaning of the word, they are asked why they are so
convinced that. God will grant what they ask—

" By Thine own promise we are sure,
The which doth evermore endure,
The very God of truth Thou art,
Who from Thy word wilt ne'er depart."

Even the difficult questions as to the delay or the
apparent denial of a response to prayer meet with believing answers. The children then repeat the Ten Commandments in verse, arranged as in Luther's Catechism,
after these they proceed to the Belief, in which we find
an ingenious alteration of the second article, the fulfilment of it being in the future—

" In the Redeemer I believe,
Whom from above we shall receive,
His feet on Satan's head to place,
Salvation bringing to our race."

In reply to the question, " What do you mean by forgiveness of sins ? " we read—

K

> " What is it God Himself hath told—
> Through the Redeemer which shall be,
> From all our sins He sets us free."

The good God is much pleased by these answers, and
promises them a reward—

> " Ye children, all who know My way,
> Keep in it ever day by day.
> My Spirit shall with you remain,
> To guide and teach, console, sustain,
> Till everlasting life ye win.
> And even in this world of sin
> Gladness and might He shall bestow.
> Great shall ye be on earth below,
> As princes, sov'reigns, nobles, magnates,
> Wise men, teachers, learned prelates ;
> And everywhere in every land
> Your names in honoured place shall stand ;
> On ye for aye My peace shall rest,
> Now and alway ye shall be blest."

The archangel Raphael then closes the act by admonishing
all to praise God with hymns and instruments of music.

In the next act it is the turn of Cain and his set.
They are at least no hypocrites, for Cain begins by
acknowledging that if the Lord questions him, he will
not know how to answer, and his wicked brothers express
in turn a still more passionate disapprobation of the
examination. Each of the brothers is the representative
of some special vice ; Nabal of drunkenness, Achan of
dishonesty, Dathan, Esau, and Nimrod of appropriate sins.
Satan encourages them by many promises, but when the
good God again enters to renew His inquiries, he hides
himself.

Every question elicits a false and contradictory reply, ([3])
till at length the good God sighs over this impious band,
who will not have anything to do with Him, but will
only follow the dictates of their own evil nature—

> " Therefore on earth shall be your place
> As a poor, rough, hard-toiling race,

> As peasants, woodmen, charcoal-burners,
> Herdsmen, hangmen, knackers, turners,
> Grooms, broom-makers, beadles, tailors,
> Serfs, shoemakers, carters, sailors,
> Jacob's brethren, rustics coarse,
> Hireling men, with one resource,
> A labouring life with little gain.
> Rude and uncouth ye shall remain ;
> And up and down shall make your way,
> Toiling wearily day by day.
> Mean and poor shall be your life,
> With scorn and misery ever rife."

Finally they shall receive eternal damnation, unless they repent and turn to God with faith, obedience, and prayer; they must therefore get Abel to instruct them in the right way.

The last act is opened by Cain in a discourse with Satan, in which he complains of Abel's great influence in the court of heaven, so that he has even been appointed bishop.([4]) Satan advises him not to tolerate this, for is he not the eldest-born? Why should he not kill his brother? Cain replies that he has already thought of doing so. When the two brothers make their offering in the field, Cain's sacrifice is rendered the more evidently worthless by his assertion that he has taken care to thresh all the wheat. As in the fourth chapter of Genesis, the murder follows. Perhaps a fratricide has never been related with such absolute lack of pathos; the brothers waste no remarks on it, and Satan helps Cain to conceal the body.

The pitying sentence of God is copied from the Scriptures. When Cain cries aloud in despair and self-reproach, the Lord makes on his brow the mystic sign, whereby his life, though that of a wanderer and a fugitive, shall yet be consecrated and protected from his brethren. Satan leads him away counselling him to self-destruction, and while the unhappy murderer disappears in the evil-haunted darkness, God causes Abel, His pious and obedient child, to be buried by the angels, and comforts Adam and Eve by sanctifying Seth as the first-born, from whom shall descend the Seed of the woman to break the bonds of the curse.

The herald then closes the play, and deduces from it four excellent lessons. In the first place, by the example of Adam and Eve, we may behold how the whole human race has been laid under a curse by God, so that even in the present day one tribulation closely follows another, and we eat our bread in the sweat of our brow. In the second place, in Abel we have a picture of all who fear God, and do what they can for the good of their neigh-bours, both bodily and spiritual. Verily, their Heavenly Father shall recompense even more unto them. Thirdly, Cain is the type of all godless men, who live without faith by the dictates of their own reason and of their fleshly lusts, plunged in vice and crime and persecuting all who would lead them to God. In the fourth place we are here shown how God is ever willing to help our human race, through the blessed Seed of the woman, by the promise of whom He hath comforted Adam and Eve—

> " The Christ He is who came to heal,
>   Whom God our Father did reveal;
>   The Son of Mary born to save,
>   Who on the cross harsh death did brave,
>   And bruising thus the serpent's head,
>   Hath wholly rescued from the dread
>   Just wrath of God our race outcast
>   Through Adam's fall. Thus, when at last
>   Past we are through this vale of sorrow,
>   That God an ever-joyous morrow
>   May give us 'mid His angel host,
>   Is that which Hans Sachs wishes most."

Besides chiming in with this good wish, the reader will readily admit that Hans Sachs has done all that it was possible to do to associate the mediæval mystery with Protestant sentiment. Only the tragedy of the murder of Abel, the second and bloody fruit of the Fall, is not treated as a tragedy, but is adventitiously affixed to an instructive catechism, which in its close, through the inappropriate answers of the sinful children, has even assumed a comic tinge. Also, while the fable on which the drama is founded contains no attempt at a definite explanation of the contrasts of human destinies, but merely deduces our hereditary inequality from a little bit of harmless vanity on the part of the First Mother and an oversight of the Creator, the poet, in his treatment of the primitive dualism of the brothers, has been led to adopt the harsh aristocratic theory which would derive the scions of every noble house from a pious and divinely favoured ancestry, and the pith of the nation, which supports and fosters the upper classes, from a race under the divine ban.

This doctrine was, however, so akin both to the naïve genius and the social standing of the bold shoemaker, that he was induced in the same year, 1553, to rearrange the same subject, and thus furnish a corrective to his own composition. This second play is quite simple in outline, being neither divided into acts nor announced by a herald. It is headed, *How God the Lord blesses the children of Adam and Eve.*(⁵)

The opening speeches are almost word for word the same, but Adam reflects how continual sorrows of many a sort follow in the track of their sin—

> " But few days past, to our sore pain,
> Hath Cain our lovèd Abel slain ;
> Right sad and heavy is our grief.
> O God ! we cry, for our relief,
> That holpen now we be and shriven,
> The promised Saviour may be given."

In the remainder of the drama the dualist conception of the former piece, the rivalry of the brothers, is laid aside. On the receipt of the news, which Adam has quite accidentally learned from an angel, Eve takes the children in hand, and she brings her four favourites to Adam to obtain his approval ; she thinks the Lord will probably be pleased with their looks. Adam praises them, but, as these are not all the children, he inquires what she has done with the rest, who ought also to receive God's blessing. Eve replies that she really cannot show them, they are too ugly and dirty; some are hidden in the hay in the stable, and some are asleep behind the fireplace; she does not mean to let them come out while the Lord is present. Adam thinks differently—

> " I would you had brought them every one.
> God heedeth not the body's fairness ;
> 'Tis sense and virtue He will bless."

He nevertheless consents to the arrangement, and he instructs the four children, who have been dressed for the occasion, how they are to behave. These are only distinguished from their "ill-formed" brothers by the superiority of their personal advantages.

As in the former play, the Lord enters with two angels, and comforts Adam and Eve by His gracious words, referring them to the Seed of the woman, who shall trample the serpent in the dust and make an end of all sorrows. Eve asks—

> " Heavenly Father, prithee say,
> Is the blest Seed here e'en to-day ?
> Of these my children is there one
> By whom this great deed shall be done ?"

The Lord answers by affirming the succession of generation to generation till the time shall come. He then asks if the children can say their prayers. They kneel, Seth begins the Lord's Prayer and the rest follow. The Lord praises and blesses them; their descendants shall increase till they shall be as the sand of the sea-shore, and shall dwell in every land. Eve then begs for a special blessing on each child, and a prophecy of what he shall become. The Lord mercifully grants her wish, and He lays His hand on the head of the first. This one shall become a great king, and princes and nobles shall be subject to him. In token thereof He gives him a crown and sceptre. The next shall become a great warrior, he shall fearlessly defend his country and his nation, the widow and the orphan. His gifts are a shield and sword with other arms. The third shall become a burgomaster and administer for the common weal, punishing the wicked and rewarding all good deeds. He receives a judicial staff. The fourth shall be a merchant and possess great riches, goods of every kind shall be transported by him from land to land, and his payments and receipts shall ever be fair and just. His portion is, therefore, a set of weights and measures. Every one shall remain in his own station whereunto he has received the blessing of God. The Lord then takes the children for a walk in Paradise.

When Eve is thus left alone with Adam, after everything has gone so smoothly, she confesses her regret that she did not bring forward the other children also. The good God would surely have made great lords of them, also through His abounding and benevolent blessing. Adam advises her to fetch them now. When the Lord returns, and is about to depart again for His heavenly kingdom, because the sun is almost set, He allows himself to be detained in order that Eve may present to Him the four boys whom she has taken out of the hay. They, however, have not learnt to pray. Eve receives a sharp reprimand for having trained them so badly; but she excuses herself as she best may by pleading the number of her children and the many fatigues of her life and Adam's. In time she will instruct them better, but meanwhile she beseeches the Lord to forgive their foolishness and to bless them also. The Lord too is willing to excuse them, and He lays His hand successively on the head of each child. The first shall be a shoemaker, so his gift is a last; the second, who shall be a weaver, receives a shuttle; the third, who shall become a shepherd, has a shepherd's pouch; and to the fourth, who shall be a peasant,

is given a ploughshare.   The gifts are accompanied by
approving remarks on the utility of each in his station to
his fellow-men.   But Eve is not satisfied—

> " O Thou most gracious Lord of heaven,
>   Why is Thy blessing so uneven?
>   Since sons they are of Adam born,
>   All equal, why hold four in scorn?
>   Since some as great men Thou hast blest,
>   Why common folk should be the rest—
>   Shoemakers, weavers, herdsmen, hinds?"

The Lord comforts her by pointing out how He has selected
every one according to his natural fitness; also how necessary they are each to each, the nobles and the common
people; and how the different ranks depend on one
another.   Eve is willing to believe all this, but to the
first it has been given to lead a princely life, while the
others will have to work hard, to eat rough food and
couch rudely, and to bow before kings, nobles, and
burghers.   One set are to have fine clothes, rich meats
and drinks, pleasure-gardens like Eden, magnificent houses
and soft beds; if the rest had the same good things, she
would be quite satisfied.   The Lord once more comforts
her—

> " One class is even as another,
>   Each rank of service to its brother.
>   'Tis true a king, knight, magistrate
>   Hath no handtoil, nor merchant great
>   Harsh labour; but beneath the sheen
>   Of riches, lurk, to men unseen,
>   Troubles a mány, weary cares
>   And dangers which their wealth prepares
>   Before them; riot, overthrow,
>   Rapine and plague, in bitter row.
>   While those in lower place who stand
>   No cares distract, a tranquil band,
>   Save how they wife and child maintain
>   By labouring hands and daily gain;
>   And aye their toil doth bring them health,
>   A sweeter sleep than that of wealth,

Well-tasted is their drink and food,
Nor ever through dull hours they brood.
Men's wits for work I have made bright,
Have fitted them as birds for flight,
Be each man on his calling bent,
And every man shall find content,
And daily bread shall daily earn.
Now to my heaven once more I turn,
'Mid angel choirs in peace to dwell ;
But peace I leave on earth as well."

The Carnival play (*Fastnachtspiel*), of which the modern German drama is a direct descendant, Hans Sachs found already existing in Nuremberg, where it had been common among the Master-singers of the previous generation. He merely elevated its rude extravagances into a finer form of satirical jesting, without, at the same time, cramping any of its luxuriant merriment. This form of the miracle play had its source in the license of the buffoons and maskers of the Carnival, when the speeches of the strolling mummers, which they had at first improvised, were loosely and carelessly strung together into pieces which they had to learn. These pieces consequently became reflections of the most ordinary popular life, of its petty needs and pursuits, of its squabbles and its amity. They were also short and slight enough to be fitted for representation in any house into which the Carnival guests might chance to enter; or they could be acted without preparation in an inn, leaving time afterwards for a merry feast. The jests at the expense of the Church are nearly always introduced only in the form of careless side-thrusts; as, for instance, when, under the favourite form of a lawsuit, matrimonial quarrels are judged with some levity by the ecclesiastical umpire. But Hans Sachs, even when according to established custom he takes the great apostles as the theme of his witticisms, displays the most genial humour in his treatment of the joys and troubles of humanity, and he always preserves a genuine earnestness beneath his banter.

In the Carnival play, *How St. Peter has a Farewell Feast with his Friends*, the Lord asks Peter how he likes His kingdom. St. Peter heartily praises it, but there is one thing which he regrets—he has not taken a formal farewell of his numerous friends, nor had a last feast with them before His crucifixion—

> "Good Lord, I pray Thee grant to me,
> If every wise it well may be,
> That for just three days I may go
> Once more to dwell on earth below,
> For three short days my friends to see,
> And feast once more right merrily."

He makes this request because it is the Carnival. The Lord gives him leave to go to see how it fares with his friends, if things are with them as in former days. While he is away, as he will not be absent long, the heavenly gate may remain closed. Peter gratefully thanks Him, and promises to see that it is properly fastened.

The first person he meets on earth is his cousin Clas with two friends. They are so terrified at the supposed ghost that they are on the point of running away, when Peter reassures them, and the four depart together to feast and enjoy themselves.

Peter next appears on the scene with a headache. It is now the ninth day; he had entirely forgotten his promise until he was reminded of it by his headache; he will forthwith proceed to heaven to entreat pardon of the Lord. The Lord has come out to look for him,(7) and sees him approach, and when Peter has pleaded his friends' good-cheer and merry company as an excuse for his forgetfulness, He inquires if in the midst of so many good things, of all this feasting and enjoyment, every one was full of thankfulness to Him, the Giver of all. Peter is not able to return a satisfactory reply; in fact no one said anything about God except one old woman whose stall was burnt; she shrieked and called so wildly on the Lord to help her, that they all laughed.

Peter is reinstated in his office ; but when another year has passed, leave is again granted him to revisit earth. This time he may stay a month. But the Lord has reflected, "Since sweet does no good, sour must help "— and so He has determined to send forth His angel, bearing plagues and troubles for mankind. When Peter comes to his cousins with permission to keep the Carnival with them for a full month, he hears only mournful and pious talk about the wrath of God, blight, famine, war, and pestilence. Upon this he returns straightway to heaven, where he is again questioned by the Lord—

"Is there still none who asks for Me ? "

PETER.

"Oh yes, most gracious Lord ! for Thee
Both young and old with fervour cry,
Early and late they weep and sigh,
In penitence would pity.win,
Owning with grief their guilt and sin.
With such true heart their cry they make,
Return, O Lord ! sweet pity take !
To heal and end their bitter pain,
Myself I cry, Lord, turn again ! "

The Lord closes the play—

"My Peter, well this wonder view,
My gracious hand I did undo,
And for the souls beneath on earth,
Sweet peace and calm content had birth ;
Glad health I gave with them to dwell,
And fertile seasons on them fell,
With corn and wine in overflow,
And each good thing in plenteous row.
But waxing only fat and bold,
My people left My grace untold,
The Giver of all good forgot,   .
The while their souls they did besot
With pleasure, av'rice, worldly pride,
And many a hellish sin beside.
Defiantly My law they brake,
And when My gospel word I spake,

> It nought availed to purify ;
> And thus no longer might I try
> With gracious gifts their hearts to gain,
> But with plague, famine, war's harsh pain
> To tame.   Since love of worldly good
> Drew them to sin, why e'en I would
> No longer in My mercy spare,
> But dragging them as by the hair,
> My memory in them rouse once more
> By griefs, diseases, troubles sore.
> So, Peter, thou may'st e'en bethink
> This medicine harsh the which they drink
> Shall for their good their ill flesh tame,
> Their souls to holy strife inflame.
> —To the redeem'd at heaven's door
> Be thou the porter as before ;
> To souls on earth leave passing toys,
> Thine are for aye the heavenly joys."

To this closing speech is added Hans Sachs' usual formula of farewell good wishes.

In some popular dialogues, which are almost dramatic in conception, the worthy Master-singer has constituted himself a special pleader for the Reformation regarded in the light in which it presented itself to a simple citizen, *i.e.*, as a re-establishment of the pure Word of God in contrast with the corruptions of the Papacy.   In his regular dramas he has not introduced the controversy between the Churches.

A later offshoot of the polemic plays of this period was the *Christian Knight of Eisleben*,[8] by Martin Rinckart, Deacon at Eisleben, whose hymn, *Nun danket alle Gott*, is sung as the national *Te Deum* at every great German Protestant festival.   The *Christian Knight* was acted by students at Eisleben shortly before the outbreak of the Thirty Years' war.   The argument shows how a king, Emmanuel, had three sons—Peter, Martin, and John. The father dies while all three are absent in different lands, Peter in Italy, Martin in Eisleben, and John, the youngest, in Switzerland.   Peter, who is the first to return, assumes the crown, in spite of his father's testamentary prohibition, and rules with great violence. Then Martin arrives, and beholding his brother's harsh deeds, he reminds him gently of his father's will. While they are arguing, John appears from Switzerland. He first endeavours to pervert the expressions of the will in favour of his own sovereignty, but failing in this, he erects his father's body as the target for a shooting-match; whichever of the brothers most nearly pierces the heart shall be king. Peter is ready enough, but Martin affectionately and reverently refuses to be a participator in so great a crime. His two brothers urge him with much harshness, till the father appears in a vision, and punishing his unworthy sons, sets the crown on the head of their deserving brother.

The decisiveness of the conclusion shows that the fable on which the drama is founded did not originate during this controversy. It is taken from the *Gesta Romanorum*,(⁹) a collection of tales in monkish Latin which dates from about the thirteenth century. In this first story a king, who is both rich and wise, has a faithless wife, and her three elder sons are not really the king's children. They are disloyal to their supposed father, and in no way resemble him. The queen has also a fourth son who is the child of the king. It comes to pass that his father dies, and the four brothers dispute the throne. They choose as umpire an old noble, who has been very greatly in the confidence of the dead sovereign, and he advises that the body should be taken from the tomb and fastened to a tree. Each of the brothers is then to try a single shot with bow and arrows, and he whose arrow penetrates the deepest is to have the kingdom. The first aims, and as he pierces quite through the right hand, he at once congratulates himself on his prospective sovereignty. The arrow of the second brother penetrates the mouth, so he feels still more certain of the throne; but when the third brother strikes the heart, he thinks his claim indisputable.

The fourth brother, as he approaches the body, sighs deeply, and says in sorrowful accents,([10]) " Far be it from me to harm the body of my father, living or dead." Upon this the great men of the kingdom and all the spectators exclaim, " Behold the true heir ! " and setting him on the throne of his father, they deprive the other three youths of all their possessions. Their evil hearts have betrayed the secret of their birth.

This parable was interpreted to signify the conduct of infidels, Jews, and heretics, as opposed to that of the sons of the true Catholic Church ; just as in its new dramatic form it was used to gratify the zealous wrath of the Lutherans against the Papal chair, and their still deeper rage against Calvin and his faction. It was the dawn of a new day when a similar fable of like traditional origin could afford its aid to the cause of moral enlightenment in *Nathan the Wise.*

Lessing had at an earlier period written from Leipzig to his anxious father, " The Christian religion is not a thing which can be received on trust from one's ancestors." He had also invoked the memory of Luther, " O thou misunderstood great man, thou hast delivered us from the yoke of tradition, but who shall now deliver us from the yoke of the letter ? " He himself was conscious of an inborn fitness for such an enterprise. While on the one hand closely related to Luther in his influence on the formation of an indigenous German literature, he had on the other hand published some *Fragments* from an un- named author, already beyond the reach of human criti- cism,([11]) which contained a grave impeachment of Christi- anity, based upon the Canonical Scriptures themselves and their supposed contradictions. Lessing, it is true, did not sympathise with the ideas expressed in these *Fragments,* but he did not care to keep them to himself, and desired to have them refuted by theologians. He had at the same time added, as his own opinion, that if it should become absolutely necessary, the infallibility of the Bible

as God's own Word might be relinquished, since it is
not by that alone that Christianity will either stand or
fall. . This admission allowed him to trace an independent
historical origin for the Apostles' Creed, as well as its
eternal origin in the constitution of the human mind;
and he had thus plunged himself into a controversy with
Melchior Götze, a Hamburg rector, a learned, bold, zealous
man, who had already denounced the *Sorrows of Werther*
as a new Sodom and Gomorrah, and had also declined
all Christian fellowship with a colleague because he was
in the habit of omitting from an old penitential prayer
the sentence, "Pour out Thy wrath, O Lord, on the
heathen who have not known Thy name!" Götze raised
against Lessing a clumsy outcry of heresy, which he
answered by crushing argumentative papers against the
pretensions of the Lutheran clergy. In the midst of the
controversy, when an attempt was being made to curtail
its freedom,([12]) an old cherished idea of Lessing's took a
more definite form in the plan of the drama of *Nathan*,
in which he appeals from professed scholars to the whole
mass of educated Germany. To his brother he writes,
"I will try one more experiment, and see if I shall be
allowed to preach without interference from my old pulpit,
the stage." The piece contains no satire on his rival, of
whom we may at most be reminded by the wrath of the
patriarch against the pride of human reason, and the
confidence with which he pronounces, "It matters not;
the Jew goes to the stake!" The controversy has been
elevated into the liberal realm of the ideal.

The drama centres, as is well known, in the parable of
a precious ring, which, if worn with proper confidence in
its virtues, has the power to render the wearer pleasing in
the sight of God and man. It has descended from father
to son for many generations, and has always created
its possessor the chief among his brethren. At length a
father has three equally dutiful sons, whom he regards
with equal affection, and to each in turn, in an hour of

weakness, he promises the ring. In order to redeem his promise as well as he can, he has two other rings made, so like the first that he cannot himself tell the difference. He then dies, after he has secretly given to each brother one of the rings, and each naturally affirms that his is the true gem; even as Christians, Jews, and Mohammedans respectively assert that theirs is the true religion.

A form of this story also is found in the *Gesta Romanorum*, but in it the father secretly favours one son above the rest, and he causes therefore two other rings to be fashioned which contain only coloured glass instead of a precious jewel. After his death, when each of the brothers imagines that he possesses the true ring, a wise elder, to whom they appeal, decides, "We will try which ring has power to heal diseases, and we shall thus discover which contains the real gem." Only one ring has the power in question, so the people are enabled to perceive which son the father has really preferred. In the three brothers are typified the three sects, Christians, Jews, and Saracens, by creation all children of God. Christians alone have the magic ring, its signs and miraculous virtues are not to be found among infidels.([13]) We have here, based on the same Catholic belief, the same critical test by which in a much earlier legend the cross which bore the Redeemer is recognised among the three crosses freshly dug up on Calvary.

But this arrangement of the fable, although it has recently also been found in a French manuscript of the thirteenth century,([14]) reads very like an orthodox revision. In an Italian collection of tales, scarcely later in date,([15]) we may probably trace the original intention of the story. The Moorish Sultan, being in need of money, resolves to find a cause of complaint against a rich Jew. He asks him, "Which is the true faith?"—thinking, "If he replies, *The Jewish*, I will accuse him of pronouncing against the religion I profess; while if he answers, *The Mohammedan*, I will say, *How can you then remain a Jew?*" The Jew, however, responds with the parable of the three rings, two of which the father, in his desire to satisfy the wish of each of the sons, has had made so like the first that he alone may distinguish the original gem. "Thus do I hold of the religions, which are likewise three: the Father which is above knoweth which is the right creed; we are the sons, and we each believe our own to be the true one." When the Sultan sees how the Jew has escaped this snare, he does not know wherewith he may find occasion against him, and he lets him depart.

This tale was of a kind to recommend itself to the taste of Boccaccio,[16] and in his graceful version of it the Sultan becomes Saladin, the Moorish hero of the Crusades, while the Jew is named Melchisedech and is represented as avaricious. Yet when Saladin intends to win his gold from him through the ensnaring question, after he has been delivered by his wisdom and the Sultan has frankly confessed his purpose, he himself proffers his treasures, and they become friends.

Lessing borrowed from the *Decamerone* not only the fable of the rings, but the person of Saladin and the *rôle* of the wise Jew, whom he names Nathan, as it were Nathanael, the Israelite indeed in whom the Saviour Himself found no guile. The scene he transfers from Alexandria to the sacred soil of Jerusalem, where at one time, under Saladin's mild rule, the three chief historical religions of the world actually co-existed, each with rights defined by charter. A second feature of the drama is also historical. In the very midst of the Crusades, the strife in which for a hundred years two of these religions contended at once for a sepulchre and for the sovereignty of the world, simultaneously with the highest development of doctrinal enthusiasm, another conception grew up and took possession especially of the Order of the Templars. This conception, which was probably encouraged both by repeated contact with a noble foe, and by the very misfortunes of those who believed themselves soldiers of the

L

cause of God, recognised a certain truth in the rival religion, and sometimes even went so far as to admit a doubt whether Christ or Mohammed were destined to be the ruler of the world.

In the *Complaint of a Knight Templar,*"([17]) a picture is drawn of the losses which the Crusaders had already sustained in territory and men, because God had forsaken His own cause. "And think not that this is all, nay, rather, He hath manifestly sworn that none who believe in Jesus Christ shall remain in Jerusalem. Sooner would He that the minster of the Holy Virgin should become a mosque. And since His divine Son who should be thereby aggrieved is content, why we must well be satisfied." Walter von der Volgelweide, himself a Crusader, wrote—

> " Is there one who can judgment give
> 'Twixt Christian, Jew, and Turk ?
> The Lord by whom we each do live,
> Who without us doth work."

The Pope, in a public bull, reproached the great Emperor Frederick II. with having asserted the counter proposition to that contained in the parable of the rings : namely, that " the World has been led astray by three deceivers, Jesus Christ, Moses, and Mohammed ; of these, two died in great honour, while the third perished on a gallows."([18]) The Emperor naturally disowned so mad a remark, and the Pope could not prove it against him. But even in those old days the idea existed.

Lessing has kept as a mainspring of his play the Sultan's endeavour to find a complaint against the Jew in order to obtain his money; but as his argument required that our conception of Saladin, as well as of Nathan, should remain pure and lofty, all anxiety about the issue of the test is removed, and even our sympathy with the Jew is not excited. Both Sultan and spectators are merely curious to see how, through his wisdom, he will evade the danger of the query. The other characters who are employed to

develop the poet's idea are entirely of his own creation, as
is also the dramatised story, in which, in relief against the
great historical background of the Crusades, the motives
of an ordinary comedy are brought into play. A Templar,
who has been reprieved by Saladin, rescues a Jewish
maiden from a burning house, and she loses her heart to
him in consequence; but Nathan's supposed daughter is
an orphaned child of Christian parents. At length the
Templar and the Jewess are discovered to be brother and
sister, and the children of the Sultan's dead brother, who
had become a Christian.

This drama, which in its technical form resembles no
other of Lessing's, is strictly a didactic poem, almost as
much so as a mediæval morality. There is no impetus in
the action, and the *dénouement* has nothing dramatic; it
does not even afford us any clear glimpse of the future
of the two young people, for whom our sympathy has
naturally been enlisted, and whose love is now moderated
to the tranquil affection of brother and sister. In fact,
through both the entire tale and the verse there runs a
slightly frigid vein—and yet the piece went straight to
the heart of the German nation. It illustrated the
noblest features of the struggle of the age for liberty of
opinion, *charity towards those of a different creed* and the
religion of humanity.(19)

When Nathan has related his parable to the Sultan, he
adds that the umpire to whom the three brothers appeal,
each fully convinced of his own claim, refuses to decide,
and gives them as his advice—

> "' Go, therefore,' said the judge, ' unless my counsel
> You'd have in place of sentence. It were thus :
> Accept the case exactly as it stands.
> Had each his ring directly from his father,
> Let each believe his own is genuine.
> 'Tis possible your father would no longer
> His house to one ring's tyranny subject ;
> And certain that all three of you he loved ;
> Loved equally, since two he would not humble,

That one might be exalted.   Let each one
To his unbought, impartial love aspire ;
Each with the others vie to bring to light
The virtue of the stone within his ring.
Let gentleness, a hearty love of peace,
Beneficence, and perfect trust in God,
Come to its help.   Then if the jewel's power
Among your children's children be revealed,
I bid you in a thousand, thousand years
Again before this bar.   A wiser man
Than I shall occupy this seat and speak.
Go !'   Thus the modest judge dismissed them.
If therefore, Saladin, you feel yourself
That promised, wiser man "——

When the Sultan upon this exclaims—

"I ? Dust !   I ? Naught !
Not ended are the thousand, thousand years
Your judge foretold ; not mine to claim his seat "

—not only theological pride, but sincere Christian faith
in humblest gratitude to God, may rejoice to feel itself in
possession of the true gem.   But the special lesson of the
piece requires that we should also recognise that a person
of a different creed, as long as his faith is sound, honestly
believes that in the religion of his fathers he holds the
real jewel, and that he is obeying the divine command in
endeavouring to verify its virtues during his own life and
to transmit it to his descendants.   And this form of veri-
fication is certainly a more assured warrant of the truth
of a religion than the one demanded by the *Gesta Romanorum,* where the true ring is approved by miracles, the
effect of which is as it were arbitrary, and the abyss between
the false and the true religion is in no way filled up, but
only bridged over.   Every unprejudiced mind is gratified
when the Jew, or any other of the personages of the drama
holding an alien creed, displays before us a sympathetic
kindliness, a readiness to do good, and a heartfelt trust in
God.   In all this it sees a proof that the moral sense is a

common inheritance of mankind, and is merely baptized by
each religion with its own name. And such of the spectators as were then unable to comprehend the entire aim of
the piece, were impressed by the lofty tone of the characters, and by simple sentences of elevated morality—
even when this morality was of the universal order already
referred to. Thus when Nathan is conversing with his
daughter, who is still under the impression that she has
been saved from the fire by an angel, he observes that
human pride is certainly gratified by the idea of the
interposition of an angel; and that it is very convenient
to be absolved from the necessity of any compensatory
service, such as a fellow-man might demand—

> "Have you not learned
> That pious ecstasies are easier far
> Than virtuous deeds; how gladly idleness,
> Concealing its true motive from itself,
> Would stand excused from virtuous deeds, and plead
> Its pious ecstasies instead?"

Recha would, however, very willingly have devoted herself
to her deliverer—knight or angel—as his reward.

Lessing hoped to play the "blackcoats" a craftier trick
with his *Nathan* than with the *Fragments*. But when
it appeared in 1779, the influence of the Pietists was
already on the wane. Herder recognised in *Nathan* a
circle of precepts of the grandest order in universal religion and in national toleration—the Age of Enlightenment found in the piece the highest expression of its
ideas.

But again a new day has dawned. Even men of
moderate opinions find fault with *Nathan* as displaying
a spirit of enmity to Christianity. There is one point
which cannot be denied. In Nathan and Saladin, whose
characters stand respectively far above the religion of
their race, Islam and Judaism find much more worthy
representatives than are allotted to Christianity; for the
Christian personages of the drama all rank far below their

religion.([20])   We have first the Patriarch, who holds both
that—

> " A villany
> In man's esteem may not be one in God's ; "—

and that every means is equally legitimate which may
enable him to avenge the injuries of the Church, and to
rule supreme in her name.   Secondly, we find Daja, a
well-meaning believer, who, while she resides under
Nathan's roof and subsists by his kindness, yet in her
eagerness to obtain a convert is not over sensitive about
the means she employs—

> "One of those fanatics,
> Who think they know the universal, true,
> And only road to God."

In the third place we have the Lay Brother with his
pious simplicity, who is but a feeble tool in the hands
of the Church ; when his better nature asserts itself, his
sentiments are only those of Nathan.   He thus excuses
the Jew for having brought up as his own the orphaned
Christian child—

> " Children
> Need love, though but a wild beast's love it be,
> In those first years, above Christianity.
> Christianity will still find time enough.
> Have but the girl in health and innocence
> Grown up before your eyes, in sight of God
> She's as she was.   Has not Christianity
> Its root in Judaism ?   It oft has vexed,
> Provoked me e'en to tears, to see how Christians
> Forget our Saviour was Himself a Jew."

When afterwards, excited by Nathan's magnanimity, he
exclaims—

> "You are a Christian, Nathan !   Yes, by heaven,
> You are a Christian !   Never was a better ! "

Nathan answers—

> "What makes of me a Christian in your eyes,
> Makes you in mine a Jew.   Happy for both!"

Lastly there are the two young people.   The disposition of the Templar is certainly noble and upright; but, as if influenced by the Moorish blood which, unconsciously to himself, throbs in his veins, he is without special piety or regard for Christianity, the more lurid flames of which he has beheld in the theological rage of the sacred warfare. He reproaches Nathan, whom he as yet only regards as a Jew—

> "Know you, Nathan,
> What people practised first this casting slurs—
> What people were the first to call themselves
> The Chosen People?   How if I—not hate,
> Indeed—but cannot help despising them
> For all their pride,—a pride which has descended
> To Mussulman and Christian,—that their God
> Must be the one true God?   You start to hear
> Such words from me, a Christian and a Templar.
> When, where, has this fanaticism of having
> The better God, and forcing Him as best
> On all the world, e'er showed itself in colours
> More black than here and now?"

And Recha, who has been baptized a Christian, but if not actually brought up as a Jewess, has had the "seeds of wisdom" sown by Nathan "pure within her soul, cannot understand what it means to fight for one's God—

> "'His God for Whom he fights!'   Can God be owned?
> What sort of God were He Whom man could own,
> Who needs defenders?"

To the sorrows of the Christian heroes, when they have been related to her by Daja, she has willingly accorded the tribute of tears, but—

> "Their belief
> I never held their greatest heroism.
> The more consoling was the lesson,
> That faith in God depends not on the views
> We entertain of Him."

Even among the characters which illustrate Islamism, the talkative Dervise, whose speeches are made much longer than the action demands, is evidently introduced with the sole intention of wresting from Christianity the exclusive credit of slighting the things of this world.   This attempt is not without its historical justification, for the intensest disdain of worldly good has been as often seen on the banks of the Ganges as in the Egyptian desert.

But all these illustrations were introduced by Lessing precisely because his drama was to be regarded from a Christian point of view.   Since the history of Christianity is stained and disfigured by a tale of persecution, he deemed it necessary to represent in persons, whom a Christian might term infidels, a noble and charitable tone of mind, which is manifested by correspondent actions. Supposing that a Jew had written *Nathan* with a purpose similar to Lessing's—if indeed we can conceive such a poem possible outside the higher regions of Christian culture—this Jewish author, while he might perhaps have made Moses Mendelssohn impressively demand of his friend Lavater to become a Jew, or to give his reasons against doing so, would, we can scarcely doubt, have selected a Christian as his type of pious wisdom.   He might perhaps have idealised into the form of a Christian Nathan the exquisite charity which allowed Lavater to feel a warm affection for Goethe, even while Goethe seemed still an antagonist of Christianity.

Nevertheless Wackernagel, one of the most careful of our German literary historians, has expressed his opinion that a flavour of bitterness pervades the entire drama, imparted by Lessing's dislike to Christianity, or, to say the least, his prepossessions against it.[21]   While tolerance towards Jews and Mohammedans is taught, intolerance towards Christianity is displayed.   The same critic is surprised at the innocent amiability of the German nation, which " is able to find a lesson in toleration, and in the ethics of Christian charity, even in a book through which

there runs a so sharply discordant note of intolerant pre-
judice." He is persuaded that this deistical equanimity
towards every form of religion only bears the semblance
of real charity; and is rather the most uncharitable of all
sentiments with its unstable intellectual conceptions of
possible falsity in its own creed, and possible truth in the
creeds of others. If we take this view, how full of bitter
humour must appear the course adopted by Frederick
the Great and Joseph II.! while an odour of the stake,
almost as strong as that which clings to a judge of the
Inquisition, may be said to cleave to Voss the Apostle of
Toleration! Wackernagel is also convinced that a believing Christian alone, who rests on the steadfast ground
of that charity which is the climax of faith, and who is
humbly conscious of the blessing which has been vouch-
safed to himself, is able to show a true tenderness for the
imperfect faith of another: a state, too, can only really
tolerate the Jews in so far as it is itself a Christian state.
But this very author is so kind as to admit and to impress
upon the admirers of Lessing—whom he regards as being
themselves indifferent to religious truth, and only affected
by the verdict of their fellow-men—that the drama of
Nathan would have been essentially a different poem, if
it had been composed two years later, when Lessing, in
his *Education of the Human Race*, had pointed out the
progressive education of humanity by divine revelation,
and had therefore accorded to Christianity its due superiority as the historical development of Judaism, while he
had at the same time set aside Mohammedanism as being
intrinsically a defective creed. If Lessing had composed
Nathan when he had attained to this later altitude, he
would not have selected for his parable the fable of
Boccaccio, but rather the legend of the *Gesta Romanorum*,
in which the ring is approved by its more marvellous
virtues.

In every strict historical inquiry, it must be admitted
that the great religions of the world have not acquired

their historical majesty through tolerance—the patient charity of Nathan—but by the aid of inspired oratory; at times either through the axe, as when Winfried hewed down the oak of Woden; or through the sword, as when the Saxons received at the hands of Charlemagne the baptism of blood. Not Paul only has been an apostle, but also Mohammed. There have been both lands and ages in which the seal of decay has become impressed on a whole world of belief; and the signal by which the new faith shall conquer has appeared, as it were, in the necessary sequence of historical development. And the acute perception of this sign, together with an eager anxiety for the everlasting welfare of the souls of a people, may be necessary to rouse the courage which shall dare even to run the risk of being devoured by those whom one is endeavouring to convert. *Nathan* would be scarcely the most suitable of handbooks for a missionary amongst savages.

But in other lands and ages different religions or sects dwell side by side, each tenacious of its limits and with rights defined by custom; and, face to face with the silent influence of a more abundant culture, but a small space is left for the ebb and flow of proselytism. In such periods the wisdom of Greece holds good, as we find it expressed by Isocrates, " Guard the religion which thou hast received from thy ancestors ; but account this ever the richest offering and the highest service, when thou thyself who worshippest art as pure and upright as thou canst render thyself."(22) To such an age of conservatism the thankful feeling is most suited, that Christ has brought to me and mine salvation here and hereafter ; but this assurance should be united with the most tolerant regard for the opinions of others. As soon as ever it is allowed to grow into the ecclesiastical dogma of exclusive salvation, which proscribes all who differ from us as lost, then must ensue the eager desire to proselytise described by Recha—

"If it be true
This is the only road that leads aright,
Can men resign themselves to see their friends
Advancing on another which descends
To death, eternal death?"

It at once becomes a solemn duty to save not merely one's friends, but all whom one can by any means influence, from the deluge of sin and from eternal death. And thus we have the enthusiasm for conversion, of which the darker side is fanatical persecution. Men delude themselves with the idea that God approves of every means which can be employed in His service, and so they burn the mortal body to save the immortal soul, if not the special soul of the particular heretic, at any rate, through the lesson of terror, the souls of many other unbelievers.

Nathan was intended as a counterbalance to this doctrinal rage; both to this and to the hateful tendency which, for the sake of the varying forms of Christian belief, breaks the bonds of affection, disturbs the harmony of families, and will not even permit that the dead should rest side by side in peace. It is undoubtedly true that so-called *free-thinkers* have been by no means always the most tolerant of people; but with them intolerance has been the fruit of an inconsistent passion for domination, while their opponents are consistent with their own principles, and are intolerant through a motive which they deem a sacred one. They believe, perhaps, "If you are not circumcised, you cannot be saved;" or, "If you do not suppress the workings of your carnal reason, you cannot be saved." Whatever opinion we may entertain of the maxim of Frederick the Great—that every one should be allowed to get to heaven his own way—we must, at any rate, admit that a wider tolerance is evinced by it than by the religious edicts of his successor. The Christian community enjoyed a far greater amount of freedom under the Saracen rule, than the Lutherans under Frederick William III., or free-thinkers under Frederick William IV.; and the Jews have not hitherto had much reason to exult in the privileges accorded to them in states which put forward a special claim to the title of Christian states.

At the same time it must be confessed that the parable of the three rings is given with as little intention of claiming for any one religion the sole distinction of truth, as of proving all three to be false; which last possibility the judge only admits as it were incidentally, in case each of the three sons should seek self alone, and thus should not maintain for his ring its miraculous power of rendering the wearer agreeable to God and man. And without stopping short at this admission he demands that, in a noble emulation of righteous thought and deed, each should endeavour to approve the worth of his own gem. That one ring should be genuine and the others but counterfeit, is an allegorical symbol, intended to illustrate the conviction of each of the three great historical religions that it alone possesses the jewel of a true belief; as well as to show that precisely because the faithful followers of each creed deem this gem to be their own, they are the more bound, not only to bear leniently with their opponents, but to acknowledge whatever truth they may be able to perceive in the antagonistic creed, which the adverse side is maintaining in its desire not to disobey the will of the common father. As Nathan affirms in his conversation with Saladin—

" Are they not founded all on history,
 Traditional or written ?   History
 Can be accepted only upon trust.
 Whom now are we the least inclined to doubt
 If not our people—our own blood ; not those
 Who from our childhood up have proved their love ;
 Ne'er disappointed, save when disappointment
 Was wholesome to us ?   Shall my ancestors
 Receive less faith from me, than yours from you ?
 Reverse it.   Can I ask you to belie
 Your fathers and transfer your faith to mine ?
 Or yet, again, holds not the same with Christians ? "

Thus the fanaticism for a single saving form of religion is replaced by a pious faith in our own creed, which to each of us has been given by God through the medium of our ancestors. Only most momentous and incontrovertible reasons can justify a breach with this faith; such reasons as occasionally possess a solitary individual, and sometimes have influenced an entire nation. It is, therefore, a most contemptible act when any one, for mere external inducements, either changes his own religion, or effects a change of faith in a mind which has as yet attained to no firmness of conviction. It is true that in these later days many Protestant princes do not consider it a matter of any importance if their daughters happen to marry into the Greek Church, though a simple citizen would regard a similar marriage as impious and a dishonour to his family. Catholicism attaches to such transactions a far greater weight, as did also the Protestant Church of the last century. Though an imperial crown was the stake of the first bridal of the kind, the wrath of the German Protestant populace was excited both against the aged sovereign who gave his granddaughter, and the theologian who exerted himself to persuade her. There will always, too, remain a division of opinion as to whether Henry of Navarre's attendance at mass was an act of self-sacrifice for the pacification of France, or an apostasy from his better self. And Henry, who was generally so light of belief, during a night of severe illness was affected by the dread that, in thus deserting his religion, he had committed the sin against the Holy Ghost. Of one thing we may be sure: Lessing never intended to assert Christianity and Mohammedanism to be equally efficacious. A mind such as his could not fail to perceive how much, even on this side the grave, depends on the religion in which a people has been brought up, nor could he have sung with the advocates of a mere human enlightenment—

> " Lo ! in a selfsame God we all believe,
> Him Christian, Turk, and Hottentot receive ! "

His treatise on *The Education of the Human Race* is itself only a tentative endeavour to embrace the various religions of the world in a historical scheme of the gradual evolution of the religious spirit through the form of progressive divine revelation. At the same time the ideas he expresses in this later work would have equally prevented his ascribing all miraculous virtue to a single ring, as is done in the narrow revised fable of the *Gesta Romanorum*. Had he accepted this as the basis of his drama, *Nathan* would have been but a pitiful production, foreign to the spirit of all true enlightenment, whether in his own age or in ours; in other words, it would have borne no stamp of its author. Neither this play, nor Lessing's powerful influence as a whole, was directed against Christianity, but only against the intolerance of its professors, founded on their assumption of being alone the people of God. But a poem which with so great a skill effected an attack on this assumption, could not, on the other hand, be expected to establish the claim of Christianity to the peaceful dominion of the world. If Lessing wrote in the sketch of a preface for his drama, "Nathan's feeling against positivism in religion has always been my own"—by "positivism" he simply meant what was then generally accepted as the meaning of the word, namely, arbitrariness and exclusiveness in a religion.

Nathan's character is still not by any means the result of any renunciation of the Jewish religion, for though he soars far above Judaism, then a historically servile creed, he never displays any consciousness of the Christian ideal, which, however lofty may be a man's own attainment, yet remains in advance of him. He does not even recognise Christianity in the form in which Lessing would derive it from the Gospel of St. John, as the Religion of Love.

Therefore *Nathan* is especially in disfavour with those who in the present day endeavour to sustain, not only the exclusiveness of a religion in which alone salvation is to be found, but also the definite interpretation of

Christianity, given by a particular theological school, and who even go so far as to regard the embracing an old friend of an opposite persuasion as a dreadful scandal, which must be atoned for by some lame apology. This kind of disfavour it shares in some measure with the whole of the German classical literature, which the nation generally regards as a chief instrument in its civilisation. Though not then actually brought on the stage for the first time, *Nathan the Wise* first obtained a success in Weimar, through the influence of Schiller and Goethe, in the end of the last century, the century of its production.[23]   In this success may be said to have been fulfilled the prophecy of Lessing's preface: " I know as yet of no stage in Germany where this piece could be brought forward.   But peace and good luck to the place where it shall first be represented ! "   During this century, though it has but seldom appeared on the programmes of the greater theatrical houses, even these have regularly re-produced it from time to time.   Then grave personages appear in the stalls, and young people are sent thither, as to hear an earnest, instructive discourse.   Perhaps in all German schools, with the exception of a few Church schools of the most modern order, speeches from *Nathan* are learnt and declaimed.[24]   Almost every boy who has received any school education knows the parable of the three rings ; and it will be found difficult to persuade either teachers or fathers that a book which their fathers placed in their hands as a treasure of religious wisdom, can be really a dangerous and unchristian work.[25]

Lessing under the mask of Nathan, and Melchior Götze, almost independently of their historical reality and their many - sided individuality, have remained deeply impressed on the German imagination in the character of fixed ideal types.   It surely can do little harm to youth to perceive in *Nathan*, and to derive from it, lessons of charity towards persons of another faith, or even towards Christians who do not maintain every article of the Lutheran Catechism; although no doubt by these lessons an opinion is strengthened, which under any circumstances it is not always easy to eradicate, namely, that it is not the letter of a man's creed alone which is the test of his moral worth, but that uprightness and piety are found among differing sects. *Nathan the Wise* is the visible illustration of the words of the Apostle, "In every nation he that feareth God and worketh righteousness is acceptable with Him."[26]

LECTURE VI.

THE CHURCH AND THE THEATRE.

As the preference accorded to secular themes constantly increased, their representation devolved upon a class of professional actors, instead of remaining in the hands of the great schools, or of honest citizens such as Shakespeare has painted in the *Midsummer Night's Dream,* or Gryphius with more rough fidelity in *Peter Squentz.* In consequence of this change, the rank assigned to the drama by popular custom was again lowered, and the stage began to pander to purposes of mere frivolous amusement, while the Church returned to her primitive opinion. Even the Old Testament precept which forbade that men should wear women's clothing was held valid; and when at length women commenced to personate their own sex, the sense that a money value was attached to their every glance, as well as the general debasement of the unhappy outcasts who joined the strolling bands, seemed even less in keeping with Christianity.[1] The sacraments of the Church were very generally denied to actors, even on their deathbeds, unless they solemnly promised that, in case of recovery, they would not resume their occupation. To many this vow was rendered easier by the absence of any hope that they should ever have an opportunity of breaking it. Real artistic inspiration could but rarely be maintained when thoroughgoing contempt was united with temporary approbation. Actors who refused the requisite promise, or who died suddenly, were buried as suicides; and thus by their exclusion from the pale of

M

the Church, and from all civic rights, a distinct social
barrier was erected, the tendency of which was to become
more and more definite, and to create its own justification.
Molière, against whom indeed the priesthood had a special
grudge, in his dying moments vainly besought the con-
solations of the Church; and the command of a king,
supreme in Church and State, was necessary to obtain
Christian burial for the privychamberlain to whom he
owed so many pleasant hours. Frederick IV., Elector of
Brandenburg, also forbade that the blessed sacrament
should be withheld from "merrymakers." In Frankfort
on Main, as late as 1753, the communion was refused to
Adam Uhlich, an actor and the author of some insignificant comedies, on the ground of his profession, although
he had not been on the stage for some years. He composed in verse *The Confession of a Christian Comedian*,
and died a lunatic. For a long time such a denial of
the sacrament and of Christian burial to an actor was
considered requisite to prove the zeal of a pious pastor.

Although the clergy could adduce no definite prohibition
from the Scriptures, their protest against dramatic performances, as being both sinful in themselves and an incitement to evil in the beholders, found its justification in a long
list of moral arguments, which were variations sometimes
on the assertion that evil, even when in the end it may be
worsted, is yet adorned on the stage with the attractive
sheen of heroic grandeur; at other times, on the counter
affirmation that there everything, even virtue, becomes
exposed to ridicule.([2])   But the root of the Church's
opposition really lay in the feeling that every secular
amusement in which she had no share would tend to
endanger the authority of the priesthood, and its power to
protect the souls of men.   When, however, modern learning
began to defend a taste which had become too strong for
suppression, the verdict of St. Thomas Aquinas himself
(note ([9]) Lecture I.), the prince of scholastic divinity, was
quoted in Catholic lands in defence of the guiltlessness of

the dramatic profession. Among the nations of the Roman communion, and especially in France from the beginning of the seventeenth century, a long literary controversy ensued on the question whether the drama is a permissible amusement for Christians. At this very period the classical works of French genius were being produced on the Parisian stage.

The chief opposition to the theatre originated in the body of thoughtful men who, under the distinguishing title of Jansenists, contemplated a religious reform of the Roman Church.(³) They considered a complete severance from all worldly interests, and a life wholly dedicated to God, to be the only safeguard of an elect soul. The poet who had written *Athalie* admonished his son to abstain from offending God and defaming the memory of his father by frequenting theatres.

Even among the Jesuits, the implacable rivals of the Jansenists, some strict moralists were to be found who maintained the sinfulness of all worldly spectacles; but, on the other hand, members of the same order argued that men might venture to yield to the allurements of the theatre, if they visited it without evil intent. The Jesuits have ever desired to be all things to all men, to the worldly-minded as well as to the devout.

Two leaders of the new learning, which was certainly far from theological, at length took sides in the clerical controversy. In an article on "Geneva" in the *Encyclopædia* a wish was expressed that this little free city, with its graceful culture and high social tone, would admit a theatre within its walls. While this admission would tend to the moral elevation both of dramatic art and of the character of the actors, it would also fill up a sensible void in this town otherwise so hospitable, and an example would be given which might prove of service to the whole civilised world. In opposition to this article, Rousseau, as a citizen of Geneva, pictured in a letter to d'Alembert the dangers of the theatre. (⁴) Like Plato, he reproached

the drama with exciting the passions, and also with
flattering popular sentiment, instead of endeavouring to
regulate it.   If reason were represented at all, it was only
that it might be derided.   The pretended spiritual elevation produced by the tragic drama would be merely an
idle excitement, which would induce men to be satisfied
with themselves and with their fine sentiments, while they
remained indifferent to their real duties : men would weep
over fictitious sorrows who had never dried the tears of
a fellow-creature.   The comic drama would promote abstinence not from vice, but simply from what was ridiculous.   Everything would be beheld in a false, exaggerated
light, and, being but a spectacle and incapable of produc-
ing any serious effect, the drama would tend to increase
every natural inclination to idleness and dissipation, and
to a forgetfulness of one's better self and one's duties;
while the theatre would become a secure retreat for
loungers, in this capacity best fitted for a great corrupt
town which can become no more corrupt than it already
is.   The players themselves, whose highest talent lies
in simulating a character which is not really their own,
and who in the exercise of their profession are exposed
to every public insult, can scarcely fail, off the stage, to
make use of some of the same arts which they have
employed on it, and they will hardly refuse to satisfy the
passions which have been roused in the theatre.   Let them
be under the ban of the Church or no, however stormy
the applause which greets them in the theatre, outside it
they will not need the excommunication of the priesthood
to become the scorn of every nation.

To this letter d'Alembert replied : ([5]) Man needs pleasure in some form in order to bear the bitterness and
insipidity of his daily life.   The stage offers him an
elevated pleasure in sympathy with human fortunes ; instead of allowing him to remain an isolated being, it
attracts him by its pictures of human life to a sympathetic
interest.   Its office is not to procure any sudden changes,

but by repeated impressions it gradually strengthens the weak and confirms the upright. What can be more effectual in fortifying us for good, than the fact that even when we actually see before us the fortunate results of vice, we are yet tempted sooner to envy the lot of virtue in adversity ? No ridicule is attached to goodness, but solely to the imperfect and pretentious imitation of it. If through the divine gift of imagination, which enables a man to penetrate the depths of an alien character and to represent it, he is rendered a hypocrite, then the poet is the greatest hypocrite of all. Though the profession of an actor is certainly surrounded by dangers, there is nothing which would do so much towards raising it as the circumstance that, instead of encountering alternate adulation and contempt, a player should be considered an artist and an honest man, as far as he has a claim to be so esteemed.

Each writer is, in fact, an uncompromising advocate. D'Alembert defended the cause of modern culture, while Rousseau employed all the instruments of this culture in advocacy of a sort of primitive Paradise, not certainly the Paradise of the Church, but an Arcadian condition painted by his own imagination. Yet when the Revolution appeared which was to bring this in its train, and the Church with her anathemas was engulphed amid the general earthquake, the theatre remained intact. The rulers of the Republic were desirous of availing themselves of its services, not only in inciting the populace, but in recommending sedate virtues replete with sentimental benevolence in the very midst of the Reign of Terror.(6) The deification of Reason in Notre Dame was itself a comedy ; and when Robespierre on the Champs de Mars burnt the Vices and proclaimed the worship of one God, he was but a player hurrying onward to the tragic close of his own drama.

In Spain, where the drama not only rested on a popular basis but gladly proffered its services to the Church, and where also the most celebrated dramatists were knights of religious orders, Brethren of the Inquisition, and priests, plays were not uncommonly represented in convents ; and a row of stalls in each of the great theatres of Madrid was in jest termed *Tertullia,* because these seats were usually occupied by noted ecclesiastics.([7])   To their artistic criticism special weight was attached.   Yet even in Spain clerical arguments were sometimes advanced against the permissibility of dramatic performances.([8])   In the very prime of the Spanish drama, when the life of Philip IV. had been darkened by the death of his Queen, which was speedily followed by that of the Infant, the zealots gained a temporary victory.   The theatres, which according to custom had been closed for the period of mourning, remained shut for five years, from 1644 to 1649; and they were then only reopened by the counsel of the Castilian Cortes, and under conditions appointed by them.   Only the Lives of the saints and the noble deeds of historic characters should be exhibited; while tales of love should be entirely excluded.   This limitation banished from the stage the greater number of the hitherto favourite plays, especially the comedies of Lope de Vega, which, according to the zealots, had done much to promote the corruption of morals, "more than a thousand devils."([9])   Exciting and alluring dances were also forbidden.   Of the perils of these we have lately had opportunities of judging on this side also of the Pyrenees. The official regulations, however, speedily fell into disuse, partly through the passion of the people for the drama, and partly also owing to the genius of the Spanish dramatic poets of the day.

As Calvin inflicted severe ecclesiastical penances on those who merely danced or even witnessed a dance at a marriage-feast, what would he have said to players in Geneva!   The same severe spirit triumphed in Scotland and appeared in England.   In this latter country the Reformation obliterated neither the Catholic forms nor a certain spirit of cheery worldliness, but it roused a threatening sentiment of opposition to them, which enrolled itself under the title of Puritanism, that is to say, pure Protestantism. The national secular drama, with its depth and humour, was a genuine national growth, produced by a combination of a knowledge of the antique drama with the influence of the old mysteries and moralities, which for a time continued to be acted, though cramped in their naïve development by the Reformation which it was their effort to serve. The rigid tone assumed by the opposition of the Church, perhaps furnishes the explanation of the fact that Shakespeare in his dramas was satisfied with the employment of moral force only. Many-sided as nature and unprejudiced as history, he sounded every depth but one of the human heart, and reproduced in permanent form what he found there. Even shapeless visions from the chill mists of the spirit world were compelled to answer to his call; but on religion he never touches, except in its most general aspect; and he scarcely ever introduces a sentence from the Bible, except in an occasional travesty intended to ridicule the Puritan perversion of the Sacred Word. We possess an emphatic declaration put forward by his comrades and himself in 1589: "These are to certify, your Right Honble Lordships, that her Maiestie's poore playeres, James Burbadge, Richard Burbadge, John Laneham, Thomas Greene, Robert Wilson, John Taylor, Anth. Wadeson, Thomas Pope, George Peele, Augustine Phillips, Nicholas Towley, William Shakespeare, William Kempe, William Johnson, Baptiste Goodale, and Robert Armyn, being all of them sharers in the Blacke Fryers' playhouse, have never given cause of displeasure, in that they have brought into theire playes maters of state and religion, unfitt to bee handled by them or to be presented before lewde spectators; neither hath anie complaynte in that kinde ever bene preferrde against them or anie of them. Wherefore they trust most humblie in your Lordships' consideration," &c.(10)

Religious fanaticism recognises no privileges of genius. While William Shakespeare was moulding a miniature world to the very image of the world of God's own creation, the Puritans were denouncing every spectacle as a pomp of the devil, such as Christians renounce at their baptism. They considered that a true Christian can have no time for the pursuit of worldly amusements, he knows that his day of grace is given him in order that he may work out his salvation with fear and trembling. He has, besides, no pleasure in such vain delights; his joys lie in attendance at Church, in fervent prayer, in the study of the Holy Scriptures, in singing of psalms, and in godly converse with pious friends. It was under the dominion of this conviction that William Prynne, a barrister of Lincoln's Inn, wrote his *Histrio-Mastix*, or "Players' Scourge," a tragedy of the theatre.[11] This work, of which the form is dramatic, undertakes to forestall the Last Judgment, and consigns to eternal damnation all actors and persons who consort with actors. Its severe sentence is supported by quotations from Scripture, and by numberless references to authorities both of the early Church and of later times. The same conviction ruled the Puritan Parliament, which, after having condemned its king to death amidst psalm-singing and speeches abounding in the phraseology of the Old Testament, prohibited all spectacles as amusements invented by the devil. Every player who continued to act in spite of the decree was to be scourged by the hangman, and every spectator was to be fined five shillings. William Prynne had to atone for his pious zeal by the loss of his ears and various amercements.[12] A little later the ecstasies of the Quakers and the revivalist sermons of the Methodists were represented on the stage for the delectation of the worldly-minded;[13] and after Shakespeare's dramas had for some time been held in abeyance by French taste, a Puritan outcry was raised in the eighteenth century that he had become the idol of Englishmen.

Luther was induced to speak a good word for the school comedies, both by his own bold artistic genius, and by his opinion of the value of these dramatic exhibitions for the improvement of the boys' Latin and for their general culture. " Christians," he says, " need not entirely shun comedies because occasionally coarse expressions and knavish deeds are found in them, as for this cause some might even refuse to read the Bible."(14) During the Carnival of 1525, he invited his friend Spalatin to be present at a comedy which was to be acted by some trained students in his house, the former cloister of the Augustine monks. Spalatin was also to remain to sup, and he was if possible to bring some pasty with him. Luther expresses his pleasure that the actions of our Lord, carefully and truthfully arranged in German and Latin pieces, were being acted in the schools, whereby the memory of them was impressed on the boys and their trust in Christ strengthened,(15) He even considers that some of the later portions of the Old Testament, such, for instance, as the Books of Judith and of Tobit, may have been originally dramas, which were only gradually converted to the prose form in which they have descended to us.(16) Melanchthon never forgot that in his boyhood he had assisted in the performance of a Latin scholastic comedy, composed by his great-uncle Reuchlin.(17)

Spener also, when Court Preacher at Dresden, commended the comedies of the excellent Gryphius as having strengthened him for good. Afterwards, however, the Pietism of which he was the founder, in its endeavour to transform Protestantism from a mere definite orthodox belief into an inward sense of the misery of sin and the need of a Saviour, declared everything which was not done in the name of Jesus, and which could not with the utmost directness be conceived as taking place in His presence, to be in itself absolutely a sin and even a denial of God and of Christ. The theatre was, of course, included in the general condemnation, which was fortified by the

same assertion that accompanied the early ecclesiastical
denunciations :([18]) that it was incapable of purification.
Spener himself headed the Berlin clergy when they
presented to the King a solemn petition demanding the
entire abolition of the theatre, especially on the ground
that in the favourite popular play, *Doctor Faustus*, Faust
abjures God and the Saviour.([19])   A spirit similar to that
of the Berlin clerical body actuated also Anton Reiser,
pastor of the Church of St. James at Hamburg.   In answer
to the complaint of the celebrated Veltheim Troupe that
the sacraments were denied to them, Reiser wrote his
Theatro-mania, showing " how the works of darkness
witnessed in the public plays are condemned by the
early Fathers and by some heathen writers."   Fuhrmann,
a Hamburg chorister, seconded this work by another
entitled " Satan's Chapel *versus* the House of God."
Fuhrmann relates how " when Veltheim's wife had a
sharp fever, in sore anguish of conscience and with the
fear of death before her eyes, she desired the Holy Sacrament, but no pastor could be found to administer it to so
vile a creature, till she solemnly vowed that she would
from that day forward forsake her evil mode of life, by
which renunciation she would render her bed of sickness
a bed of praise.   The which would truly have been the
case, but she did not keep her vow and soon fell back to
her former ways."([20])

The defence of the theatre was undertaken not only by
persons who had a pecuniary interest in it, but the animosity of the orthodox party against the Pietists led some
of the clergy to defend both the actual religious drama,
in so far as it might tend to the edification of their fellow-
citizens,([21]) and also the opera which at that time prevailed in its full splendour.   Pastor Elmenhorst, who
himself wrote some operatic texts, pointed out how the
modern opera differed entirely from the heathen plays which
the Fathers had justly denounced, since nothing vain or
idolatrous took place either on the stage or off it, and even

immoderate drinking was not permitted.([22]) The Theological and Judicial Faculties of Rostoch and Wittemberg, to whom the case was referred in 1693, condemned certain secular pieces, such as *Theseus* and *Alceste*, on account of their representations of heathen gods and amorous adventures unfavourable to morality; but they approved of operas on Biblical subjects, a large number of which were to be found, the natural result of the descent of the opera from the old mysteries. Méhul's *Joseph in Egypt* has survived to this day, and our own century has seen Auber's *Prodigal Son* produced in all its brilliancy, though, perhaps, scarcely with a hope that it, too, will live for future generations.

Frederick William I. banished from Halle, in 1715, all "comedians, jugglers and rope-dancers," because through them the students were only tempted to "ill lives and idleness." But when the Theological Faculty, in their pietistic legislation, wished to renew this sentence under the Philosopher-King, Frederick the Great, he wrote to his minister, "The players shall stay, and as a punishment the Methodist Francke sha himself go to the theatre, and the manager shall give him a certificate that he has done so."([23])

A second quarrel of the clergy with the Hamburg theatre took place immediately after the period when Lessing, though he had not succeeded in establishing in Hamburg a German national drama, had yet shaped for all future time the laws which should govern such an enterprise. A declining pietism had allied itself with a declining orthodoxy against the common enemy; and the Hamburg candidates for the priesthood were not only bound to subscribe all the articles of the Lutheran faith, but also on no account to enter a theatre. It was rumoured that some farces, which had been printed anonymously in 1768, were the work of Schlosser, now Pastor of Bergedorf, who had written them in his student days when he was a candidate for holy orders. Götze, the pastor who has been rendered immortal by his controversy with Lessing, at once publicly stated his sense of scandal at such an authorship.([24])   As the standing of the theatre no longer permitted him to condemn it unconditionally, he was only able to denounce all clerical countenance of it, while for lay Christians he instituted so many conditions, on which alone it could be permissible, that they amounted to a prohibition.   Aware of the opposition which he would be sure to encounter in Hamburg, not only from those who regarded the theatre in the light of a pastime, but from all who had imbibed Lessing's theory of an ideal stage, Götze referred his case to the Theological Faculty of Göttingen.   Their sentence put forward, in a clear and logical style, a number of precepts for the fitting conduct of a Christian; as, for instance, that since time is in such close connection with eternity, it becomes very sinful to squander it, not only in vicious pleasures, but even on harmless amusements; also every expenditure on a mere luxurious gratification is to be accounted an offence against Christian benevolence, nay an absolute injustice to the necessitous, to whom this superfluity is due by divine right.   By partly modifying the application of these principles, a certain leniency is observed in the condemnation of the authorship of dramatic pieces of a harmless order during the period of student life; but if a pastor should be unable to prevent the facts of such youthful lapses becoming notorious, he must publicly state his regret for them, either before a body of his colleagues or in a printed paper.   Dramatic representations are certainly admissible for the laity, but they must be free from everything antagonistic to Christian morality; they must portray only elevated characters, and have nothing to do with love and love affairs.

Such was the verdict of this learned body at a time when *Macbeth*, *Richard III.*, and *Romeo and Juliet* were not only written, but had become, through Lessing, well known to the Germans.

Schiller, when he first began to cherish an ideal of the future of the German drama, asserted the moral influence of the stage;([25]) and after the fashion of the culture of the day he bestows only a slight contemptuous side-glance on the objections of the clergy:—" If morality were no longer taught, if religion no longer commanded faith, if laws no longer existed, we should still shrink in horror from Medea when she descends the steps of the palace after the murder of her children. We should still be affected by a wholesome shudder, and each beholder would still be silently glad of his own good conscience, when Lady Macbeth, in her terrible sleep-walking, washes her hands and calls on all the odours of Arabia to destroy the hateful scent of death. Just as certainly as a visible scene has more power to influence us than mere dead letter and calm recital, even so certainly the effect of the stage is deeper and more enduring than that of law and precept." Its mission is to reveal what is hidden, and to betray the secrets of evil-doers. On it Truth sits in judgment, as incorruptible as Rhadamanthus. Her jurisdiction begins where the domain of human law ends. " When the bondage which binds the eyes of justice is tempered with gold, and she herself luxuriates in the offerings of crime ; when the vices of the great mock her impotence, and the arms of authority are bound by the fear of men, then the stage takes up the fallen sword and balance, and summons crime before a terrible tribunal. The realms of imagination and historical truth, of the past and of the future, are all subject to its sway. Dauntless villains who have long mouldered in the grave appear, in answer to the poet's all-powerful invocation, to retail to the horrorstruck learner of a later day the lessons of their evil lives." In the drama the great hear the truth, virtue is exhibited in her native beauty and vice in her inborn repulsiveness, while to folly a mirror is presented ; thus the stage becomes a school of practical wisdom. Men worn with work find in the drama a noble relaxation, while " the sad in their tears for alien sorrows, find relief from their own griefs, the joyous learn a lesson of sobriety, and the careless of thoughtfulness." To these benefits Schiller adds the influence of the drama for the consolidation and culture of a nation. "If we once succeed in establishing a national theatre, we shall become a nation." The drama teaches a man to understand his fellow-men, and is thus a school of charity and justice. Since, too, in the theatre men of every rank and occupation share the same sentiments and are united by the bond of identity in sympathy, which, as it were, obliterates even the self-consciousness of sex, so "each, enjoys the transports of all, which seem to gain in strength and beauty from the reflex glances of a hundred eyes, till at length in the mind of the spectator one feeling triumphs above all the rest, the consciousness that he too is a Man." Already the thought must have been fermenting in the mind of the poet which was afterwards to lead him, a scholar just emancipated from the harsh teaching of the Kantian system, to attempt to propagate, through the direction he tried to give to the theatre, a moral culture which he had never sought in the Church, and a doctrine of the redemption of humanity by art.

He was, at the same time, by no means unconscious that the German theatre of the day was but very little in correspondence with his ideal. It was much less a school of morality than an idle pastime; indeed, at times it served as an actual incitement to vice: "As long as the victims of passion are personated by the daughters of sensuality, so long will scenes of grief, fear, and horror serve principally to exhibit the marketable wares of a slim figure, small feet, and graceful movements. But let the Theatre take comfort in comparing herself with her greater sisters, Morality, and—I venture but timidly on the parallel—Religion. Though these come to meet us in consecrated garments, they, too, are not above the assoilment of the coarse, foul multitude."[26]

It was in sympathy with the ideal purpose just described

that Joseph II. dedicated the Royal Theatre of Vienna "to the spread of good taste and the elevation of morals." Iffland, who had been intended for the pulpit, and who ·always retained some traits of his destined profession, spoke the sense of the body of which, for so many years, he was the conscientious leader, when he asserted that the true actor regards himself as a public teacher. And in Prussia, in 1808, the theatre was associated with the Academy of Sciences among the institutions serviceable for education, and placed under the superintendence of the Ministry of Education and Public Worship. It is true that, two years later, in 1810, it was subjected to the surveillance of the police, together with other institutions for the convenience and entertainment of the people. But again some years afterwards, when one of the court clergy spoke of it as a mere pastime, Frederick William III. rejoined, "I attach more importance to it; I consider it an agreeable medium for moral instruction, and as such rank it among other establishments for the purpose."

Werner's *Luther* was acted by Iffland in a style which was at least calm and dignified, however little he may have possessed of the material to render him a fitting representative of Luther.[27] Although many persons strongly objected to the *rôle*, it made a considerable impression, and a *Moses* by Klingemann, and a *John Baptist* by Krummacher, were offered for the theatre. Also Dräsecke, then a pastor at Bremen, wrote a pamphlet *On the Representation of Sacred Subjects on the Stage.*[28] In this he divided sacred subjects into two classes. In the first class he included all that is elevated and moral in the life of humanity; in the second, everything definitely *religious*, that is to say, all that immediately concerns man's relations to the Deity. A question, he affirms, can only be raised with regard to this latter class: sacred themes are capable of dramatic representation because they can find expression through visible form, and through action and character; they offer an interest of an elevated order, and are susceptible of an ideal beauty of illustration. Since the painter may interpret a religious subject in form and colour, and the sculptor in clay and marble, why may not the dramatist do the same in word and action? It cannot with propriety be argued that it is impossible to separate the actor from his performance, while in every other form of art the work remains distinct from the worker. The actor does not pretend to offer his individual self as the representative of the sacred person, and even the less intelligent among the spectators, in spite of every effort at theatrical illusion, do not in the least confound him with the person he represents. At the same time the drama, like every other form of art, has its particular limits, and just as there are physical phenomena for the proper representation of which the theatre is too small, so there have been moral events too majestic for reproduction on the stage. Thus above its sphere, from a moral point of view, would be the giving of the law from Mount Sinai, the scene on the Mount of Olives, the Crucifixion, the Resurrection, and the Ascension. On the one hand these events present themselves to us as ideal types, embracing the sublimest conceptions of the human mind; and we prefer to cherish them in the silent and sacred depths of our imagination, rather than to see them translated into an all too corporeal form shorn of their divine splendour. On the other hand, as absolute distinct facts, they lie so far beyond all the usual bounds of human experience that they can only appear as it were crippled on the stage, and, thus crippled, they lose all their artistic worth. But, independently of such mystic and superhuman events, religious grandeur is a property of actual human life. A Luther, defiant of papal anathemas, standing fearlessly before Diet and Emperor; a St. Paul at Rome, Athens, or Jerusalem, toiling for the New Faith, and ready to encounter martyrdom; a John Baptist, preaching on the banks of the Jordan, and equally unwavering in his mission in the palace or in the dungeons of Herod—all these lie within the realm of the stage, if only poet, actors, and audience are not unworthy. The drama, contemplated from its artistic side, is full of solemn earnestness, but even before the altar the divine may be desecrated by unholy hands.

The comparison is not well chosen, although Goethe's influence on the Weimar actors was at one time so powerful that Amalie Wolff said that, on the day appointed for a rehearsal, she felt as if she were about to receive the communion.[29]

There has been, as far as we know, no religious persecution of an actor, as such, during this nineteenth century, not even in this latter half of it, although the Pietism which has now joined forces with the orthodox section of the Lutheran Church ought, logically, to condemn as sinful the vain love of the theatre. One might think, also, that the priestly spirit, which has lately arrogated to itself some ground even in this Church, could scarcely fail to grasp the keys of heaven in order to exclude actors. But in spite of the present decline of the European drama, the pathology of the German branch of which has but recently been put forward,[30] the principal German evangelical gazette has not even attempted to write down the Sunday representations of the Court Theatre. This fact may be explained partly by the force of modern culture, and partly by the respectable standing of actors on the stage of the present day, as well as by the recollection of the lofty artistic aims embraced by the German theatre during the golden age of its union with the great national poets. We may see by this example how a point which was once held vital by the Church,—or, rather, which her clergy, in uneducated narrowness but sincere good faith, thought it necessary to insist upon as a proof of their Christian zeal, —by the mere silent force of progressive culture, may become gradually untenable, and be relinquished almost without a struggle.

Christianity is no religion of barbarians, but is com-

N

patible with the highest culture, to which indeed it acts as a
pioneer.   As regards the expenditure necessary for a really
artistic stage, we may remember that it was Judas who once
said, "Why was not this ointment sold for three hundred
pence, and given to the poor?"   At the same time the arguments affecting all other forms of human life, and especially
all culture of which the aim is purely secular, must be
applied to justify or condemn the theatre.   It can scarcely
fail to appear a home of sin and temptation to every one
who considers this earth a mere vale of tears, and accepts
the priestly picture of man's life as designed solely that he
may prepare for immortality by crushing the mortal flesh,
instead of rather subduing and permeating it by the spirit.
Almost all educated men of the present day recognise the
fact that conversion and perversion are equally outside
the sphere of the stage.   It is true that there are insipid,
flashy, and even vicious dramas, which tend to encourage
effeminacy and levity in the spectators; but in their influence we see the results of dramatic exhibitions as they
ought not to be.   On the other hand, dramas with a distinct moral, such as in Germany were produced by Iffland
with a strong colouring of middle-class sentimentality, or
by Kotzebue with a considerable admixture of questionable scenes, have no proper value as works of art, and
have never really affected the spectators.   Dramas of
genuine poetic worth and elevated moral tone may assist
in invigorating and ennobling the character of a nation;
but every one who apprehends the nature of a sincere
conversion, in the grave Christian sense of the term, will
mistrust a change produced by the stage, even while
admitting that the Spirit of God, which speaks to man
through divers means, may employ even the speeches of
an actor to pierce an obdurate heart.

What Schiller asserted and prophesied of the drama is
true of poetry generally, and it is on the stage that her
triumphal procession passes before us in the most visible and
impressive form, in the closest union with all creative and

pictorial art. Dramatic representations, like poems, are
their own justification, even if it should be admitted that
they serve for nothing further than visibly to illustrate the
power of poetry ; and every cultivated nation should seek
to possess an artistic stage, since, in common with poetry
generally, though it may not be a means of salvation,
it exercises an influence which may become either wholesome or hurtful. The dramatic form, even when only
half complete, that is to say, while the drama remains
unacted, is unquestionably a powerful means of dis-
seminating particular ideas and feelings among a nation.
Voltaire made his characters express principles elsewhere
proscribed and persecuted by the State. We find in the
Spanish dramas speeches bold enough to excite our surprise that it was possible to utter them under the surveillance of the Inquisition. Lessing acted wisely when, in
the midst of his theological discussions, he again mounted
his old platform, the stage ; and *Nathan* affords a more striking sermon on tolerance than was ever preached in favour
of the opposite. With what force, in a time of oppression,
might not the Marquis Posa assert his gospel of freedom
not only before princes but before peoples! Thus, more
especially in periods when the mind of a nation is fettered,
and the pulpit no longer exercises its divine right of
sanctuary for the truth, that is to say, for the Word of God,
as freely given through Christ, the stage becomes a platform for an oratory which is certainly often not without
its own dangers. We are then reminded of the complaint of
Isocrates, " Since the establishment of democracy no one
is allowed freedom of speech, except the players who have
not your interests at heart."[31]

The clergy, to whom, in Protestant countries at least,
no form of human society is forbidden, need not be excluded from the theatre. Even the part of the Protestant
clergyman has found some place on the stage without
exciting any opposition. This is chiefly perhaps because
the character can hardly be employed except as illustrat-

ing the priesthood in its ideal form as a force to rebuke, to aid, to console; and since the appearance of Pastor Moser in the *Robbers*, this is the sense in which it has actually been represented. If Herder did write dramas, even as Calderon the priest wrote *autos*, can we discover anything unchristian in the fact? At the same time even heathen priests admonished Julian the Apostate not to show himself in the theatres. In those days it was not the tragedies of Sophocles that were represented. It is a debased stage and frivolous plays which a clergyman should not honour with his presence, or rather which he must not demean his calling by countenancing. And where pre-judices founded on old-fashioned custom would sustain a shock at the sight of a clergyman in the theatre under any circumstances, he is in duty bound to avoid that which is in itself innocent, even as St. Paul once enjoined on his converts abstinence from meats offered to idols. He can read what he may consider worth reading. Any direct professional benefit he may derive from the stage may be rated very low; the cause of Christianity may once have been furthered by religious dramas, but can never be served by clerical comedians. Goethe has expressed, through Wagner, the thought of a shallow culture—

> " I've often heard it said at least
>   An actor might instruct a priest."

True culture replies with Faust—

> " Yes, if the priest an actor be,
>   Which sometimes happens certainly."
>   —*T. Martin.*

The public use of the drama in its proper form is to cheer and elevate, or in other words we may say, as a counterpart to Plato's objection, *to purify the passions.* It is necessary, not that a man should be without affections, but that his affections should be refined, and become passions, pure and noble.

The moral influence and artistic significance of the stage are indissolubly connected with the seats of civic splendour and regal power, while the old-fashioned travelling bands, which are still occasionally to be met with, can seldom long escape the old disorderliness and squalor. They may at best serve to develop a theatrical talent, or to afford occasional harmless amusement. But even in the larger theatres great artistic pieces cannot be given every evening, and dramas which offer a mere light relaxation after the day's work have also their claim. It is a well-known fact that Frederick William III. in his latter days was a very frequent attendant at the theatre, and that he was quite satisfied with insignificant pieces. He was a pious man, and much interested in the Church, yet he once gave the following as his experience :—" Most preachers excite themselves in the pulpit in a mere empty oratorical style. It is a frightful idea to have to sit for half an hour and hear nothing but unmeaning stuff quite past bearing." When in his book of orders he would only allow an hour for the Sunday service, of which not more than half an hour was to be given to the sermon, his faithful bishop, Eylert, took courage to object, "Your subjects will say, Sire, the King can remain three hours or even more in the playhouse, but he never favours us with so long a time in the church." The King answered kindly, "I am glad to find you so frank. At the same time, you must forgive me for saying that is rather an unmeaning remark of yours. You have compared two things which are not in the least alike. In the theatre one is amused; in the church one prays and seeks to be edified. Now it is easy to be entertained for hours, but one can only be earnestly devout for a short time."(32) Perhaps this may really be the case generally speaking, even though minds of a special order have during long hours of prayer recruited their strength either for heroic deeds or for a life of silent self-sacrifice. The question then arises whether it may not be possible to combine amusement with edification, or, as our forefathers would have said, "amuse ourselves in a godly manner?" Why should we not even be able to find

edification in the very form of amusement in question, even
as the Middle Ages found it in the mysteries, which to
them were a living realisation of the ideas and pictured
forms, under the shadow of which all Christian people have
grown up, and which they can never cease to regard with
an affection which has in it something personal ?

Yet to us moderns the representation of the sacred
narrative will always have in it something that jars on
our taste, if for no other reason than because the actor
who to-day represents a prophet or a still higher personage, may to-morrow be assigned the *rôle* of an ordinary
mortal or perhaps of a villain; an actress may be to-day
the Madonna, to-morrow Lady Macbeth, or even the
Dame aux Camélias.   Artistic, and to a still greater extent popular, criticism becomes hardly possible when the
person represented is one before whom we naturally bow
in reverence; and it is also in fact impossible absolutely to separate the actor from his *rôle.*   The great duke
Carl August considered it inadvisable, on account of the
ironical remarks which would be excited, that his favourite
Caroline Jagemann the Younger should even act the Maid
of Orleans in Schiller's drama, which for that reason was
not immediately produced on the Weimar stage.   Such
sacred pieces could only be acted by amateurs, who might
regard their performance as a sort of religious service, and
even then they could only be given on particular festivals
and not in the ordinary theatres.   Under these conditions
something of the mediæval sentiment might again be
awakened, when actors and audience felt themselves, as it
were, one congregation, and united in prayer and praise.
And with all this, the influence of these Scriptural dramas
might remain a questionable one.   The proverb, "Seeing is
believing," would hardly apply to dramatic representations
of the sacred story unless the spectator were already a
believer.   Though wrapt perhaps in a somewhat vague
halo, the personages of the Bible will always appear far
grander to a devout imagination than it is possible to

picture them on the stage. Even at Oberammergau we shall find it difficult to forget that the great central figure is in reality a carver of crucifixes, and the Madonna only the sexton's daughter; while, if any sanctity were to be acquired by the representation of sacred persons, on the other hand, how dangerous would become the part of a Judas. There would certainly be less ground for objection in any place where the play has its origin in ancient custom, and among a simple Catholic people who are already familiarised in their worship with a rude realisation of the divine, and are thus less likely to be offended by the mixture of sacred and secular. The success of the Oberammergau Passion play may perhaps incite to imitation, but such an imitation will hardly be possible, and at any rate can only possess real vitality where it is a revival of an old tradition, and the resumption of a custom which has been merely held in abeyance by the civil arm.

At the same time among us moderns, indifference to religion and religious earnestness will be equally enlisted against the Scriptural drama. To the one the New Testament story will offer too little interest, to the other it will be too sacred a theme for the stage ;([33]) and it is, in fact, a part of the more complete artistic development of the drama that its office is now to illustrate the conflict of the passions and all the entangled web of human interests. Both the heroes of religion on their spiritual altitudes, and the martyrs in their Christian resignation, have done with these human interests, and the Son of Man ever held them in subjection.([34]) Then Christianity is an historical religion resting on a sacred written record, the inviolable nature of which, at least for Protestantism, leaves no room for the free exercise of fancy, which might give the fitting mould to the poem or the drama. Even in the mediæval mysteries the Biblical words are repeated again and again with an unchanging monotony; and it is only by the massiveness of the whole conception, and by the introduc-

tion of Old Testament types, that some compensation is
afforded for the free play of creative imagination.

The history of St. Paul too, in so far as we are accustomed to regard his words as the utterances of the Holy
Spirit, partakes of the same inviolable character; as does
that of Luther for those of his followers who see in him
the inspired founder of a new religion. Although the
earlier heroic and the later tragic years of the latter easily
lend themselves to a dramatic conception, it will always
be difficult for an alien mind to do him justice; while in
the memory of Protestant Germany the story of his life
is present in such distinct historical outlines, that poetry
will hardly earn any gratitude by attempting a dramatic
arrangement of these; as, for such an attempt to be crowned
with success, some transformation of the material would
become necessary. Besides, while we are unwilling to
see professional actors represent persons whose names we
are accustomed to hear with reverence in our churches,
amateurs will hardly prove equal to the task.[35]

The same considerations do not apply to subjects from
the Old Testament. Why should not the mournful end
of Saul's career afford material for a tragedy, as it actually
did to Alfieri, even though such an undertaking should
involve a slight departure from the ecclesiastical principle
of an absolute reproduction of the Old Testament story?
Such events can scarcely be termed in any special sense
religious, but belong rather to the domain of secular history, and there are even some among them which have a
peculiar value as historical records, the horrors of which
are altogether too harsh and unsoftened for dramatic
purposes. In this class we may include the crimes of the
house of David, which only the bold genius of the Spanish
dramatists, or the simple *naïveté* of Hans Sachs, might
dare to offer for the stage.[36]

But since religion is the property of our common
humanity, and as it were its flower, it often happens that,
even when the stage has no definite religious aim, the

poetry of the drama demands that a self-conquering, self-renouncing hero should pass away in a dim mist of religious glory. The story of Faust has an indestructibly religious tone, whether Faust is saved, or is eternally condemned, as in Marlowe's tragedy or in the German puppet-shows. In these, in spite of the Hanswurst,([37]) who in the last night when he is watchman indulges in many sly jokes, the impression remains on us so strongly that, when he calls the hours which announce the gradual approach of the midnight doom, the sound of his voice causes a shudder. In saving Faust, Goethe has preserved the religious significance of the story, although the actual theological interest, as we may see in the scene on Easter Eve and in Gretchen's agony, becomes subordinate, and assumes the form peculiar to the Roman communion, even as regards the mere jest about the wide jaws of the Church.

The devil has kept a firmer hold than the Hanswurst on the modern German drama. He is certainly a theological personage, but in his capacity as the ideal personification of evil he is also a poetic one; whether according to mediæval tradition he is treated as the comic personage, as by Hans Sachs; or as the incarnate Spirit of Evil, as by Goethe, who with a quiet irony gives to Mephistopheles the devil, a sort of human personality. In a Carnival play by Hans Sachs the Evil One inclines to take some repose, and in order to be sure of having a wife who will be faithful to an old husband like himself, he marries an old woman; but she makes his earthly home so hot for him that he cannot stand it any longer, and prefers to return to hell. It does not, on the contrary, seem to have entered into Goethe's plan to give his evil spirit a comic tinge through any exaggeration of his qualities, though this has lately been done by a celebrated actor. In the summer of 1857 the good people of Dresden were much amused by a farce in which Prince Hönigschnabel, a devil of the kind drawn by Heine, " a dear charming creature," only with a rather dark complexion and with pretty little horns like those usually bestowed on Moses, appeared in an elegant frockcoat surrounded by a gay company. In answer to the astonished question as to what had become of the old devil with his tail, he was made to say that he had cut off the last tail from his uncle as entirely out of date, his own kingdom was the embodiment of peace, of the motto "Live and let live." The belief in the personality of the devil will scarcely be promoted among a populace generally by such farces, especially when they are given in a royal theatre; though Vilmar, an authentic literary historian, affirms that he saw with his own eyes, in no metaphorical sense, the devil show his teeth from the abyss, and heard his mocking laughter echo underground.[38]

The downfall of a national religion offers a rich field to dramatic invention, and the tragic fate of Judaism has afforded material for a whole series of dramas.[39] Goethe once thought of selecting as the basis of a tragedy the encounter between Christianity and a culture doomed to destruction by a combination of causes both political and religious, and certainly the necessary extinction of the old mythology with all its beauty before the religion of the Cross has in it a highly tragic element. Schiller suggested, perhaps, the most suitable hero for such a tragedy when he spoke of composing a drama on Julian the Apostate.[40] His intention was certainly to annoy the *blackcoats* after the manner of Lessing; but in any really historical conception of the noble-minded Apostate, some justice must have been dealt to Christianity. That neither of these great poets carried out their idea is, perhaps, owing to the difficulty of giving any definite representation of the Christian religion on unconsecrated boards without offending modern sentiment.

It is, however, impossible entirely to exclude prayer from the domain of tragedy; for in moments such as those with which tragedy has to deal, prayer becomes the natural expression of the agonised or rescued soul, and is, as it were, its poetry. The admonitions of ecclesiastical bodies at the close of the seventeenth century had at the end of the eighteenth been replaced by prohibitions evincing a quite ludicrous dread of any religious allusion. In Catholic Germany, where people had become scrupulous about letting a priest appear on the boards which formerly the saints were allowed to tread, the king's confessor in Schiller's *Don Carlos* was transformed into his chancellor, while the massacre of the Huguenots became a fray of the Guelphs and Ghibellines. Körner relates that when *Hamlet* was being acted in Dresden, at the place where he has to say, "Look you, I'll go pray," the censorship of the theatre directed that this sentence should be altered to, "I'll look after my own affairs." Christian reverence indeed demands that subjects which have become in a peculiar sense associated with our religious belief should, as far as possible, be avoided; the Lord's Prayer, for instance, could not properly be repeated on the stage. Herder thought it very edifying when Schiller introduced the sacrament, but the Great Heathen, as the stricter religious party termed Goethe, showed more delicacy of sentiment, and would not allow the scene to be acted; while the confession of Mary Stuart, in which she acknowledges her guilt before God at the foot of the scaffold which she ascends innocent of her imputed crime, he allowed to be so integral a part of the plan of the drama that it could not be omitted. Any imitation of the giving of the sacred elements, in itself a symbolic and representative act, would jar on our feelings, even though it may be quite true that the representation of the first institution of this very sacrament at the Last Supper is viewed with edification at Oberammergau. On the other hand, religious functions will be the more readily permitted on the stage in so far as, together with their religious side, they have another which appeals to our universal humanity; we may instance a marriage or funeral procession and a coronation. So world-wide a subject as

Christianity cannot be entirely ignored in every drama; but where any religious machinery is required, it might be as well to allow the arches of a cathedral to form a vista in the background, or the clang of bells might announce the religious service which itself should not be given on the stage. Although the modern drama has its root in a subsoil of Christian culture, we ought still, in the spirit of Lessing's modest hope, to desire that some day a *Christian drama*, in the more accurate sense of the term, may again have power to touch the hearts of the public. By a Christian drama we mean one in which the principles of Christianity shall rule both the intricacies of the plot and the catastrophe. Existing pieces like the *Marvellous Magician*, the *Steadfast Prince, Polyeucte*, and *Athalie*, may perhaps be taken as arguments for the possible success of such an undertaking; and we may even derive some encouragement from the influence of *Nathan* itself. The Christianity of this new drama should lie in the ideas it illustrates, and in the motives of the action, and only in a very minor degree in any appropriation of that which is in a peculiar sense the property of the Church, her sacred history and her forms of worship.

The Church and the Theatre are, in fact, at present so completely dissociated, that even our mentioning them together carries with it an air of paradox. The Theatre is not excommunicated; but in furtherance of its own completer development it has emancipated itself from the rule of the Church. The general closing of the playhouses on the great festivals and in Passion Week, however little in keeping with the sentiment of an earlier age, quite accords with a modern feeling which has become habitual. In Rome they are not opened during the entire Lenten fast. It was among the minor causes of the unhappy estrangement of Herder and Goethe that the latter did not think it possible to dispense with the services of the Weimar students in forming the choruses of the operas, and in arranging for the performance of subordinate dramatic parts; while Herder, solely on educational grounds wished to deny to the young men an amusement so incompatible with their studies.([41]) But the order of a contemporary archbishop of Paris, that opera singers should not be permitted in choirs, shows an intentional deepening of the existing gulf between the Church and the Theatre; even though in some other places, precisely on account of the Catholic ritual, this gulf had often to be spanned. In Italy the clergy were obliged to be contented with merely excluding operatic melodies from the churches.

It is perhaps indeed in the universal speech of music that the more doctrinal side of Christianity may most readily again find its dramatic expression. While it was almost with a sense of scandal that I heard for the first time in Meyerbeer's *Huguenots* the band break into the melody of Luther's Hymn, there is a great propriety in the idea of suggesting the character of militant Protestantism by this its Reformation chant of war and triumph; and the sublimity of the strain, in the midst of the glitter of the secular music, has a very impressive effect. The Lutheran Church, too, at one time appropriated so much both of the melody and texts of popular songs, that a similar piracy on the part of a secular composer ought hardly to create much surprise. But if any one were to attempt to close a drama, we will say for example Werner's *Luther*, by singing the actual hymn in question, the effect, so far from being impressive, would rather offend our taste. We should not be edified by hearing a hymn on one day in the theatre which we were to sing on the next in our churches. At the same time, it is in the department of music that we may trace a revival of the mystery in the form best suited to the taste of the age. In the oratorio we have the dramatic effect without any attempted representation of sacred personages, which would be out of keeping with our more refined culture. This representation is replaced by the music and the chanted words. Bach's *Passion*, Handel's *Messiah*, Haydn's *Creation* with its picturesque secular tone, so admissible in a piece designed to illustrate the making of a world, Mendelssohn's *St. Paul*—all these are genuine mysteries, and have justly claimed to be reinstated in the churches, their original home.

One of our profoundest theologians has conceived the State as a moral community embracing every human concern, in which, as is actually the case in a Christian state, as soon as the Church assumes an overpreponderance, she advances to her ruin ; and from this conception he has gradually developed an idea of the future union of Christian ritual and the stage.([42])　We do not need to look forward to an age of fuller spiritual culture to imagine such an union, which we may rather see in the rude form of the mystery, even as the period when the State was the representative of the national religion also lies in the past. The vital force of religion in Christian countries has determined the current of human life in favour of a separation between Church and State.　Even as we trace in these, as far back as our vision can reach, the two fundamental principles of all human fellowship, in the State the justly ordered public association, in the Church the effort to form mankind into a religious community ; and as, too, each of these rests on its separate historical basis and protects and strengthens the other, thus will the Christian form of worship, which centres in the Word of God and in the simple sacred rites ordained by Christ, remain distinct from art, and only gather artistic forms around it in so far as these are immediately directed to the divine service and are an expression of the religious spirit.　But in the Theatre the poet will cause ever new pictures to pass before the successive generations of mankind, portraying for them all the changing varieties of human life, whether those which shall then exist or those which he may find in the memory or traditions of the nations.　With them he will combine the contrasts of feeling and fate, and the story of the conflict of the ideal with the real.　If the Theatre is to be the mirror of humanity, it has no need of the Church in her limited capacity as an institution for divine worship, while the Church has still less need of the Theatre. This latter is neither a portion of the sacred building, nor a chapel of Satan, nor yet is it fitting that it should assume with regard to the Church a magnificent position like that of the Royal Theatre of Berlin, which is situated between two ungraceful, half-modern, half-antique churches. The Church, as the brotherhood presided over by the Spirit of Christ, is necessary to the salvation of mankind; the Theatre is only the instrument of an ennobling culture and a means of harmless relaxation. The true union of the two forces does not lie in their identification, but in a friendly distinction of their respective offices, which shall tend to promote the welfare of both.

NOTES TO LECTURE I.

—◆◆—

1. GREEK Tragedy indisputably arose out of the national worship. This fact may be reconciled with the tradition that the wandering car of Thespis was the first Athenian theatre, only by supposing that Thespis anticipated later times in his attempt to divest the drama, as an entertaining performance by professional players, of its sacred meaning. This, however, still remained embodied in the choral songs.

2. *Lactantii Institt. div.*, vi. 2 :—"Comicae fabulae de stupris virginum loquuntur aut amoribus meretricum ; et quo magis sunt eloquentes, qui flagitia illa finxerunt eo magis sententiarum elegantia persuadent. Item tragicae historiae subjiciunt oculis parricidia et incesta regum malorum et cothurnata scelera demonstrant. Quid de mimis loquar corruptelarum praeferentibus disciplinam, qui docent adulteria, dum fingunt, et simulatis erudiunt ad vera ! Quid juvenes et virgines faciant, cum haec et fieri sine pudore et spectari libenter ab omnibus cernunt ! Qui hominem quamvis ob merita, damnatum, in conspectu suo jugulari pro voluptate computat, conscientiam suam polluit. Hos tamen ludos vocant, in quibus humanus sanguis effunditur. Adeo longe ab hominibus secessit humanitas, ut, cum animas hominum interficiant ludere se opinentur. Quaero, an possint pii et justi homines esse, qui constitutos sub ictu mortis ac misericordiam deprecantes non tantum patiuntur occidi, sed et flagitant ; quinetiam percussos jacentesque repeti jubent et cadavera ictibus dissipari, ne quis illos simulata morte deludat."

3. *Constitutiones Apost.*, viii. 32 [θεατρομανία]. *Concil. Illiberatanum,* a. 305, can. 62, 67—*Acta Sanctorum:* August. Trev., p. 119 *sq.*

4. Χριστὸς πάσχων. *Gregorii Nazianzeni tragedia, ed.Bladus,* Roma, 1542 ; and often reprinted in Gregory's works. The tragedy in the original, with metrical German translation, literary and historical

O

introduction, and explanatory analysis, was edited by A. Ellisen, Leipzig, 1855.

5. *Confess.*, ii. 2 :—"Rapiebant me spectacula theatrica, plena imaginibus miseriarum mearum et fomitibus ignis mei. Congaudebam amantibus, cum sese fruebantur per flagitia. Cum autem sese amittebant, quasi misericors contristabar ; et utrumque delectabat tamen." III. 3 :—"Cum mihi theatrici carminis certamen inire placuisset," &c.

6. In the Homilies on St. Matthew especially (*ed. Montfaucon*, t. vii. p. 60, 99 s., 113 s., 226, 422 s., 673, 712), there will be found numerous invectives against fequenters of theatres. A then favourite spectacle (*Majuma*) is above all anathematised. In it there occurred a scene of women bathing, similar to that in the *Huguenots*, but managed with less regard to decency. The very precise descriptions of what was to be found in these "show-rooms of immorality, lecture-rooms of lust, and schools of revelry," prove that the "Goldenmouthed Father" was by no means unfamiliar with their interior appearance. [The feast of Majuma was abolished by imperial edict in 399. For the relation of the Byzantine Church to the stage, see Hazlitt's *Warton*, iii. p. 294.]

7. *Concil. Arelat.*, A.D. 412.

8. Augustin : *De consensu Evangg.*, i. 33 :—" Per omnes civitates cadunt theatra inopia rerum, quarum lascivo et sacrilego uso constructa sunt."

9. Thus Thomas Aquinas (*Summa*, ii. 2, qu. 168, art. 3), expounds the office of a player as being serviceable for the enlivenment of men, and as not being blameworthy, if the player lead an upright life.

10. *Conc. Aquisgranense, a.* 816, *can.* 83, *concilia German*, ed. Harzheim, i. p. 476):—"Quod non oporteat sacerdotes aut clericos quibuscunque spectaculis in scenis aut in nuptiis interesse, sed antequam thymelici ingrediantur, exsurgere eos convenit atque inde discedere."
[Klein (iii. 635) quotes a French chronicler who affirms that Louis le Debonnaire (778–840) never broke into a laugh, even when *thymelici, scurræ, et mimi* came forward at festivals to amuse the people. It is important to notice the existence of these popular actors, especially in France and England, where they became the rivals or coadjutors of the clergy. The condemnation of actors found in John of Salisbury (1110–1180), *Polycraticus*, I. viii., evidently refers to

these popular players and not to the performance of miracle plays by the clergy.]

11. There is an indefinite tradition of dramas composed in the Frisian language by Abbot Angilbert in the time of Charlemagne. Fragments of dramas in Latin verse, dating from the ninth to the eleventh century, are preserved in the Munich Library. [The existence of these early fragments is somewhat apocryphal : see Wilkens, p. 168.]

12. This is not Helena von Rossow, nor is *white horse* nor *white rose* the signification of her name, though we doubt whether it is better represented by her own description : "Ego clamor validus Gandershemensis," taken from the old German "Hruodswind." [The last explanation is given by Jacob Grimm, who is cited by Klein, iii. p. 648. Klein, however, himself considers that the name is equivalent to Roswitha, *i.e.*, white rose. In the original preface to her comedies the name is written Hroswitha, not Hrotswitha, and is therefore probably not the same as "Hruodswind."]

13. Discovered in the Benedictine convent of St. Emmeran in Regensburg by Celtis, who, as Gottsched observes, was not a little surprised, "when he read how a German woman, six hundred years ago, was able to write in Latin, and even in Latin verse. Hroswitha's dramas were published first by him in 1501, and afterwards by Schurzfleish in 1717. They have been introduced to the French nation by the Academician, Charles Magnin : *Théatre de Hrotsvitha Religieuse allemande du X. Siècle traduit en français avec le latin revu sur le Msc. de Munich, précédé d'une introduction et suivi des notes*, Paris, 1845. See A. Barack, *Die Werke der Hrotsvitha*, Nuremb. 1856. [For Hroswitha and the questions raised by her dramatised legends, see also especially Köpke, *Ottōniche Studien*, ii., and Klein, l. c. There is no reason for supposing that Hroswitha's plays were ever acted ; nor does it appear that Terence's plays were acted at this epoch.]

14. [For the dramatic character of the Mass, cf. Ward, i. p. 18, ff. Mr. Ward shows that we have in the Mass "a dramatic action in part pantomimically presented, in part aided by both epical and lyrical elements." The pantomimical action in the Mass is supplied by the action of the officiating priest, the epical by the portions of Scripture read to the congregation, the lyrical by the anthems and antiphons and by the processional chants and hymns. There is no doubt that the service of the Mass has very materially affected the religious plays which were originally grafted on it. But the close connection between religion and the drama is not due ultimately

to the composition of the liturgy. Christianity is based on the life of a Person. This life itself supplies materials for a drama of the highest kind, and is linked in various ways with events and characters of Old Testament history, which are also fit subjects of dramatic art.]

15. See *Uffizio della Settimana Santa secondo il rito del Missale e Breviario Romano*, Roma, 1853.

16.   " Die heiligen drei Könige mit ihrem Stern
         Sie suchten den Herrn, sie hätten ihn gern.
         Sie kamen vor Herodes Haus,
         Herodes sprach zum Fenster heraus.

        " Ihr lieben drei Weisen, kommt rein zu mir,
         Ich will euch geben Wein und Bier,
         Ich will euch geben Heu und Streu,
         Auch sollt ihr haben die Zehrung frei.

        " Ach nein, ach nein, wir müssen fort,
         Wir haben ein kleines Kindlein dort,
         Ein kleines Kindlein, ein' grossen Gott,
         Der alle Dinge erschaffen hat."

Given by Weinhold (p. 132) from Sömmerda. Every student of Goethe knows that poet's graceful travesty of these lines for a masque, in which Corona Schröder acted the beautiful White King.

17. *Chroniques de Sire Jean Froissart*, l. iv. c. 1.   The angels sang—

         " Dame enclose entre fleurs de lis,
          Roine estes vous de Paris,
          De France et de tout le pays,
          Nous en rallons en Paradis."

18. Dlugossi, *Hist. Polon.*, i. 94. P. C. Hilscher, *De Dominica Laetare rituque idolum mortis illa die ejiciendi*, Leips. 1690, 4. J. C. Zeumer, *De Dom. Laet. vulgo Todtensonntag*, Jena, 1701, 4. [The fourth Sunday in Lent is in Germany termed Sonntag Lätare, and was observed with special festivities.] C. H. F. Kruse, *Ueber das Fest des Todtaustreibens und Sommersingens* (Zeitschr. für hist. Theol., 1838). Witzchel, *Ueber der Sommergewinn in Eisenach* (Zeitschr. für hist. Theol., 1852). [Kruse gives the following account of the custom, which may be interesting to English readers :—" In Silesia, on Mid-Lent Sunday, the feast is celebrated, ' des Todtaustriebens und des Sommersingens.' This festival contains the traces of very

ancient customs, and is therefore sufficiently interesting to repay some notice both of the ceremonies observed at it and of their probable origin. It is chiefly to be found now in country places only, . . . but I have understood that it was celebrated as late as 1819 in Breslau by some persons of the lower class. . . . I can give some account of the festival in the neighbourhood of Kreuzburg from information collected by myself when I was in Silesia. The mode of celebration is as follows :—On Mid-Lent Sunday, early in the morning, the young girls of the place collect branches of fir from the neighbouring woods, which they ornament with strips of red, blue, and yellow cloth, or sometimes with ribbons, and these boughs so entwined they call *Summer*. Above the boughs they generally fix a small doll. Thus provided, they promenade the streets of the towns and villages singing hymns in celebration of the sufferings of Christ, and other songs of which the subjects are much less morally elevating. The people give them bread, butter, eggs, money, and trifling presents, which they divide fairly among themselves, singing in return verses expressing their gratitude. They continue thus parading the streets till three or four o'clock in the afternoon. Then follows the ceremony of the 'Casting forth of Death.' For this the youths, or occasionally some of the men of the neighbourhood, go to the woods, where they hew off a great pine branch, and roll it round with straw and oakum till it assumes something of the shape of a man. Then the schoolboys put on it a face made of painted paper. Every peasant will offer a piece of straw to help. Then the *Popel*, as this figure is called, has to be dressed. First some old hat or cap is placed on its head, and round the neck, instead of a cravat, is wound a rope of straw. Then comes an old jacket, then a pair of trousers made of scraps of bright coloured cloth, while sometimes the attire is rendered quite complete by a pair of shoes or boots. When the puppet has thus been decked out in the midst of noise and shrieks of laughter, the young men attempt to carry it off to souse it in the nearest brook, but this the girls will not allow. They come running up and try to prevent the drowning, their efforts causing much noise, accompanied by shrieks, pushing, and blows. However, the girls cannot get the better of the youths, who all defend the one who is carrying 'Death ;' and in the bustle of the struggle the party approach ever closer and closer to the brook, where the figure is undressed and thrown into the water in spite of every endeavour on the part of the girls to prevent this. Then the whole crowd set off to rush home, singing perhaps a few songs, and screaming noisily. The evening is passed in dancing, feasting, and singing."

In Trebnitz it was thought that the person who might chance to be the last to reach his home would die that year. Before leaving the village Death was exorcised from the last house in which some one had died. The straw figure was not allowed to remain in the brook, but was taken out by the youths. In Breslau, at the time Kruse wrote, the "Sommersingen" was still kept up by children without the other observances, and he quotes the verses they were in the habit of singing. One of the sources given by him for the festival is the same as that mentioned by Dr. Hase—the casting forth of the images of the old gods on the introduction of Christianity. At the same time he ascribes to this merely a minor influence in the sustenance of the traditional custom. At the end of his article he sums up the result of his inquiries.

"1. The casting forth of Death and the welcoming of the summer by song are the last remains of an old heathen new-year festival, which was intended at once as a tribute of honour to the dead, and a celebration of the reawakening of the productive forces of nature. The feast is by no means entirely of Christian growth.

"2. The groundwork of the main idea of the festival and of the customs observed is to be sought both among the nations of Southern Europe and of Northern Africa, and in the farthest East.

"3. It seems to have been imported from the south, and its degree of kinship to the Italian, Greek, Egyptian, Indian, and Persian festivals, which were celebrated about the same time of year, could only be traced through an exhaustive examination of the customs of the Slavonic race. The root of the ceremony must be sought in India."]

19. [Some old popular customs, such as the wandering of the Wise Men on Christmas Eve, may have been derived from pagan ceremonies ; but the religious play itself, as Professor Hase intimates, cannot be traced to a heathen origin. The Christmas play was due neither to the Roman Saturnalia nor to the Scandinavian Yule feast, though the latter name was afterwards applied to Christmas. For former surmises as to the origin of the religious drama, see Warton, iii. p. 95, ff. ; Collier, ii. p. 55.]

20. See Grieshaber on the Easter Sequence, *Victimae paschali*, in its relation to the religious drama of the Middle Ages, Karlsruhe, 1844.

21. *Synod. Dioeces. Wormat.*, A.D. 1316, c. 2 (*Concilia German.*, ed. *Harzheim*, iii. p. 258).

22. For the sake of theatrical convenience this generally is not introduced, in spite of the Scripture, until after the Resurrection.

23. [The interest in the persons introduced into the scenes properly

belonging to the Easter festival would naturally lead to the inclusion of all those parts of the Gospel history into which they had entered. It was perhaps this personal interest, rather than a desire for theological completeness, which led to the first expansion of the Easter play, until it even includes the scenes of the Christmas play, and cannot well be distinguished from it.]

24. The Church's strain, "Orietur stella ex Jacob," is met by the response of Virgil, *Ecl.* iv. 5-7:—

> " Magnus ab integro saeclorum nascitur ordo,
> Jam redit et Virgo, redeunt Saturnia regna ;
> Jam nova progenies coelo dimittitur alto."

Thus in the annual service of St. Paul at Mantua, it is said of the Apostle, as he passed on to Posilippo—

> " Ad Maronis mausoleum,
> Ductus fudit super eum,
> Pie rorem lachrymae ;
> Quem te, inquit, reddidissem,
> Si te vivum invenissem,
> Poetarum maxime ! "

25. For pictorial illustrations of this legend, see Piper, *Mythologie d. Christl. Kunst*, Weimar, 1847, i. p. 485, ff.
[" Lebeuf mentions a Latin Mystery written so early as the time of Henry I. of France (1031–1061). In this Virgil is associated with the prophets who came to offer their adorations to the new-born Messiah, and at the conclusion he joins his voice with theirs in singing a long Benedicamus. A fragment of what may be a German translation of the same Mystery, copied from a MS. of the thirteenth century, will be found in Dieterich's *Specimen Antiquitatum Biblicarum*, p. 122. But here Virgil appears as an acknowledged heathen; and he is only admitted with the other prophets from his supposed predictions of the coming Messiah contained in his *Pollio*."—Warton, i. p. 217, *note.*]

26. In the German *Prophecy of the Sybil* (see Mone, *Schausp.*, i. p. 313) Seth is only sent for a fruit of Paradise, not of any particular tree. In the Christmas play given by Jubinal (ii. p. 17, ff.), Adam sends him for the oil of mercy, a kind of oil of extreme unction to keep off Beelzebub, who is seen lurking in the background with his halter. It is only later in the play, in obedience to a divine command, that Seth plants the twig on the grave, and in this case it is from the Tree of Knowledge. It is to produce the Tree of the

Cross, and thus overshadow death by life.   There is some depth of
fancy in this legend ; the Tree of Knowledge turned to a right
account acquires a deeper significance, and becomes the Tree of
Eternal Life.   In a play of the Fall of Man (given by Schönemann
at p. 48), the angel bestows on Seth three seeds from the Tree of
Paradise, from which grow three trees—a cedar, a cypress, and an
olive tree.   The first is a symbol of the Father, the second of the
Son, the third of the Holy Spirit.   The sending of Seth is borrowed
from the *Gospel of Nicodemus*, c. 19.

27. Mone, *Schausp.*, p. 27, ff.   *Der Sündenfall und die Marien-
klage.   Zwei niederdeutsche Schauspiele aus Handschr. d. Wolfenb.
Bibl. hrsgg. von Otto Schönemann*, Hanover, 1855.   Pichler, p.
115, ff.

28. Weinhold has (p. 91) a duet between Jodl and Riepl, the
rustic names for George and Rupert.   It is from Upper Carinthia,
and runs thus :—

> " *J.* Auf auf Riepl, heb dein Schedel !
>   Schau was gibts für frömde Göst !
> *R.* Halt dein Maul du grober Kerl,
>   Hoan mi glei glögt ins Nöst.
> *J.* Dort gibts Engel ganz scharweis
>   Fleugen um wie die Flödermaus.
> *R.* Hast mei Jörgl glei wol trôfen,
>   Der uns hat das Heil verkündt.
> *J.* Sein mir nit umsonst herglôfn
>   Sehn schon auf'n Heu das Kind.
> *R.* Darf ichs küssen ?
> *J.* Kanst nit wissen !
> *R.* Wann's dö Mutter küssen last
>   Von an so kolschwarzen Gast.
>   Bist der wahre Herrgôts Bue,
>   Bleib heunt dô, kriegst Krapfen gnue !
> *J.* Mein Heiland wie hart muest löben,
>   Underm Vieh fangsts Löben oan !
> *R.* Voder, Mueter thuts acht göben,
>   Dass dem Kind nix gschehen koan.
> *J.* Ihr muessts Kind zudöcken fein,
>   Dann dem Ochs fallts â nit ein !
> *R.* Dank dir dass so guet bist gwösn
>   Und hast üns den Gfallen thoan,
> *J.* Hast uns gwöllt vom Tod erlösn,
>   Beten dich von Herzen an.

R. Bleib halt fein gsund, mein kloans Liebl,
    Wann' woas brauchst, so komm ze mir.
J. Kannst in mein Dienst stehen ein,
    Wann darzu wirst gross gnue sein."

29. In Munich this picture is ascribed to J. van Eyck, but Berlin criticism gives it to Rogier van Brügge. See Kugler, *Gesch. d. Malerei*, 2 Q., Berlin, 1847, b. ii. p. 124.

30. L'Enfant, *Hist. de la guerre des Hussites*, Amst. 1731, 4, ii. p. 440. Flögel, *Geschichte der komischen Literatur*, iv. p. 291.

31. *Mystère de la Nativité.* See Jubinal, ii. p. 1 *sq.* The scene with the shepherds, and the *Jeu des trois rois* which is followed by the Flight into Egypt, are, however, here only adventitious additions.

32. *Adam, drame anglo-normand du XII. siècle publié pour la première fois d'après un manuscrit de la bibliothèque de Tours, par Victor Luzarche*, Tours, 1854. In the *Gottinger gel. Anzeiger*, 1856, at p. 24, Adolf Ebert points out that the epilogue, which is of unparalleled length (362 lines), although given with the play in the MS., which is itself a compilation, yet really belongs to some other piece, of which the subject was probably the Last Judgment.

33. He recommends himself to her on his first appearance by the assertion that he knows all the secrets of Paradise, and that he will instruct her in some of them. She is at once curious to hear them, but he demands from her the promise that she will never speak of them to any one. She promises, and he then finds fault with Adam for being so dull (*fols*). She adds that he is also rather hard (*durs*). The devil thinks he will soon become more yielding. Eve replies, " *Il est mult francs* " (He is quite his own master). On this the devil responds, "*Ainz est mult serf* " (Nay rather quite in subjection). "Thou art weak and a gentle creature, fresher than a rose and whiter than snow. It was unjust of the Creator to make thee so soft and Adam so hard ; but, in spite of all, thou hast the most wit, and a mind set on high things." In this style he continues to delude her.

34. Parfait, iii. p. 53, f.

35. [The oldest remains of the early *officia* out of which the mystery was developed were discovered at Freising in Bavaria, and at Orleans, Limoges, and Rouen. They are printed in Weinhold and Du Meril, and discussed by Wilkens, pp. 5, ff., 168, ff.* In Germany,

* The Orleans services were first printed by Mr. Wright, *Early Mysteries.*

as well as in France, the mysteries appear to have sprung up independently. No early English offices such as those which form the basis of the play in France and Germany have been hitherto discovered, although such usages must have been common : cf. Hone, p. 222, *note.* But at the time when miracle plays or mysteries were gradually growing up in Europe, England was undergoing the changes which followed the Conquest. The introduction of the miracle play into England was probably due to French ecclesiastics. The earliest play acted in England, the *Ludus de S. Katharina,** about the year 1110, which was probably in Latin, was composed by a Norman monk ; the first dramas from the pen of an Englishman, those of Hilarius, were also in Latin, and were written in France not many years later. The mysteries, however they were implanted on English soil, soon reached their full development. Traces of their existence are found in the end of the twelfth century, but they received the greatest impulse from the institution of the festival of Corpus Christi in 1264.† The earliest mystery extant in English is probably the *Incredulity of St. Thomas,* written for performance by the Scriveners' Guild at York, and evidently forming one of a series of plays on the New Testament. It is one of the peculiarities of the English mysteries that they are combined into series in which the whole course of Divine Providence from the Creation to the Day of Judgment is placed before the spectator. Three such groups have been preserved, known as the Chester Plays (which have been ascribed to so early a date as 1268), the Towneley or Widkirk, and the Coventry Plays. For a full and interesting account of these, and the question connected with them, see Collier, p. 65, ff. For the actors of the English mysteries, or miracle plays, see note 50.]

36. Weinhold, p. 51, ff.

37. *Ludus paschalis de adventu et interitu Antechristi. Erutus e cod msc. Tegernseensi a P. Bernardo Pez.* In *Pezii Thesaurus Anecdotor. noviss.,* Aug. Vindel., 1721, t. ii. p. iii. p. 186 *sq.* See *J. G. V. Engelhardt, de ludo paschali qui inscriptus est: de adventu et interitu Antechr.,* Erlang. 1831, 4 (programme of Easter play). Fr. Kugler, *De Werinhers saec. XII. monacho Tegernseensi,* Berol. 1831. I was tempted to picture to myself as included among the Hypocrites in the army of Antichrist, the mendicant orders as they would appear to a wealthy and learned Benedictine of the period. In this case the piece would have belonged to the thirteenth century, and to the reign of Frederick II. But present researches point to

---

* See p. 22.

† Both Piers Plowman and Chaucer refer to them as familiar usages.

Wernher, a monk and deacon in Tegernsee, as the probable author. This Wernher composed also, about 1172, a German epic poem on the life of the Virgin, of which a fragment and an old imitation are preserved. If he should prove to be the author of the *Antichrist*, it must belong to the reign of Frederick I., and the patriotic monk Waldo and other heretics probably served as models for the hypocrites.

[The only other known play on the subject of Antichrist is contained in the Chester Mysteries, the twenty-third in that series. The Chester play has no political bearing. The Tegernsee play of Antichrist is also printed by Mr. Wright, *Chester Mysteries*, vol. ii.]

38. That this play was very generally known we are led to suppose by the verses borrowed from it in the *Ludus scenicus de nativitate Domini*, a collection of German and Latin hymns from Benedictine records of the thirteenth century, published for the Stuttgart Literary Union by Schmeller: *Carmina Burana*, Stuttg. 1847, p. 80, ff.

39. Latin, "Gentilitas."

40.
> "Haec est fides, ex qua vita,
> In qua mortis lex sopita.
> Quisquis est qui credit aliter,
> Hunc damnamus aeternaliter."

41. "Sequentur Apostolicus a dextris et Imperator Romanorum a sinistris." This sentence has caused Jubinal, generally a most trustworthy authority on the miracle play, to fall into the mistake of ascribing a Protestant tendency to this piece (t. i. p. 16) : "Le pape se trouve désigné sous le nom de l'Antechrist." It is certainly true that the design of the piece is more to magnify the Emperor than the Church, and the Pope is merely an enthroned mute.

42.
> "Sicut scripta tradunt historiographorum,
> Totus mundus fuerat fiscus Romanorum,
> Hoc primorum strenuitas elaboravit,
> Sed posterorum desidia dissipavit."

43. "Cum jam tota Ecclesia subdita sit imperio Romano," signifies absolutely more than this, but the context will only admit of the meaning given.

44.
> "Nostro consilio mundus favebit totus.
> Nos occupamus favorem laicorum.
> Nunc per te corruat doctrina Clericorum."

45.   " Deponam vetera, nova jura dictabo."

46.   " Et cum Teotonicis incantum proeliari
     .   .   .   Teotonicorum furor
     Extollit cornua contra religionem."

47. *Les vierges sages et les vierges folles.* See Mommerqué, p. 1 *sq.*
From the chant at the commencement this would appear to have
been an Easter play :—" Ubi est Christus meus Dominus et Filius
excelsus ? Eamus videro sepulchrum ! Quem quaeritis in sepul-
chro o christicole, non est hic. Surrexit sicut prae dixerat," &c. ; with
the response : " Adest sponsus, qui est Christus : vigilate virgines ! "
After the short drama in the words of the Scriptural story, the prophets who prophesied of the Redeemer follow in a long procession
which ends with John the Baptist. The list includes Virgil as *vates
gentilium*, as well as the Sybil and Nebuchadnezzar—this last because
he saw the Son of God walking with the Three Children in the fiery
furnace. This series of prophets does not, however, appear to be
rightly placed at the end of the drama, though it is very properly
connected with the hymn—

> " Omnes gentes congaudentes
> Dent cantum leticie
> Deus homo fit de domo David
> Natus hodie."

That this piece may therefore be part of a Christmas play is very
properly urged by Weinhold (p. 71), but when for that reason he
regards the prologue on the grave of the Saviour as not belonging to
the drama of the *Virgins*, the reverse of the argument might be
applied to the scene in which the prophets appear. If the parable
of the Virgins is only part of a longer piece, it may be an introduction to a mystery of the Last Judgment, which might certainly have
been performed as an Easter play.

48. Innocent III., A.D. 1210 (*Gregor. Decret.*, l. iii. tit. 1, c. 12) :—
" Interdum ludi fiunt in Ecclesiis theatrales, et non solum ad ludibriorum spectacula introducuntur in eis monstra larvarum, verum
etiam in aliquibus festivitatibus Diaconi, Presbyteri et Subdiaconi
insaniae suae ludibria exercere praesumunt. Mandamus quatenus,
ne per hujusmodi turpitudinem Ecclesiae inquinetur honestas, prae-
libatam ludibriorum consuetudinum vel potius corruptelam curetis e
vestris Ecclesiis extirpare."   *Concil. Trevir*, A.D. 1227, can. 6 (*Conc.
Germ.*, t. iii. p. 529) :—" Non permittant Sacerdotes ludos theatrales
fieri in Ecclesia et alios ludos in honestos." The Diocesan Synod of
Utrecht (A.D. 1293) went still further (see *can.* 11, *Conc. Germ.*,

t. iv. p. 17) :—" Ludos theatrales, spectacula et larvarum ostensiones in *Ecclesiis* et *Cimiteriis* fieri prohibemus."

[The statement in the text requires some modification. Pope Innocent's edict was intended to apply to Italy and to France, as well as to Germany. In France the Feast of Fools and the Feast of the Ass, in which the priests had taken part, seem to be specially reprehended. The German mysteries hardly come within the scope of the edict. In the same way, a decree of the Synod of Worms, 1316 (see note 59), forbids the clergy to be present at shows, processions, or performances of jugglers (*speculatis, pompis, joculatoribus*); and other similar prohibitions have been found. These decrees refer to secular performances, or, at all events, to performances by secular actors ; for special mention is made of masking and mummery, which were never employed in the German religious plays, although they were an essential part of popular performances and of the Fastnacht-spiel. Cf. Wilkens, p. 252, ff.]

49. " Popule meus, quid feci tibi aut in quo contristavi te," &c. Pichler, pp. 17–28.

50. [The *Ludus de S. Katharina* was acted, as has been said, by the pupils of a conventual school. But another class of players had been introduced into England by the Conquest. Minstrels (French, *menestrels*, from the Latin *ministerium*) and *joculatores* came over from France, and were welcomed in the monasteries by the French-speaking inmates, while they made themselves acceptable to the people by shows and stage tricks (see Ward, i. p. 15, ff.). These actors are known to have aided the monks in the performance of plays (Collier, ii. p. 70). No doubt they helped to supply materials for a professional class of actors in later times. The author of the *Manuel des Pechiez* supplies evidence that in the thirteenth century the clergy themselves were actors as well as writers. But before long the acting of the plays passed chiefly into the hands of the trading companies. At Coventry, for example, each portion of the collective series is assigned to some company; *e.g.,* the Smiths' Company acted the Trial and Crucifixion, the Cappers' Company acted the Resurrection and Descent into Hell, the Shearmen and Taylers' Company undertook the Birth of Christ, the Adoration of the Magi, the Flight into Egypt, and the Massacre of the Innocents. Special guilds also devoted themselves to the acting of the plays, such as the Guild of the Holy Trinity (Sharp, p. 165) and the Guild of the Lord's Prayer (*History of Early English Guilds*, Early English Text Society, 1870). The parish clerks also took a prominent part. In London, Clerkenwell was the scene of their performances. Until the miracle play fell into disuse, the trading companies and guilds seem principally to

have maintained them. The mixture of secular with ecclesiastical players doubtless helped to change the character of the English plays, and to provoke the censure which from the beginning of the thirteenth century began to be directed against them.]

51. *" Wir wollen halten ein Osterspiel,*
        Das ist fröhlich und kost nicht viel."

Quoted by Hoffmann from a Viennese manuscript of 1472 (ii. p. 298).

52. I have certainly only been able to find a distinct reference to this space as a common ground for all in a MS., of comparatively late date (sixteenth century), of a large Passion play at Donaue-schingen, which is interspersed with stage directions for the perform-ance. In the sketch which accompanies the MS., besides eighteen separate spaces, there is a hill in the middle, intended to serve as the common stage for the Last Supper, the Scourging, the Crowning with Thorns, and other parts of the play. Mone (*Schausp.*, p. 154, ff.) is of opinion that this common ground was customary, and he has completed the plan of the Donaneschingen MS. by placing the seats of the audience in a semicircle on each side of the stage—that is to say, as in an amphitheatre. But of this no trace is to be found, and the nature of the action is against such an arrangement. For combats and circus sports, where the performers have to approach from all sides, the amphitheatre is suitable ; but where a consecutive story has to be represented in action and speech, the action must be directed towards spectators in front, while it is impossible for a large audience to hear the player's words unless placed in front of him. The Romans invariably observed this distinction between the theatre and the amphitheatre, and in Pompeii the two buildings stand in close proximity. Plays were certainly sometimes acted in ancient amphi-theatres, and I have seen one occasionally in the amphitheatre at Verona ; but in the use of this amphitheatre we have only an instance of the employment of a convenient spot as a summer theatre, a tem-porary wooden stage having been erected in the centre, and the space for the audience limited to the ranges of seats immediately opposite, while by far the larger portion both of the arena and the outer circle remained untenanted in empty grandeur.

[Each group of actors to whom a special part was assigned, appears to have taken up its quarters for the day on the stage, on its own special *Burg*. In France, also, the players remained all day in their quarters on the stage. Much light has been thrown on the manner of arranging the stage by the Lucerne plays of the fifteenth century (see Wilkens, p. 239).

In England, during the thirteenth century, plays were often per-formed in church ; and this practice had not ceased in 1542, when

Bonner prohibited it in his diocese. So late as 1572 it appears that interludes were occasionally played in churches. But from an early date, perhaps from the thirteenth century, in towns the chief performances were transferred to the streets and public places. The manner of the representation has been fully described by Sharp in his dissertation on the Coventry Mysteries. A movable stage was employed, called a *pageant*, a name probably derived from *pango, pagina*. The same term was used to designate the plays themselves, although it was afterwards applied to a different kind of performance. The scaffold is said to have consisted of two rooms—a lower, in which the performers attired themselves, and a higher, in which they acted. The lower stage was sometimes used to represent hell, with the devils rising from it and falling into it. The scaffolding was thus not so elaborate as that used in France, where three stages were usually erected, and sometimes a much larger number. As many as nine are mentioned (see Collier, ii. p. 78, ff.). The English plays commonly required more than one scaffold. A separate scaffold, like the German *Burg*, was often assigned to those who undertook a particular portion of the play, and the adjoining space was also used for parts of the performance—*e.g.*, where a waggon, or horses, or a number of people were introduced. As in Germany, some of the spectators looked on from the adjoining houses. The so-called *Guary* plays of Cornwall were performed in spaces enclosed by circles of stones, forming a kind of amphitheatre (*Plân an guare*, or plain of sport and pastime). Remains of these still exist (Norris, ii. p. 454).]

53. It is from the Paradise of these stages that we derive the name of the upper gallery of theatres [Ger., *Paradies*: Engl., *The Gods*], which very often does not much resemble paradise.

54. In the *Adam* discovered at Tours it is naïvely remarked that when the devil has carried off a soul into hell there shall be a great noise made with pans and kettles, "so that it may be heard without," also "a great smoke shall be made." Of purgatory I have nowhere found any trace. [Hone and Sharp give interesting facsimiles of old woodcuts representing the jaws of hell, as depicted in the mystery plays.]

55. In the Easter play at Donaveschingen the cock also, which crows for Peter, had its own pillar opposite to the one where Christ was scourged.

56. In the stage directions we generally find, " surgat e loco suo." In Germany this is, in later pieces, replaced by, " soll her für gan."

57. See note 5.

58. Mone would explain this by supposing that the audience were in the habit of moving towards the part of the stage on which the play was then being acted, in which case noise and bustle could not be avoided. Such a moving audience is certainly conceivable, when we think of a crowd of children before a travelling marionette theatre, but not when we hear of festal assemblies of thousands. Also probably most of the divisions of the stage were small, so that the whole could be seen at once. Bechstein (*Thüring. Mysterium*, p. 11) imagines that the repeated injunction to be silent, which in the play of the *Ten Virgins* is given by the angels, who here act the part of choir-leaders, was addressed to the persons who spoke or sang, and that even the Christ would have to submit to an angel's command—" Sile." As if the actor would not of himself stop speaking when he had finished the sentence of his part which he had committed to memory !

59. Wackernagel (*Gesch. d. deutschen Literatur*, p. 300) traces the derivation of the word from the Latin (*ministerium*) instead of from the Greek (μυστήριον). The original intention of these plays as religious services would be still more strongly brought out by this derivation, as *divinum* must of course be understood. The spelling *mystère* cannot affect the argument, as it is frequently alternated with *mistère*, and, besides, may have had its source in the prevailing mistaken impression of the origin of the word. But one cannot understand why the central syllable should be so uniformly dropped in the name of the play, as both in the religious vocabulary and in the vulgar tongue of the French nation the word *ministère* is commonly met with. In the Greek Fathers μυστήριον is used for every sacred function, especially when any such function was typical, and contained for the believer a deeper secret meaning beneath the visible sign. Chrysost. *in* 1 *Ep. ad Corinth., Homilia* vii.: Μυστήριον καλεῖται ὅτι ουχ ἅπερ ὁρῶμεν πιστεύομεν, ἀλλ᾽ ἑτέρα ὁρῶμεν καὶ ἑτέρα πιστεύομεν.

Isidore of Hispalis was the first who endeavoured to establish the distinction of *sacramentum* in a sentence in the book of canonical law issued under the name of Gregory I. Gratian, p. ii. c. 1, qu. 1, c. 84:—" *Mysterium* ob hoc dicetur, quod secretam et reconditam habeat dispensationem ; *sacrificium* autem quasi sacrum factum, quia prece mystica consecratur pro nobis in memoriam dominicae passionis ; *sacramentum* vero est in aliqua celebratione, cum res gesta ita sit, ut aliquid significare intelligatur quod sancte accipiendum est." In a decree of the Synod of Worms, A.D. 1316, it is said of the raising of the crucifix from the sepulchre, the foundation of the Easter play—" Ut resurrectionis mysterium peragatur debita cum devotione." The opinion of Funkhanel, " that the name of mystery was at first given only to such sacred plays as treated of the Crucifixion, the Burial, and Resurrection of the Saviour, but was afterwards made to include every sacred drama," is proved by the origin of the mysteries in the worship of the Church, to which the commemoration of the birth also of the Son of Man naturally belongs. But Funkhänel also suggests the question whether any mention of the festivals of the Church under the name of mysteries occurs in the Fathers. I do not remember any instance in point—indeed such a use of the term could only be conceived as compatible with their view of the subject, in so far as for us to expect to find the name sacrament or mystery employed for Easter or Christmas in connection with the events commemorated on these festivals. Thus in a Christmas sermon of Leo the Great (*Opp. ed. Ballerinii*, t. i. p. 73): "Nota quidem sunt quae ad sacramentum pertinent solemnitas hodiernae."

60. Another example may be found in the allegory of a lawsuit between *Nature humaine* and *Dame Débonnaire* (Mary) on the proposed death of *Dame Débonnaire's* son *Innocent*. In this play, which was acted in Paris in 1544, the suit is four times urged—before Noah, before Moses, before the *Cour Souverain*, and lastly, before the *Roi Souverain*. *Dame Débonnaire* loses every time, and finally *Innocent* is given up to *Envie Judaique*, and *Gentil Trucidateur*.

61. The derivation of this appellation has been traced to the old term for a judgment hall, "Basilica." Also to the influence of the Basilica has been ascribed the frequent recurrence of the forms of a trial in the mediæval miracle plays, but "plaidoyers" were also common in the disputations of the schoolmen.

62. An arrangement of this story is found in Hans Sachs under the Greek title of *Hekastus*. See Flögel, iv. p. 198, ff.
[This piece is reprinted in Hawkins' *Origin of the English Drama*, vol i., and most recently in Hazlitt's *Dodsley's Old Plays*, vol. i., with the old frontispiece. The full title runs thus:—" Here begynneth a treatyse how the hye fader of heven sendeth deth to somon every creature to come and gyve a counte of theyr lyves in this worlde, and is in maner of a morall playe." Mr. Collier (ii. p. 227) thinks it " one of the most perfect allegories ever formed," and attributes its composition to a very early period, perhaps to the reign of Edward IV. If the play be of this date, it cannot be intended, as Hone conjectures (p. 228), to attack Lutheran doctrine, although the prominence assigned to Good Works might have been distasteful to the Reformers. The moralities flourished with the greatest luxuriance on English soil. Mr. Collier prints an analysis

of the earliest extant in MS., which he assigns to the reign of Henry VI. An interesting sketch and analysis of the moralities is given by Mr. Ward, i. p. 61, ff.]

63. *Le mystère du Chevalier, qui donna sa femme au diable, mis en ryme françoise et par personnaiges.* There is no date to this MS. See Flögel, iv. p. 240, f.

64. [It is necessary to distinguish between the species of play here termed mysteries, miracles, and moralities, respectively. But the name "miracles" or "plays of miracles" was the common designation both of mysteries and of miracle plays. The term " mystery " does not seem to have been used in England until Dodsley in 1744 introduced it. The author of *Piers Ploughman's Crede* calls them *miracles*, and Chaucer denominates them *plays of miracles* (Collier, ii. p. 54). Mr. Collier retains the term *miracle play* as the comprehensive designation of mysteries and miracles.]

65. *Mystère des Actes des Apotres,* by the brothers Gréban, of whom one was a canon at Le Mans, the other a monk. This play is in nine parts. It is founded on the Gospel of St. Luke, and is interspersed with jests and legendary tales. From 1450 it was frequently acted in French towns, and the performance seems to have occupied a week. See *De la lecture des livres franc. comme amusement*, Paris, 1780, t. i. p. 360, ff.

66. In an Ascension play given by Mone (i. p. 55), Christ thus frames His question : " What do people say of the Son of Man, and eke of His Mother ?" Peter replies, " I say for certain that Thou art the Son of God from the kingdom of heaven ; and Thy Mother, she is for all the world its Woman-Saviour."

67. This caused in the sixteenth century a division into " mystères sacrés " and " profanes," as we see in a decree of the Parliament of Paris in 1548.

68. Mone, ii. pp. 9, 40, f.

69. From a MS. of the fourteenth century belonging to the Benedictine Abbey of Kremsmünster (Hoffmann, ii. p. 284, ff.). The end is lost. See Flögel, iv. p. 290, f.

70. Giov. Villani, *Historie Fiorentine*, viii. 70.

71. It is really thus termed "prologue final." The prologue begins the play of St. Dorothea :—

> " In allen diesen dingen,
>   Daz ein ieglich mensche will beginnen,
>   Sô sol er ze dem ersten got ruofen an
>   Des allerbesten des er kan,
>   Daz daz ende werde gut
>   Mit minre sünde uñ mit merrem gut :
>   Des helfe uns got ze disen dingen,
>   Daz uns alhie müeze wol gelingen,
>   Uñ din heilige juncvrou Dorothê,
>   Daz uns der helfe werde mê.
>   Nû singe wir alle disen leis :
>   Nû bite wir den heiligen geist.
>   *Et cantat omnis populus.*"

72. *Chronikon Sanpetrinum* in *Mencken, Scriptt. rerum Germ.*, iii. p. 326 (*Ann. Reinhardsbrunnenses*, given by Wegele, p. 302, f.). J. Rothe, *Thür. Chronik.*, given by the same, p. 1633. After five days of suffering and violence, the Landgrave was paralysed by an apoplectic stroke, but he languished in gloom and pain till the 16th November 1324. The play is said by the Sanpetrinum Chronicle to have taken place on the Monday after *Misericordias Domini* [second after Easter], but Rothe places it on the previous Saturday. On this Sunday there was held in Eisenach the *Dedicatio Praedicatorum* (the Preachers' Indulgence), otherwise known as " Der Brüder Kirmesse " [Kirmesse, or Kirchmesse, is commonly used for a wake or a country fair]. A monk preached and dispensed indulgences from a cask placed on the open square in front of the Dominican cloister. From this custom was derived the local proverb that the weather in spring cannot be trusted till the monk is out of his cask. If the Saturday seems a likely day for the play, which might have served as a prelude to the monkish festival, yet the near date of the Sanpetrinum Chronicle, which was completed in the year 1355, is a warrant for the performance having actually taken place on the Monday ; and it may have been in no way connected with the other celebration, for the Dominicans are not mentioned as having conducted the action, nor was the spot chosen for it in front of their cloister (C. H. Funk-hänel, *Ueber das geistl. Spiel von den zehn Jungfrauen*).

73. Frederick Stephan, town-councillor of Mühlhäusen (*Neue Stoff-lieferungen für die deutsche Geschichte*, Mühlh. 1847, part ii.).

74. *Das grosse thüringische Mysterium, oder das geistl. Spiel von den zehn Jungfrauen. Aufgeführt zu Eisenach*, 24 *April* 1322. *Nach*

der einzigen (Mühlh.) Handschr. hrsgg. v. Ludwig Bechstein, Hal.
1855. Godeke claims to have discovered the identity of this play
with the one of which the performance at Eisenach is recorded.
Bechstein's researches assign a contemporary date to the MS.

75. In the middle-high-German text :—

> " hat vns got syn riche beschert,
>   ich weiz wol daz iz vns nummir sente peter gewert."

76.   " Eia liebes Kind mein,
>   Ich bin ja doch die Mutter dein,
>   Und gedenke an das Ungemach,
>   Das mir durch deine Marter geschach,
>   Da ein Schwert durch meine Seele ging.
>   Was ich je pein durch dich empfing,
>   Das lohne mir mit diesen Armen,
>   Und lass dich über sie erbarmen ! "

[Dr. Hase gives here, as will be perceived, the modern spelling.
Most of the extracts from old German plays are similarly adapted.]

77. According to the stage directions :—" Post hec fatue vadant
inter populum cantando planctos."

78.   " Ach der jämmerlichen Fahrt !
>   Dass je ich Mensche ward !
>   Wehe Mutter über dich, dass du mich trugst,
>   Dass du mich geboren nicht alsbald erschlugst !
>   Eh noch ein Christenname mir war kund,
>   Dass ich nicht hinstarb als ein Hund."

The metre changes in these lines in order to give intensity to their
pathos ; first to the metre of the *Nibelungen Lied*, then to that of
the *Walter Lied*.

79. It is for this reason that we cannot suspect this piece of any
Protestant tendency, nor of being intended as an argument for the
Dominican followers of Augustine against the Franciscan favourers
of Mariolatry. It is not the lack of faith alone, but also of good
works, which causes the condemnation of the foolish virgins. God's
mercy through Christ helps them as little as the intercession of the
Divine Mother. The opposition of the Preaching Friars to the
Minorites had reference entirely to the belief of the latter in the
Immaculate Conception of Mary, which only in our days has become
a dogma necessary to salvation. In a Dominican cloister, on the very

eve of the Reformation, no hesitation was shown in supporting the traditional opposition of the Dominicans to the belief in question by the aid of miracles performed by the Blessed Virgin herself. Minds of a Protestant or revolutionary tendency were in the fourteenth century more at home in the Franciscan than in the Dominican order. By this latter such men were burned as far as their power extended.

80. Adam Ursinus in his *Thüring. Chronik.* (Mencken, iii. p. 21). He says also of the vain intercession of the Virgin and the saints : "Diss war etwas czu hart vnd czu heftig gespielet, denn maria vnd alle gottis heiligen bitten vor keynen verdamten nicht, denn sie wollen nichts anders denn das got will." Admitting this, and presupposing a knowledge of what we must conclude to be the will of God in this case, the intercession of the saints could not fail to appear here unavailing, especially to a Catholic mind.

81. "Ihr mögt euch wol besinnen bei unsrer Niederfahrt,
   Und wollt ihr Gottes Hulde gewinnen, so seid vor Sünde
   mehr bewahrt ?"

82. The legend of Theophilus was translated into Latin by Paulus Diaconus, and it was also celebrated by Hroswitha in a Latin poem. (See *Acta Sanctorum*, February 1, p. 480). [Cp. Dasent, *Theophilus in Icelandic, Low German, and Other Tongues*, London, 1845.]

83. See the lines once so common in France.

   "Sainte Marie Magdelaine,
   Fu ensi de ses péchiés sainne
   Au diable fu retolus,
   Par repentir Theopilus."

84. Mommerqué, p. 136 *sqq.* Published in Low-German by Ettmüller, Quedlinb. 1849.

85. *Apotheosis Johannis VIII. Pontificis Romani. Ein schön Spiel von Fraw Jutten, welche Babst zu Rom gewesen*, Eisleben, 1565.

86. In the second part of the necessary preface, p. 80, ff.

87. A rude farce on the subject by Flins, was acted in Paris in 1794, apparently the same as one which was again brought on the stage in 1848. In the mystery we find comic passages, but in nearly every case the humour is unintentional.

88. This song, which is chanted first by Unversün, and then by

the other devils in chorus, is very simple, and almost the same as one in an Easter play acted at Alsfeld :

> " Luciper in deim throne
> Rimo, Rimo, Rimo.
> Warstu ein Engel schone,
> Rimo, Rimo, Rimo.
> Nu bistu ein Teufel grewlich.
> Rimo, Rimo, Rimo."

89.   " Maria Mutter reine
> Aller Sünder ein Trösterin,
> Ich klage dir gemeine,
> Dass ich ein Sünder bin.
> Des weine ich, dass Blut so roth
> Mein' Augen Thränen giessen,
> Das lass mich, Frau, geniessen,
> Und bitt' für mich dein liebes Kind."

90. This contradiction in the poet's scheme is due to the continuation of the story, which, however, he cannot drop, as by it the external subjection of the female pope to the law of a higher necessity is set forth. A Pilgrims' Guide to Rome (*Mirabilia Romae*), dated 1475, in announcing that the stone statue of the woman-pope with her child might be seen at a ruined church, between the Colosseum and San Clemente, already inserts this touch—"An angel has set before her the choice of being condemned for ever in the other world, or of bearing on earth the disgrace of her crime."

91. My attention was first drawn to the brilliant dramatic effect of this conclusion by E. Devrient (*Gesch. d. deutschen Schauspielkunst*, i. p. 85). Hans Sachs has used " the history of Joan of England the Pope " in a rhymed story for controversial purposes. Joan, who is represented as a wicked, debased woman, corrupt in soul and body, rules the whole papal suite at her pleasure, in spite of the assertion that the papacy can never be at fault, "as some flatterers aver."

92. Jubinal quotes a chronicle of 1495, preserved in the Royal Library at Paris (i. p. 43 *sqq.*). " *La vie de Monseigneur S. Martin* " was acted " en façon que à la voir jouer le commun peuple pourroit voir et entendre facillement, comment le noble patron dudit Seure en son vivant a vescu saintement et devostement." Satan, too, came off very well, for he appeared the next day with his costume in good order, and thus addressed Lucifer :—

" Mille mort te puisse avorter,
Paillart, fils de putain cognu,
Pour à mal faire t' en orter
Je me suis tout brûlé le cul."

93. The fact that in not a few MSS. *Dominica persona* is always written over the speeches of Christ, but only *Figura* over those of God the Father, perhaps shows that in reverent fear, notwithstanding the usual boldness of the stage, the part was merely recited.

[In the earliest French and German *officia* the most sacred personages were not brought on the stage at all. At Christmas neither the Virgin nor St. Joseph were personated at the Adoration of the Magi, who were received by two priests in dalmatics, representing midwives. At the Massacre of the Innocents, the Christ-Child appeared in symbolic form as the *Agnus Dei.* On Good Friday, Christ was again symbolised by the crucifix buried in the grave. The Resurrection, the proper Easter ceremony, was not acted, but only intimated by the appearance of the priests who sustained the part of the angels at the sepulchre. The Virgin and St. Joseph were introduced for the first time as speaking personages in the Flight into Egypt. In Germany the Infant Christ was first represented as speaking in the cradle of Bethlehem, where a verse in praise of his mother was assigned to Him. See Wilkens, p. 34.]

94. Printed first in 1483, in Low German.

95. Hoffmann, ii. p. 265, f., 302 ; Mone, *Schausp.*, i. p. 27 ; Alt, p. 367 ; Jubinal, ii. p. 317. · [See also Ward, *History of the English Drama.* The grotesque element in the mysteries has often been exaggerated. In amount it is relatively small ; in the Donaueschingen play it is altogether absent. The introduction of this element is due to the growth of national life. As greater interest was felt in the religious drama, those parts of the action which gave scope for popular handling became prominent, and a likeness to the secular theatre was insensibly introduced. Characters to which only a passing reference is made in Scripture were brought on the stage because they were susceptible of popular treatment, and new characters were created for the same reason. Thus the dealers in ointment and perfumes, from whom Mary Magdalene, and the Foolish Virgins, and Joseph of Arimathea purchase their wares, are well-known personages in the German mysteries. The introduction of servants and of domestic scenes gave occasion for some amount of buffoonery. This was especially the case in England, where the performance of the plays passed almost entirely out of the hands of the clergy. In the Chester and Towneley plays Noah's wife is represented as a shrew ; and she was

doubtless a favourite character, as Chaucer speaks in the *Miller's Tale* of—

> "The sorrow of Noe with his feleshippe,
> Or that he might gete his wife to shippe."

Even the relation between St. Joseph and the Virgin was treated humorously. Cain with his servants, and the Shepherds in the Towneley plays, furnished illustrations of the manners and feelings of the lowest class of labourers. In the Harrowing of Hell, as the descent into hell was called (harrow, *i.e.*, harry), taken in the first instance from the Gospel of Nicodemus, both the devils and their victims were the subjects of many farcical scenes. No single addition afforded so much of the grotesque element in the English mysteries. Any characters or allusions could be brought in ; thus in the Chester plays bad brewers are attacked, and a woman is placed among the lost because she "brewed so thynne." But, notwithstanding this element, it is well observed that the chief interest of the religious play in England, as in Germany, was not comic, but tragic, and did not suffer from the introduction of the grotesque. In Germany the direct dogmatic teaching of the religious play was developed simultaneously with this popular side. The Corpus Christi and Whitsuntide dramas, in which religious teaching was most prominent, were of later origin than the Easter and Christmas plays, and were introduced when grotesque incidents had come into fashion.]

96. See the birth of *Madame S. Geneviève*, during which the angels sing in Paradise *Virginis proles*, while the *Chamberière* makes her comments to the mother (Jubinal, i. p. 170).

97. I only know this piece through Alt, p. 389 :—

> "Père eternel, vous avez tort
> Et devriez avoir vergogne,
> Votre fils bien-aimé est mort
> Et Vous dormez comme un yvrogne."

GOD THE FATHER.

"Il est mort ?"

THE ANGEL.

"D'homme de bien."

GOD THE FATHER.

"Diable m'emporte qui en savais rien."

98. Parfait, ii. pp. 5, 70.

99. Jubinal, ii. p. 21.

100. Schönemann, pp. 84, 86, f.

101. Mone, *Schausp.*, i. p. 97.

102. Jubinal, i. p. 93 *sqq.*

103. *Mystère de la vengéance de Jesus Christ*, A.D. 1437. See *La lecture de livres franç.*, i. p. 365.

104. Parfait, iii. p. 18.

105. *Miles christianus*, which tells of the knighthood of a repentant sinner (Mone, *Schausp.*, ii. p. 413).

106. I do not know that it can be proved that the farce was made to follow the mystery in any case by a regular rule, as the Satyr play followed the Greek tragedy, but merely in some such way. The chronicle which describes the spectacles in Paris on the occasion of the knighting of the sons of Philippe le Bel, relates that the joys of the blessed in Paradise and the pangs of the condemned in hell were to be seen on different stages, and that the performances concluded with the comic piece of the *Procession of the Fox*. In Seure, on the day appointed for the representation of *La vie de Monseigneur S. Martin*, the weather proved too inclement for the play ; but towards evening the sky cleared, and the actors of the mystery performed *La farce du Meunier*, chiefly on account of the many strangers assembled in the town. On the next day the mystery was represented.

[Farce and *Fastnachtspiel* were not of common origin with the mystery, or ever had more than an accidental connection with it. Ribaldry and extravagance of all kinds were the staple of these compositions, while they were marked deviations from the general character of the mystery. The *Fastnachtspiel* seems at first to have been often nothing more than coarse banter. Like the religious play, it sometimes took the form of a lawsuit ; and it appears probable that the lawyers of Germany, like the Clercs de Basoche in France, were responsible for these productions. One or two specimens have been preserved, which touch on religious topics. See Gervinus, ii. p. 337, ff.]

107. *Mystère de la Sainte Hostie.*

108. *Le Martire St. Estienne* (Jubinal, i. p. 20).

109. See the Easter play given by Hoffman, ii. p. 313 :—

> " Ich bin newlich kommen von Pareis,
>   Uf erztei habe ich geleget meinen vleiss
>   Wol vier und vierzig jar,
>   Was ich euch sage, das ist nicht wahr," &c.

110. The quack doctor asks what wages he will demand :—

RUBIN.

> " Herre, mein lon ist gar stark :
>   Ein pfunt pulze und ein gebraten quark.

DOCTOR.

> " Rubein, ich will dir den quark geben,
>   Dass du das jar nicht must überleben,
>   Und einen vladen darzu,
>   Den da machet die ku."

111.
> " Wir han verlorn
>   Der uns zu Troste ward geborn,
>   Der reinen Jungfrauen Sohn,
>   Wir haben verlorn Jesum Christ
>   Der aller Welt ein Tröster ist."

112. A Scriptural authorisation for it was also discovered in the words of the Vulgate concerning the conversation of the disciples on the road to Emmaus (Luke xxiv. 15) :—"Et factum est dum fabularentur." Æcolampadius, *De risu paschali.* Fussli, *Beitn. z. Kirchen und Ref. Geschichte*, b. v. p. 447. *Hist. polit. Blätter*, 1839, b. iv. part 6.

113. Dante has taken a deeper view of the tendency which rendered such a custom possible : *Parad.* xxix. 109 :—

> " Non disse Cristo al suo primo convento :
>   Andate e predicate al mondo ciance,
>   Ma diede lor verace fondamento :
>   E quel tanto sono nelle sue guance
>   Si, che a pugnar, per accender la fede
>   Dello Evangelio fero scudi e lance."

114. This custom was intended to commemorate the children of Bethlehem, as having suffered for the Babe Christ.

115. Du Fresne, *Gloss. ad Scriptores med. et inf. Latinit. v. Cervula.*

Culendae. Tiliot, *Mémoires pour servir à l'histoire de la fête des foux,* Laus. 1751.

116. Massmann, *Literatur der Todtentänze*, Stuttg. 1830. In the Spanish *Danza general de la muerte*, which appeared as early as the middle of the fourteenth century, the frailty of human life is illustrated in solemn theological style. Schack, *Gesch. d. dramat. Lit. in Spen*, i. p. 23.

117. In the Easter play given by Hoffmann, ii. p. 300 : "Die Juden tanzen zu Pilato und singen jüdisch." P. 302 : "Die Ritter tanzen zum grabe *cantando:* Wir wollen zu dem grabe gan !" In a Tyrolese Easter play, the soldiers go round and round the grave, almost in regular measure, while singing :—

> "Wir wollen umb das grab gan,
> Jesus der wil aufstahn !
> Ist das war, ist das war,
> So werden gülden unser har !"

The five foolish virgins dance, and Mary Magdalene.

118. In an Easter play given by Mone, *Schausp.*, ii. p. 60, f.

119. In an Easter play given by Mone, *Schausp.*, i. p. 79 :—

> "Ich bin ein ledig junges wip," &c.

120. In a mystery of the Passion found at Arras (Ebert, p. 57) :—

> "A tous je suis habandonnée," &c.

121. Mone, *Schausp.*, ii. p. 190, f. Hoffmann, ii. p. 248.

122. Mommerqué, p. 609 *sqq.*

123. Mommerqué, p. 481 *sqq.*, from the *Roman de la Manekine.*

124. "Chose moult desguisée et qui trop est contre raison."

NOTES TO LECTURE II.

1. *Heregia dels Peyres*, by Anselm Faidit of Avignon.

2. *Le jeu du Prince des Sots et Mère Sotte, mis en rime française par Pierre Gringore et joué par personnaiges aux Halles de Paris le Mardy gras de l'année* 1511.

3. *Auto da Feyra.*

4. The *Herren-Fastnacht* was a week before the *Bauern-Fastnacht*, the ordinary mediæval Shrove Tuesday.

5. *Der Todtenfresser.*

6. Faber, then Grand Vicar of the Bishop of Constance, afterwards the opponent of Zuinglius at the disputation at Zurich in 1523.

7.   " Lieber Priester sag mir an,
      Was mag doch das sein für ein Mann,
      Ist er ein Türk oder ist er ein Heid,
      Dass man ihn so hoch auf den Achseln treidt,
      Oder hat er sonst gar kein Fuss,
      Dass man ihn also tragen muss ? "

COURTIER.

" Sieh mal und du selbst Petrus bist,
      Weisst denn nicht wol wer er ist !
      Das soll mich billig Wunder ne'n,
      Doch will ich ihn zu erkennen ge'n.
      Ist der Grösst in der Christenheit,
      Er ist ein Papst zu Rom und weiter me
      König in Sicilien und Tinacrie,

Herr der Inseln Sardinien herum,
Corsica, das Land Bivarium,
Thusca Herzog, auch zu Spolet,
Benesin er auch mit Gewalt inu het,
Darzu ist er auf Erd' ein Gott,
Dass du voraus wissen sollt,
So er doch dein Statthalter ist
Und der aller heiligst Christ."

PETRUS.

" Das sind mir fremd und unerhört Sachen !
Wie könnt' ich doch ein Statthalter machen
Ueber solche Land und Lüt,
Ich halt doch auf Erdreich nüt.
Woher kommen ihm die reiche Land
Zu seinem Gewalt und grossen Stand !
Ich weiss auch nicht gar wohl darvon,
Dass ich je gen Rom sei komn,
Bin ich in solchem Gepracht da gesessen,
So hab' ich sein wahrlich ganz vergessen."

8. " Huren und Buben und was zum Krieg gehört, richlich, hoch-
prachtlich."

9. Printed in Meyen in 1524. A reprint may be found in the
valuable memoir on Church History and Art by C. Grüneisen—
*Niclaus Manuel: Leben u. Werke eines Malers, Dichters, Kriegers,
Staatsmannes und Reformators im* 16. *Jahrh.*, Stuttg. 1837. In this
memoir we find also a dialogue by Manuel on the sickness and final
testament of the Mass written in 1528. A cardinal tells the Pope
the dreadful news which has come from Germany, that the Mass,
the very foundation of the Papal power, is in a bad way. The Pope
knows a sure resource. He will call together some bold fellows who
will affirm that all who oppose it are the most virulent of heretics
and desire to deprive Christ of all honour. The cardinal has, however, already made use of this expedient, sparing no cost, but in
vain. The poor Mass has taken the affair to heart, and lies sick
unto death. Then physicians and apothecaries are called in, and
the account of their consultations and of their final experiments is
full of wit and irony. This piece is not, however, properly a drama,
nor intended for representation, but only a dialogue in imitation of
Lucian, such as Ulrich von Hutten had brought into favour.

10. The Bernese physician, Anshelm, and Bullinger, pastor at
Zurich.

11. B. Waldis, *De parabell vom verlorn Szohn*, Ryga, 1527, 4. With regard to his stay in the Rome of the period, Waldis calls to mind a wise counsel which, he affirms, was given him there in a merry company—

> " Wo ihr wollt bleiben lang in Rom,
> Müsst euch nit stellen allzufromm.
> Habt ihr euer Tag von Rom nit gehört,
> Wie man sagt im gemeinen Sprüchwort,
> Dass einem zu Rom keine Sünd nit schad
> Allein so er kein Geld mehr hat,
> Das ist der allergrösste Sünd,
> Welch nit der Bapst vergeben künd."

A. Höfer, *B. Waldis Parabel v. verlornen Sohn, Ein niederdeutsches Fastnachtsspiel*, Greisswald, 1851. F. L. Mittler, *H. Heinrichs v. Braunschw. Klagelied, Mit einem Nachwort über B. Waldis*, Cassel, 1855. Fried. Dedekind, pastor at Neustadt on the Leine and at Lüneburg, who died in 1598, wrote, " *Der christl. Ritter, aus dem 6. Capitel der Epistel S. Pauli zu den Ephesern. In ein Geistlich Spiel gefasset.*" This piece was rearranged and reprinted in Ulssen in 1590, having been first printed in 1576. Dedekind also wrote, *Papista Conversus, Ein Neues Christlich Spiel von einem Papisten der sich zu der rechten warheit bekeret vnd darüber in Gefengniss vnd gefahr des lebens kompt*, Hamb. 1590.

12. *Tragödia Johannis Huss, welche auff dem Vnchristl. Concilio zu Costnitz gehalten, allen Christen nützlich vnd tröstlich zu lesen* (von J. Agricola), Wittenb. 1537. [The burning of John Huss was also the subject of an English tragedy by Ralph Radcliffe, who, " opening a school at Hitchin in Hertfordshire in the year 1538, obtained a grant of the dissolved Friary of the Carmelites in that town ; and converting the refectory into a theatre, wrote several plays both in Latin and English, which were exhibited by his pupils " (Warton, iii. p. 309). For the controversial plays in England see below, note 18.]

13. Rivander, *Lutherus Redivivus*, Bischofswerda, 1592. The main aim of this piece would place it in the same class as the *Calvinische Postreuter* (see note 21). In Jena as late as 1732 " *Der gestürzte Goliath oder die über das Papstthum triumphirende Wahrheit* " was represented by students.

14. *Tetzelocramia, eine lustige Comödie von Tetzels Ablasskram, wie Gott der Herr denselben, jetzo vor* 100 *Jahren durch sein erwähltes Rüstzeug Dr. Mart. Lutherum in Kraft des heiligen Evangeliums*

umgestossen, lauter und rein wider die Antichristischen Römischen Greuel in Deutschland zu predigen angefangen u. weit u. breit hat erschallen lassen, zum Jubeljahr u. Freudenfest 1617, *Gott zu ehren u. männiglich zum Nutz gemacht*, by M. Heinrich Kielmann, Conrector of the Royal School at Stettin.

15. *Pammachius, ein kurzweilig Tragedi, darin aus wahrhaftigen Historien fürgebildet, wie die Bäbst u. Bischöff das Predigt- u. Hirtenamt verlassen, u. beide über mächtige Land u. Leute u. über die Blöden fürstliche Regierung wider Gottes Wort erlangt u. bisher geübet haben, welche das heil. Evangelium widerficht. Beschrieben im Latein zu Wittenberg durch Thomas Kirchmayer (auch Naogeorg genannt) von Straubingen, der christl. Jugend deutscher Nation zum Besten in deutsche Reime versetzt durch Joh. Tyrolf in Cala an der Saale* 1538.

[Bishop Bale "is said by himself to have translated the tragedy of *Pammachius*, the same perhaps which was acted at Christ's College in Cambridge in 1544, and afterwards laid before the Privy Council as a libel on the Reformation" (Warton, iv. p. 74).]

16. C. Grüneisen (see an article in the *Zeitschr. für hist. Theolog.*, Leipzig, 1838, 1) discovered an old printed work in the Munich Library with the title, *Eyn Comedia, welche zu dem königlichem Sall tzu Paryess, nach vormelter gestaldt vñ ordenunge gespielt worden. Anno* M.D.XXIIII. Then follows a German abridgment, not the piece, and the German words indicate a Latin original. The book closes: "Therefore at the ending of the play every one was moved to laughter."

17. Masenius, *Speculum imaginum veritatis occultæ*, Colon. 1664. J. H. Majus, *Vita Reuchlini, Francof. et Spiræ*, 1687.

18. [This was, properly speaking, a "Morality" in Latin. It was written in Latin, and was acted by the scholars of St. Paul's School, under the direction of John Rightwise, their master, who was probably the author of the piece. The performance took place at Greenwich in presence of the King and the French ambassadors. Among the characters were Religion, Ecclesia, Veritas, Heresy, False Interpretation, Corruptio Scriptoris, as female characters; SS. Peter, Paul, and James; the Dauphin and his brother, Luther and his wife, the former dressed "lyke a party freer [friar] in russet, damaske, and blake taffata," the latter "lyke a frow of Spyers in Allmayn in red syllke" (see Collier, i. p. 104, ff.).

During the agitation which preceded the Reformation, and while it was winning its way, popular feeling and opinion often found vent in the miracle plays, moralities, and interludes. The subjects of the two latter species of play were chiefly moral, but from their popularity they were fit vehicles for expressing both political and religious sentiment. The plays, like the popular songs and ballads, exercised a great influence, and were too strong to be entirely repressed by the edicts which were repeatedly issued against them. Both sides made use of them with alternate sanction until the proclamation of Elizabeth (May 16, 1559), which ordered that no dramatic production should be licensed which touched matters of religion or governance of the estate of the common weal. Religious plays continued to be acted for some time longer. But this proclamation, as well as the impartial dislike of the Queen for Catholic and Puritan extravagances, must have helped to bring the religious plays to an end, and to promote the development of the secular stage, which had already begun.

In the reign of Henry VIII. the earliest of Heywood's interludes, *A mery Play between the Pardoner and the frere, the curate, and neybour Pratte*, written before 1521, was directed to exposing the tricks and impositions of pardoners and friars. But the faults of the clergy had often been attacked before the Reformation can be said to have begun. The plays of Bishop Bale (d. 1563) were the most important attempts (Mr. Collier considers them the first extant attempts) to use the stage in support of the Reformation. Bale began life as a Roman Catholic, but had become a Protestant, and was promoted by Edward VI. to the see of Ossory. His four surviving plays— (1.) *The Three Laws of Nature, Moses, and Christ ;* (2.) *God's Promises ;* (3.) *John the Baptist Preaching in the Wilderness ;* (4.) *The Temptation of Christ*—were first printed abroad, probably before 1540. The second of these he calls a *tragedy* and the fourth a *comedy*. They were all, properly speaking, miracle plays, and are usually considered to have been the last miracle plays composed in England. According to Warton (iv. p. 74), "a low vein of abusive burlesque, which had more virulence than humour, seems to have been one of Bale's talents." But some allowance should be made for the habits of thought of the time. At all events, Bale warmly advocated the doctrines of the Reformation. His most remarkable production is the play of *King John*, which, as Mr. Collier says, unites the characteristics of a religious miracle play and of a historical drama, and is quite unexampled in the progress of the English stage. England is represented as a widow, who entreats the King to amend the evils inflicted on her by the clergy, but is thwarted by Sedition. Various other abstractions are introduced to represent the different powers in Church and State ; and in order that there may be no possibility of mistaking the meaning of the play, directions are given that Usurped Power shall dress for the Pope, Private Wealth for a cardinal, and Sedition for a monk. The King when poisoned by

Dissimulation exclaims that "there is no malice like to that of the clergy." All is finally settled by Imperial Majesty, and Sedition is hung.

This play, which was discovered about forty years ago, and edited by Mr. Collier, is of composite character. The main portion is considered by Mr. Ward (*History of Dramatic Literature*, i. p. 99) to belong to the reign of Edward VI., though Queen Elizabeth is prayed for in the end of the piece, which seems a later addition. In the year 1549 it had been found necessary to forbid all dramatic performances for three months; and in 1552 a stringent proclamation was issued forbidding players to play and printers to print without special license from the Privy Council (see Collier, i. p. 411, ff.). This prohibition was due to political motives and did not prevent the exhibition of plays favourable to the Reformation. Bale ascribes a play of this kind to the King himself, but the work mentioned by him was probably a later treatise in prose entitled *De Meretrici Babylonica* (see Hazlitt's *Warton*, iv. p. 151). But there are two moral plays of this date which advocate the doctrine of the Reformation—*Lusty Juventus*, reprinted by Hawkins, and *New Custome*, printed in Dodsley's *Old Plays*, i., ed. 1825. Mr. Collier thus analyses the former :—"It begins by representing Juventus in a state of grace, through the exhortations of Good Counsel. The Devil soon afterwards enters and employs his son, Hypocrisy, to seduce Juventus, which he does by assuming the name of Friendship, and by calling in the aid of Fellowship and Abominable Living, the latter a harlot. Good Counsel finds Juventus in the lowest state of vice and debauchery and reclaims him, while God's Merciful Promises undertakes to procure him forgiveness." The name of Wevor at the end of the piece may be that of the author. In *New Custome*, the principal personages are New Custom and Light of the Gospel, Protestant ministers, and Perverse Doctrine, a Popish priest.

In the first year of Queen Mary's reign it was ordered that no plays should be performed without her license. But Protestant feeling was so strong that this prohibition was evaded. In 1556 all plays were therefore forbidden. This prohibition, however, was probably not extended to London. Dramas intended to inculcate the dogmas of the Romish Church were performed in the capital during the later years of Mary's reign. Mr. Collier mentions a remarkable play existing in MS., which professes to have been "made in the year of our Lord 1553, and the first year of the most prosperous reign of our most gracious sovereign Queen Mary the First." It is entitled *Republica*. England is signified by this name, and is represented as a widow who suffers much at the hands of Avarice, Insolence, and Oppression, *i.e.*, the Reformation. At the end

Q

Nemesis (the Queen) is introduced by Justitia, and restores the old faith.

If, as is most probable, Bale's *King John* is to be referred to the reign of Edward VI., the religious play ceases with the reign of Mary to be used as a weapon of controversy. Bishop Bale is usually considered the author of the last English miracle play ; but one or two dramas, such as the *Tragedie of Abraham's Sacrifice*, written by Beza about 1550, and translated by Edding, and the *Life and Repentance of Mary Magdalen*, were issued from the press in the reign of Elizabeth. But the religious drama was now on the wane, although it no doubt lingered long in some parts of England. A few traces of its continuance will be mentioned in a note at the end of the chapter.]

19. *Lucii Pisaei Juvenalis Monachopornomachia datum ex Achaja, Olympiade nona.* Lennius was obliged to quit Wittenberg on account of this satire on Luther, and in addition was consigned *cum infamia.*

20. Given under the title of *Declamatio in Theophoria* by Dr. A. Rein (*Vier geistl. Spiele des 17 Jahrh., Nach einer Handschr. des städt. Archivs zu Uerdingen*, Crefeld, 1853).

21. *Der Calv. Postreuter von Anno 1590 an bis 92 Jahr, wie sie ihre fulsche verführerische Lehre haben wollen an Tag bringen u. die wahre Vnuerfelschte Lutherische Lehr vnterzutrucken sich unterstanden, wird hie kürzlich vermeldt. Gestellt durch einen Liebhaber Göttlichs Worts J(org) N(igrinus) A(us) B(attenberg) I(n) S(einem) P(athmos),* 1592. *Ander Theil,* 1594, 4.

22. *Phasma hoc est : Comoedia posthuma nova et sacra de variis hæresibus et hærisiarchis, qui cum luce renascentis per Dei gratiam Evangelii hisce novissimus temporibus exstiterunt,* 1592. *Jetzund dem gemeinen Mann zu Nutz, Lehre, Warnung, sich für solchen Ketzereien zu hüten (denen nun " die Jesuwider " beigefügt sind) einfältig in deutsche Reime verfasst durch M. Arnoldum Glasern, der II. Schrift Studiosum,* Gryphisswalt, 1593. Also J. Bartel, Leipzig, 1607.

23. *Triumphus Concordiæ Consensus repetiti dramaticus (dem dreieinegen Gott u. dem ehrwurdigen Deutschmann zugeeignet),* Viteb. 1676, 4.

24. His representation as a bishop caused his papal rank to be very generally forgotten. Two priests or monks, or sometimes two kings, accompanied him ; the procession took its way to the church,

where the pastor preached a sermon to the school, or in some particular places the Bishop harangued the boys. In the afternoon in
many towns a mere bacchanalian procession ensued, in which the
Bishop rode, while in the evening there was a feast. Here and
there we find the *Episcopus puerorum*, the "children's bishop,"
derived from the old Children's Festival on the Innocents' Day.
This procession began to be abolished by local prohibitions towards
the end of the seventeenth century.

25. *Eine kurtze Comödien von der Geburt des Herrn Christi. Von
den Prinzen und Prinzessinnen des Churfürst. Hofes aufgeführt.
Nach der Handschr. nebst geschichtl. Einleitung hrsgg. von* J. G.
Friedländer, Berl. 1839. The author appears to have been one
George Pondo (Pfund), sacristan at Cologne on the Spree.

26. She died three years later as the wife of Johann Ernst III.,
Duke of Eisenach, in Saxony, with her motto on her lips, "Gott
wend mein Elend."

27.   " Von Himmel hoch da komm' ich her,
          Ich bring' euch eine gute mähr ! "

28. Schorus died at Lausanne in 1552. See *Huberti Leodi.*
Annal., l. xiii. Bayle's Diction. *Schorus*, Flögel, iv. p. 297, f.

29. Information on this subject has lately been in request for
the programme of school festivals. The latest piece written for
such an occasion, to which is added a learned sketch of the general
history of the plays, is by Heiland (*Ueber die dramatischen Auffüh-
rungen im Gymnasium zu Weimar*, Weim. 1858, 4).

30. Gottsched, who afterwards endeavoured to reform the scholastic drama, remarks, "Only such as are able to act their parts in
the school comedies with particular grace and liveliness will ever
become popular preachers, good schoolmasters, or agreeable courtiers " (*Hofleute*).

31. By Cornelius Schonaeus, a pastor at Haarlem (*Terentius
Christianus*, t. i., 1592 ; t. ii., 1595).

32. By Puschmann of Görlitz, a master-singer of the school of
Hans Sachs, and like him a shoemaker, who afterwards became
a "follower of the ancient German art of poetry and song," at
Breslau. His "great comedy of the pious patriarch Jacob with his
dear son Joseph, and his brethren, the whole and complete history

briefly handled so as to occupy at most four hours in acting," was formally approved in a memorandum of the Pastoral Body of Göttingen, in spite of some *obscœna verba et gesticulationes*, but the apology was added, "that the poor man in these bad times had therewith tried to keep himself right." In 1583 it was acted by honest citizens with an accompaniment of music and song, and an entrance fee was demanded (Hoffmann von Fallersleben, *Spenden zur deutschen Literatur*, ii. p. 5, ff.).

33.   " Frau Venus gross ist dein Gewalt
           Bei allen Menschenkindern.
       Vor dir bleibt weder jung noch alt,
           Du bringst ihr' viel zu Sünden.
       Mit scharfen Pfeiln dein blindes Kind,
       Durchdringt der Menschen Herz Geschwind,
           Und nimmt sie gar gefangen."

The author, Paul Rebhun, once resided in Luther's house, and later became schoolmaster in Plauen, then minister in Oelsnitz (*Ein Geistlich. Spiel von der Gottfürchtigen und keuschen Frawen Susannen*, Zwickau, 1536, 4. 5 *Acte mit Chören in der Art der Griechischen Tragödie, am ersten Fastensonntage* 1535, *zu Hahla aufgeführt*). Rebhun also wrote *Die Hochzeit zu Kana*, Zwickau, 1538, and other plays from the Bible, in the German language, of which he had great command, and in old-fashioned rhythm. Heiland (p. 7), mentions two performances of the comedy of Susanna in a church, *i.e.*, at Weimar during Lent 1565, and at Rostock in 1606. He quotes fifteen versions of this favourite subject.

34. Heiland (p. 4) from the *Tilsiter Gymn. Programm*, 1853. This prohibition, which is dated 1585, forbids also the admission of anything which may be prejudicial to Christianity.

35. *Christus patiens.* I have at hand only the edition issued at Tubingen by Professor Matthias Hiller, *Tragoedia notis illustrata*, Tubingen, 1714, 12. This play is an imitation both of the epic poem *Christias*, written in 1536 by Archbishop Vida, and of the early Christian drama of Gregory Nazianzen. The Saviour's introductory monologue gives a short sketch of His life, from His birth in the manger of Bethlehem to the eve of the crucifixion ; then follows a choral interlude sung by Jewish women ; then Peter repeats a monologue full of remorse for his denial of the Lord, which is supposed to have already taken place. The only action in the piece is during the judgment of Christ, who is arraigned by Caiaphas before Pilate, and the entire story of the Passion is told by two messen-

gers. These do not relate it, as in the Greek, to the heart of the mother distracted with grief, but to the chorus of Jewish women, while the play closes at the sepulchre with the gradual elevation of Mary's faith to a glad anticipation of the future. The esteem in which this play was held before it faded from the public memory seems to have been due to the style of the Latin employed, which is full of plays on words. The editor, without renouncing his admiration for the author, justly remarks: "Scripto hoc mentem pascere Christianorum, non oculos voluit, nec ad hujusmodi sacra profanum admittere vulgus, cujus tota voluptas stat in sensibus et maxime natat in oculis." H. Grotius himself says, "Audivi, qui non ferrent in scenam produci salutis nostrae mysterium. Quasi id ageretur, et non potius παραφράσεως genus esset, ea quae sacrae literae διηγηματικῶς enuntiant δραματικῶς proferre, quod et Patres olim et Pastores hodie in homiliis faciunt."

36. Heiland (p. 16, f.), *Actus de capitali Christi judicio,* also called *Drama de condemnatione Salvatoris ;* written in 1700 by Grossgebauer, rector at Weimar. The Arnstadt schoolpiece was written in 1635 by the rector, Stechan.

37. *Hruod-peraht,* the god of bright fame ; an epithet applied to Woden.

38. David Trommer's *Nickerischer Poesie,* Dresd. 1670, p. 28, ff. ; Flögel, iv. p. 9, f. ; Weinhold, p. 13 ; J. K. Schröer, *Deutsche Weihnachtsspiele aus Ungarn,* Vienna, 1858.

39.
    " Macht auf, ihr Seelen, euer Thor
    Und lasset den Herrn Christum vor,
    Macht auf die Thüren wer nur kann
    Und nehmet euern Heiland an !

    "Zeuch ein du neugebornes Kind,
    Weil dir die Thüren offen sind,
    Zeug ein und lass uns Kinderlein
    Dir, heiliger Christ, befohlen sein.

    " Sitz Heiland, nieder auf den Ort
    Und gönn' uns auch ein gnädigs Wort,
    Dein frommer Mund erhebe sich,
    So preisen auch die Kinder dich ! "

40.
    "Zeuch hin, du werther heilger Christ,
    Wo du in deinem Reiche bist,
    Zeuch hin, da tausend Engelein
    Um deinen heilgen Scepter sein !

" Bewahr euch Gott, du ganzes Haus
Und treib alls Ungemach heraus,
Bewahr euch Gott, ihr Kinderlein
Und führ euch in den Himmel ein ! "

41. Heiland quotes (p. 10) from some Latin petitions of the
Weimar students that they may be confirmed as "actio comica
eaque sacra," who owe their origin to reverend antiquity, and their
increase to the holy man Luther and other celebrated persons.
The procession was customary in nearly all neighbouring towns.

42. Heiland, p. 9, f.

43. One of these complaints (*Curiöser Bericht wegen der schäd-
lichen Weynachtslarven, so man insgemein heiligen Christ nennet*, hrsg.
v. M. M. Dresd. u. Leipz., 1702) contains an account of the custom :
"In order that it may be perceived what is meant, observe that I speak
of the custom which prevails before and during Christmas-tide ;
to wit, that long before Christmas Day masked persons go about
sounding horns and calling themselves the squires of the Lord Christ,
or else St. Martin or St. Nicholas, and so do frighten the children,
causing these to beseech them greatly, whereon they give to them
some small gift. As soon as the holy festival draws nigher, these
errant persons become more numerous, till at length on the Holy
Eve the entire sacred host (*das gantze Himmlische Heer*) fill the
houses and streets. Then the new-born Christ is brought in with
crown, sceptre, and beard, as if the lovely babe Jesus had been
born into the world in such guise. The Christ is accompanied by
His angels, by St. Peter with the Keys, by the other apostles, and
perhaps by Rupert or evil spirits. This ghostly company is brought
before the little ones, who are half dead with fear, and the chief
imp, Knecht Rupert, begins a harsh plaint against them. The holy
Saviour, who is therewith much angered, interrupts him, and will
at once go away ; but the angel Gabriel with Peter and other saints
of the company make excuses for the children. Hereupon the Holy
Lord is appeased, and causing fine Christmas gifts to be brought, He
promises mercy to the naughty little ones. They, deceived, are full
of devotion, which is all addressed to this delusive appearance that
they see before them. The holy Christ is greatly honoured
on account of the gifts, the saints around Him on account of
their powerful intercession, and Rupert because he has been easily
appeased and has remitted their punishment."

44. 1678–1708. Gervinus, *Gesch. d. poet. National-Literat.*, iii. p.
457, ff. ; Palm, *Chr. Weise*, Bresl., 1854.

45. *Die Klugheit der Obrigkeit in Anordnung des Bierbrauens.* See Papst, *Arnst. Programm*, 1846.

46. Frère Nicolai, in an account of his travels through Germany, published at Berlin in 1784, has given the programme of one of these performances at Vienna in the year 1725. The piece is entitled *Abrahami gegen Gott und Isaaci gegen seinen Vater Gehorsamb.*

47. In the programme mentioned above it is merely said, "Auf öffentlicher Schau-Bühne vorgestellst von einer Hoch-Adelichen, Wohlgebohrnen, Wohledlen, Edlen, Ehr- und Sinnreichen Jugend der Andert, und Ersten Schull in *Gymnasio* der Gesellschaft *Jesu.*" See Schlager, *Wiener Skizzen aus dem Mittelalter, Neue Folge*, published at Vienna in 1839.

48. As belonging to the play of the *Sacrifice of Abraham* the programme gives, first, as introductory piece (*Vorspill*), "The sea-nymphs determine, because of Cassiopeia's pride, to deliver her daughter Andromeda to the whale, and so they give her to Mercury to bind her to a rock." As an interlude (*Unterspill*) in the same piece, "Mercury binds Andromeda to a rock, while the whale looks on with open jaws." Afterpiece (*Nachspill*), "Perseus carries off as his bride the unbound Andromeda, whom he has rescued from the whale."

49. This well-known motto of the Jesuits closes the Viennese programme immediately after the rescue of Andromeda.

50. In the first part, printed in 1624, "*Englische Comödien u. Tragödien d. c. sehr schöne u. auserlesene geist- u. weltliche Comödi- u. Tragedi-Spiel, sammt dem Pickelhäring*," we find the *Comedy of Queen Esther and the Haughty Haman*, the *Comedy of the Prodigal Son*, in which Hope and Fear are gracefully introduced as persons, together with the *Comedy of Fortunato and his Wishing-Hat*, a *Comedy of Somebody and Nobody*, the *Tragedy of Julia and Hippolyto*, a *Merry Farce of the beauteous Maria and the aged Henry*, &c., &c. The second part, printed in 1630, contains only secular pieces. [The English comedians were English actors who came over to Germany, probably some time before the year 1600, and were the first regular professional actors who performed in Germany. See Gervinus, iii. p. 104 ff.]

51. [It may be interesting to notice the phrase used by Professor Hase, *Haupt- und Staats-Action*. The same expression occurs

in Goethe's *Faust*, in the night scene at the beginning of Part I., in the conversation between Faust and Wagner :—

> " Und höchstens eine Haupt- und Staats- action
> Mit trefflichen pragmatischen Maximen,
> Wie sie den Puppen wohl im Munde ziemen ! "

It is translated " puppet-show play " by Mr. Hayward : " A puppet-show play with fine pragmatical saws, such as may happen to sound well in the mouths of the puppets ! " Mr. Bayard Taylor renders it " Punch-and-Judy play." He has the following note on the passage :—" The German phrase ' Haupt- und Staats- Action' was applied about the end of the seventeenth century to the popular puppet-plays which represented famous passages of history. It seems to have been originally invented by some proprietor of a wandering puppet-theatre, and may therefore be equivalently translated as a ' First-Class Political Performance.' The phrase was afterwards applied to plays acted upon the stage, and Goethe even makes use of it to designate Shakespeare's historical dramas. In the puppet-plays the heroic figures (Alexander, Pompey, Charlemagne, &c.) were in the habit of uttering the most grandiloquent oracular sentences ; they were as didactic in speech as they were reckless and melodramatic in action."]

52. *Martin Luther oder die Weihe der Kraft, Eine Tragödie vom Verfasser der Söhne des Thales*, Berlin, 1807.

53. A. Pichler, *Ueber das Drama des Mittelalters in Tyrol*, Innsbruck, 1850. In an Easter play given at p. 153 the Gardener addresses the Virgin—

> " Dass du mir niedertritst das Kraut !
> Get rasch in bose haut,
> Und get aus dem garten
> In die schul zu den gelarten,
> Oder ich smier euch eure glieder,
> Dass euch in drei tagen nit lust herwider."

54. This censorship was especially directed towards the suppression of the comic parts ; and members of the clerical body, and scholars who had hitherto superintended the performances, were forbidden any longer to have anything to do with them. The plays were not to commence until after the afternoon service, and they were to terminate with a collection for the poor.

55. Pichler, p. 75. On page 76 he gives the memorandum quoted below, which also bears date 1816.

56. For each of the later performances I have consulted a favourable and comprehensive account given by a competent eyewitness— Guido Gorres, *Das Theater im Mittelalter und das Passionsspiel in Oberammergau* (*Historisch polit. Blätter*, 1840) ; Eduard Devrient, *Das Passionsschauspiel in Oberammergau und seine Bedeutung für die neue Zeit.* Illustrated by F. Pecht. Leipzig, 1851.

57. [Montgelas, a native of Munich, of Savoyard extraction, administered various departments of the state under Maximilian Joseph from 1799 to 1817. He was a successful statesman, but retired from office when the King decided to grant a constitution to Bavaria.]

58. The receipts are employed to cover the costs of the performance, to indemnify the players for the loss of their time, and to pay the debts of the community. In 1840 the entrance fees were computed at 24,000 florins. In Spain, in 1252, an edict of Alphonso the Wise forbade the performance in villages of miracle plays for the sake of worldly gain. See Schack, *Gesch. d. dramat. Lit. in Spanien,* i. p. 113. [Two-fifths of the proceeds have in late years been set aside to indemnify the players. A part of the large sum received at the last performance has been expended in colossal marble figures of Christ and the Apostles, intended for the summit of the Kreuzberg, which overlooks the village.]

59. *Das grosse Versöhnungsopfer auf Golgatha oder die Leidens- und Todesgeschichte Jesu, nach den vier Evangelisten, mit bildlichen Vorstellungen aus dem alten Bunde, zur Betrachtung und Erbauung, mit allerhöchster und allergnädigster Bewilligung vollständig aufgeführt zu Oberammergau. Musik von Dedler.* Landshut, 1840–1850.

60. In the performance of 1840, two angels.

61. E. Devrient, *Das Passionsschauspiel in Oberammergau,* p. 16, f. : "It makes on us the most surprising impression when we see the Saviour, the most familiar theme of our imagination from our childhood, the figure which has stood before us in innumerable works of art, now move in our sight in living form ; when we hear Him instructing the people as they offer their praises, and answering the attacks of the scribes. We cannot admit the thought of any desecration of our idea of the Redeemer ; on the contrary, to His spiritual form such a convincing reality is given by His visible existence among men, that I found all which I had imagined of His life and sufferings now for the first time acquire an actual vital force."

62. Weinhold, p. 372. Secular farces formerly alternated with the miracle plays at Liesing.

63. It is thus employed in a MS. which has reached us from Vordernberg in Upper Styria, and which, though bearing the date of 1847, is really at least a century older. The piece, too, is itself a rearrangement of an earlier drama, which is given by Weinhold at p. 302, ff.

64. "The peasant plays in Styria and Carinthia rapidly approach extinction. It is true that here and there of late they have displayed some fresh energy, but this seems rather to resemble the final gleam of an expiring lamp. Their day has passed." Weinhold, p. 373.

65. [In England, as in other Protestant countries, the miracle plays became extinct rather from natural causes than from authoritative prohibition. The Christmas play had not such popularity in England as in Germany, and there was much in the Easter play to excite the hostility of Protestants, while the Corpus Christi plays would be wholly condemned. The critical spirit awakened by the Renaissance was, however, their worst enemy. After the Great Rebellion, when all plays were forbidden, no formal attempt was ever made to revive them.

There are authentic records of the continuance of the miracle play until the end of the sixteenth century. Strype affirms that the *Passion of Christ* was performed in London in 1556, and in 1557 on the day that war was proclaimed against France (see Warton, ii. p. 233). Miracle plays were also acted at Tewkesbury in 1586, and Archdeacon Rogers, who died in 1595, saw the Whitsuntide plays at Chester in the preceding year. So late as the reign of James I., Prynne, in his *Histrio-Mastix*, affirms that the play of the *Passion of Christ* was given at Ely House, Holborn, before the Spanish ambassador, Gondomar.

An act was passed in 1647 for the permanent suppression of all stage plays, which gave the final blow to the miracle play. But after the Restoration, although these plays were never formally revived, it was long before they entirely disappeared. Borlase thinks that the Cornish plays continued to be acted until the middle of the last century. Hone, p. 230, quotes two papers from the *Tatler* of May 14, 1709, and from the *Spectator* of March 16, 1711, which show that scriptural and apocryphal subjects were still exhibited in puppet-shows. "The English puppet-show," according to Hone, was formerly called a *motion*. Shakespeare mentions the performance of mysteries by puppets; his

Autolycus frequented wakes, fairs, and bear-baitings, and "compassed a motion of the Prodigal Son," so that the puppet-show to which Steele refers was a genuine survival. Hone and Mr. Halliwell also, in *Coventry Plays*, p. 407, quote a printed bill of the latter end of the seventeenth century (also given, too, in Strutt's *Sports and Pastimes*), which states that "at Crawley's show at the 'Golden Lion,' near St. George's church, during the time of Southwark Fair, will be presented the whole story of the old Creation of the World, or Paradise Lost, yet newly revived, with the addition of Noah's flood," this being also the subject of the puppet-show sportively mentioned in the *Tatler*. It is possible that even now the same kind of exhibition might be found in some remote spots where country fairs are still kept up. It is said that in 1824 two of Bale's plays, or some imitation of them, were still acted at the Market Cross at Bury (Warton, iv. p. 74, note). A friend has also informed me that in Yorkshire villages puppet-shows are still, or at least were recently, exhibited on the time-honoured theme of Noah and his vixen wife, and the Flood. These are but shrunken offshoots from so large a stem, but they show how hard it is to efface the last lingering traces of a popular and deeply-rooted custom.]

NOTES TO LECTURE III.

—◆◆—

1. Although the following sketch of the Spanish drama only takes into consideration the works of Lope de Vega and Calderon, A. F. von Schack (*Geschichte der dramat. Literatur u. Kunst in Spanien*) has shown that these two great poets only form the apex of a pyramid of scarcely inferior predecessors and contemporaries. Schack's careful researches have enabled me to repair the deficiencies in my own knowledge of Spanish literature. Valentine Schmidt (*Die Schauspiele Calderon's, dargestellt und erläutert*) has shown even greater acuteness in his analysis of the marshy subsoil, already undermined by despotism and fanaticism, from which grew the gorgeous flowers of Calderon's poetry with their intoxicating sweetness. The use I have made of the information and suggestions contained in the works of A. W. von Schlegel, Tieck, von Münch-Bellinghausen, v. d. Malsburg, &c., will be easily perceived. On the other hand, F. A. Huber's essay on the *Nationality and Literature of Spain*, while it professes to pay special attention to the drama, merely gives us the information that the stage is in the highest degree Catholic ; and adds that we may look for a reaction in Spain similar to that of the sixteenth century, but this time in the direction of a more evangelical form of Catholicism.

2. Born 1489, died 1557. [Gil Vincente belonged to the western portion of the Peninsula. He was, as Professor Hase has mentioned in, the former lecture (p. 53), a Portuguese. Besides his sacred pieces, he wrote also secular plays. His works were collected and published at Lisbon by his son, Louis Vincente, and had some reputation.]

3. *Auto de la Sibila Casandra.*

4. In the sixteenth century these were also known as *Farsa sacramental.*

5. *Las Cortes de la muerte.*

6. The Spanish plays of the sixteenth and seventeenth centuries are all entitled *comedies*, without any distinction for either tragedy or farce. They have three acts, which are termed *Jornados—Day's-work*—in imitation of the mysteries, where, however, the term had a more practical meaning. The *Autos*, with a very few exceptions, have no such division, and contain only a single act.

7. *Ni Amor se libra de Amor*, acted at Toledo.

8. The character and plot of some few *Autos* is given by Schack, ii. p. 393, ff. ; iii. p. 251, ff. See also Schlegel, *Dram. Kunst u. Lit.*, iii. p. 353, ff.

9. *La limpieza no manchada.* One of the plays wrongly attributed to Calderon is also entirely directed towards the exposition and popularisation of this difficult article of faith, which remained for Pius IX. to erect into a dogma necessary to salvation. V. Schmidt, p. 473, f.

10. [The Spanish clown or harlequin.]

11. The Countess d'Aunoy was an eyewitness of this play. See the letters from her given by Schack, iii. p. 20.

12. *Comedias divinas y humanas.*

13. *Comedias* or *Vidas de Santos*, called also *Comedias de ruido* or *de teátro*, on account of the stage expenditure which was sometimes demanded for the production of these marvellous legends of the other worlds, upper and lower.

14. *El Serafin humano.*

15. *El Cardinal de Belen.*

16. *El animal profeta.* See *Gesta Romanorum*, c. 18. [For a notice of the *Gesta Romanorum* consult Note 8, Lecture V.]

17. *Don Quixote.* [From the English version published by Gall & Inglis, Edinburgh.]

18. *La fianza satisfecha.*

19. *El niño inocente de la guardia.*

20. *El Ateista fulminato.*

21. *El Burlador de Sevilla y Convidado de piedra.* This play was certainly written before 1620, as in that year it was already transplanted into Italy, and the author, whose real name was Gabriel Tellez, had already entered, at the age of fifty, the convent of the Brothers of Mercy in Madrid. The story of Don Juan Tenorio had been transmitted in Seville entirely by oral tradition, and the monument of the slain commandant had been there plainly to be seen in proof of it, but at the date of the drama had been removed to San Francisco in Madrid.

22. *Comedias de capa y espada*, comedies of hat and sword; light dramatic pieces.

23. Calderon's more celebrated *Comedias divinas* belong, however, to his youth. He was born in 1600, and in 1651 he took minor religious orders. In 1663 he joined the congregation of St. Peter, composed exclusively of priests born in Madrid, and was elevated to the post of chaplain of the congregation. In 1681 he died in that office. He composed with equal assiduity after taking orders, and thus wrote for sixty-six years out of his entire term of eighty-one.

24. *El Purgatorio de San Patricio.* See *Legenda Aurea*, c. 50; *Acta Sanctorum, Mart.*, t. ii. p. 588, *sqq.* [*Legenda Aurea:* "Written by Jacobus de Voragine about the year 1260; an inexhaustible repository of religious fable."— *Warton.*]

25. See the legend of Cyprian and Justina, *Legenda aurea*, c. 142. Calderon probably drew his knowledge of the story from Surius, *de probatis Sanctorum Vitis*, Sept. 26, in which the version is taken from Simeon Metaphrastes, and the little-known magician of Antioch, who at seven years old is dedicated by his parents to the evil one from whom he derives his power, is confounded with the great Bishop Cyprian of Carthage. Perhaps we may find in this mistake the origin of the poet's idea of causing Cyprian not to appear to the outer world as a magician, but as a philosopher, wavering in his faith in Paganism. In the legend the confusion of the Cyprians allows Cyprian to retain his bishopric, and converts Justina into the abbess of a nunnery, while both die in 280 in the reign of Diocletian, a curious chronological puzzle! The earliest source of the legend lies in a confession of Cyprian (*Acta Sanctor.*, Sept., t. vii. p. 195, *sqq.*), which, it seems, was known to St. Gregory of Nazianzen (*Orat.* 18). In this he tells how as a child he was initiated into all the mysteries of Greece; how he completed his education in the magic art in Memphis and Chaldea; and how finally in Antioch he performed, by the assistance of the devil,

many apparently good works, which earned for him unbounded honour.

26. *Nat. His.*, ii. 7, Quapropter effigiem Dei formamque quaerere imbecillitatis humanae reor. Quisquis est deus si neodo est alius (ac Sol) et quacunque in parte totus est sensus, totus visus, totus auditus, totus animae, totus animi, totis sui.

27. In the legend the magician Cyprian says to the demon whom he has summoned, "Amo virginem de Galilaea ; potesue facere, ut ipsam habeam et voluntatem meam secum perficiam ? " The demon answers haughtily, "Ego qui hominem de paradiso ejicere potui, Cain fratrem suum occidere procuravi, Judaeos Christum occidere feci, et non potero facere, ut unam puellam habeas et ea juxta tuum placitum fruaris ? " When, however, this first spirit has fled at the sign of the cross, Cyprian, scorning so feeble a power, calls upon a greater demon, the chief of all the spirits of evil. Satan begins his work more cleverly than in the drama by appearing to Justina in the form of a maiden, who also has made to God the vow of eternal chastity. This counterfeit maiden relates how she has become doubtful of the excellence of her vow, for hath not God said, " Be ye fruitful and multiply and replenish the earth"? " I fear therefore that if we are obstinate, and reject our part in the will of God, our tribulation shall be great and our reward but small." On this Justina's inclination asserts itself, but she conquers both her own desires and the arts of the devil entirely by the sign of the cross.

28. Rosenkranz thinks that, "In the *Marvellous Magician* Calderon has set himself the difficult task of representing every movement of the spiritual process which transforms a Pagan self-consciousness, already undermined by philosophic doubt, into a Christian self-consciousness ; without at the same time introducing the theological system of the Church in such a way as to break the continuity of the story, or allowing the action to become the mere empty reflection and outward show of such a change. Everything breathes the breath of life. The self-centred Spirit of Evil, existing for its own sake alone, Calderon has depicted with peculiar power, especially in one respect : he has caused the devil to reveal himself as such to Cyprian only by slow degrees." Genius decidedly here both set to itself and performed its philosophical task in complete unconsciousness !

29. *La devocion de la cruz*, edition of 1635.

30. *El principe constante.* See *Leben des standhaften Prinzen*, published in Berlin in 1827, from the chronicle of the Prince's secre-

tary, Alvarez, and other documents. The Infant Don Ferdinand of Portugal, who was born in 1402, died in 1443, after the ineffable sufferings of a six years' captivity in Fez. In the historical narrative his death is thus described, " The Infant lay there with his hands raised to heaven ; his open eyes were filled with tears, and around his half-open mouth there hovered a strangely-sweet smile, such as could only be a reflection of the sublimest joy and the most heartfelt peace." His bones, which were brought back to Portugal in 1473 by Alphonso V., rest in the chapel of the convent of Batalha. Above the altar is seen the Prince's statue in the wretched garb of his slavery, with the inscription :—

Sanctus Princeps Ferdinandus
Infans Lusitaniae
Obiit Fessae apud Mauros obses
A.D. MCCCCXLIII. V. Junii.

31. *La Virgen del Sagrario.*'

32. *La Sibila de Oriente* was composed for the ceremony of the Raising of the Cross. It is taken from *Josephi Antiq.* i. 7, *sqq.*, and from such parts of the Old Testament story as can be made to apply.

33. The Queen of Sheba, having fallen asleep on Lebanon beneath this tree, recognises in it the future Tree of the Cross. In the ordinary Greek legend the Tree of the Trinity is an amalgamation of pine, cypress, and cedar. The idea is derived from Isaiah lx. 13, and has been transplanted into the region of the miraculous.

34. *La Aurora en Copacabana.*

35. *El gran Príncipe de Fez.*

36. In the Koran the glory of Mary and her birth are related from the apocryphal gospels in a much more marvellous strain than by the true evangelists. But the idea of the immaculate conception is foreign to the Koran, and was first discovered in it by Catholic eyes.

37. *La cisma de Inglaterra.* See Val. Schmidt, *Ueber die Kirchentrennung von Engl.*, Berlin, 1819.

38. Though Shakespeare, in his *King Henry VIII.*, represents the King's conscientious scruples as having actually been the reason of his separating himself in great sorrow of heart from the gentle Queen Catherine, yet the course of the action shows that the poet

understood pretty clearly the real cause of the separation, which he allows to be expressed by one of the subordinate characters—

LORD CHAMBERLAIN.

" It seems the marriage with his brother's wife
Has crept too near his conscience."

SUFFOLK.

" No, his conscience
Has crept too near another lady."

— *Act* ii., *scene* 2.

39. Calderon found nearly all these calumnies ready to his hand in Nicolai *Sanderi de origine ac progressu schismatis Anglicani*, lib. iii.

40. Lope de Vega himself names this mixture of tragedy and farce, of Seneca with Terence, a *monstrosity;* but it had its origin in the traditional claim of the populace to be *amused,* which was best gratified by an intermingling of earnest narrative and broad fun. It also occurs to the poetic imagination of de Vega that a similar variety exists in nature of which beauty is the issue.

41. *La vida es sueño.*

42. [Professor Hase gives his own poetic version of these lines. Throughout the drama the same note of the illusiveness of life resounds incessantly, as in some previous verses also translated by Lewes—

" What is life ? 'Tis but a madness.
What is life ? A mere illusion,
Fleeting shadow, fond delusion,
Shortlived joy that ends in sadness,
Whose most steadfast substance seems
But the dream of other dreams."

The idea frequently recurs also in other dramas of Calderon's, and is introduced with singular grace in Polonia's hymn in the *Purgatory of St. Patrick.* Several of Calderon's plays have been translated into English, the best-known versions, with the exception of a few extracts by Shelley, being those of D. F. MacCarthy : *La vida es sueño, El Mágico prodigioso, El Purgatorio de San Patricio, La devocion de la cruz,* and many shorter pieces have been rendered by this author. Calderon's dramas are commonly in blank verse very largely interspersed with rhyme, whole speeches and frequently whole scenes being rhymed.]

R

1. *David combattant, triomphant, fugitif,* 1566. *Saul le Furieux; Tragédie prise de la Bible, faite selon l'art à la mode des vieux poëtes tragiques,* 1568. *Les Juives* derives its name from the chorus of Jewish women. Its subject is the downfall of Zedekiah and his house after the conquest of Jerusalem by Nebuchadnezzar. See Ebert, p. 161, ff.

2. [*Le Cid. Don Sanche d' Aragon,* and Corneille's lighter pieces from the Spanish, were written later.]

3. *Polyeucte, Martyr, Tragédie chrétienne,* 1643.

4. *Art poétique,* iii.—

> " Une troupe grossière
> . . . Sottement zélée en sa simplicité
> Joua les Saints, la Vierge, et Dieu par piété
> Le savoir, a la fin dissipant l'ignorance,
> Fit voir de ce projet la dévote imprudence,
> On chassa ses docteurs prêchants sans mission,
> On vit renâitre Hector, Andromaque, Ilion."

5. *Examen de Polyeucte :* " L'illustre Grotius a mis sur la scène la Passion même de Jésus-Christ et l'Histoire de Joseph ; et le savant Buchanan a fait la même chose de celle de Jephté et de la mort de saint Jean-Baptiste. C'est sur ces exemples que j'ai hazardé ce poëme."

6. See the enlarged edition of Surius, *Vitae Sanctorum,* Cologne, 1617, under date of January 9 (t. i. p. 136, *sqq.*). The version in Surius is borrowed from Simeon Metaphrastes.

7. [Nibelungen-lied, i. 13 (Lettson's translation)—

" A dream was dreamt by Kriemhild, the virtuous and the gay,
How a wild young falcon she trained for many a day,
Till two fierie eagles tore it : to her there could not be
In all the world such sorrow as this perforce to see."

The dream is afterwards fulfilled by the murder of her husband.]

8. The legend lays particular stress on this illustration of the noble doctrine of the Church. Polyeuctus is anxious lest our Lord should fail to recognise him as His own if he should appear before Him without the mystic sign, that is, if he should die a martyr without being baptized. His Christian friend reassures him by citing the thief on the cross.

9. Veltheim's company, then much celebrated.

10. Devrient, *Gesch. d. Schauspiel,* i. p. 234, ff.

11. [Racine was born in 1639 ; *Phèdre* appeared in 1677.]

12. Perhaps Madame de Maintenon was hardly reminded of the oppressed Huguenots by Esther's prayer for the condemned Jews ; although she might well have recollected that in her own youth she had sung Marot's hymns in a Huguenot circle.

13. Alt, p. 603, f.

14. If these lines are really borrowed from a speech of the Duke of Guise to a Huguenot who tried to assassinate him during the siege of Rouen, then it has been truly remarked (in the edition of the works of Voltaire published at Gotha, ii. p. 140) that they can be esteemed in his case but a grand piece of hypocrisy ; inasmuch as he was a party leader who slew many innocent victims, in the endeavour to cover his ambition beneath a veil of religion. At any rate Voltaire has made a noble use of the speech in his poem.

15. *Le Fanatisme ou Mahomet le Prophet, Tragédie. Représentée, pour la première fois, le 9 Août* 1742.

16. *Œuv. de Voltaire,* t. iii. p. 132, *sqq.*

17. *Traité sur la tolérance à l'occasion de la mort de Jean Calas,* Paris, 1763.

NOTES TO LECTURE V.

1. In Book III. of his own collection of his pieces, made first in 1561, and often reprinted, *Clägliche Tragedien, liebliche Comedien vnd schimpf Spil, Geistliche vnd Weltliche.* The preface adds, " Weil ich noch aufs allen meinen gedichten mir bissher vorbehalten, den meisten theil meiner Comedi, Tragedi vnd spil, als ein besondern lieben heimlichen schatz, weil ich sie den meisten theil selb hab agiren vnd spielen helfen, hab ich dise meine lange vorbehaltene Comedi, Tragedi vnd spil, weltlicher inn der zal sind 102, zu gestelt dem Erbarn Jörg Willer Truckerherrn zu Augspurg auch diss mein dritt vnd letztes Buch zu trucken. Diss hab ich in drey theil abgetheilet, *zuerst* die geistlichen spiel aus altem vnd neuem Testament, Figur, geschicht der König vnd Prophetn auch Evangelia vnd ander geistlich materi, dadurch die gotseligkeyt, forcht vnd liebe Gottes inn die hertzen einzubilden vnd pflantzen. Der *ander* theil weltlich alt Histori, auss den Poetn vnd geschichtschreibern, die zu anreitzung der guten Tugendt, vnd zu abschneidung der schendlichen laster dienstlich sindt. Zum *dritten*, die Fastnachtspiel ; mancherley art, mit schimpflichen schwencken gespicket (doch glimpflich ohn alle vnzucht) die schwermütigen hertzen zu freuden ermundern—solche Comedi oder spil welche auch zum theil vorhin in etlichen Fürsten- vnd Reichstetten, mit freuden vnd wunder der zuseher, gespielt worden sindt. Also guthertziger Leser hast du mich gar, mit allen meinen werken, mancherley art der gebunden gedicht so ich vngefärlich in 47 Jarn gemacht hab— nimb an mit gutem geneigten hertzen, diss mein letztes Buch, darmit ich, mein 66 Jar vnd alter mit Gottes gnaden nun zu rhu setzen wil."

2. See the scholarly *Epistola ad nobilem et generosum Comitem Johannem de Weda, Francof.,* 1539, in *Corpus Reformatorum,* t. iii. p. 653, *sqq.* Melanchthon brings forward this narrative, which is apparently from a poem by Alberus, a priest of Brandenburg, in

order to prove that the distinctions of rank have been ordained by
God, and that in each rank every one should strive for the adorn-
ment of virtue, "unicuique elaborandum esse, ut virtute suam
personam tueatur." The classical Latin of the story contains no
trace of the realism and humour which Hans Sachs has introduced.

3. Achan replies to the Lord's question whether he hopes for
eternal salvation—

> "Ich weiss wohl, wie es steht auf Erden,
> Wie's dort zugeht das weiss ich nicht,
> Doch wenn mich Gott dazu versieht,
> Dass ich auch selig werden söll,
> So werd ich selig, thu was ich wöll."

THE LORD.

> "Esau, was hältst vom Opfer du
> In deinem Herzen, das sag mir zu!"

ESAU.

> "Ich halt Gott werd das ewig Leben
> Uns von des Opfers wegen geben,
> Darmit wir es Gott kaufen ab,
> Dass er uns darnach mit begab,
> Wo anders ein ewigs Leben ist."

THE LORD.

> "Nimrod sag mir zu dieser Frist,
> Was hältst du von dem ewig Leben?"

NIMROD.

> "Das will ich dir gleich sagen eben:
> Was meine Augen sehen glaubt das Herz,
> Nicht höher schwing ich es aufwärts,
> Ich nehm Ehr, Gut, Reichthum dermassen,
> Und will dir deinen Himmel lassen."

The germ of the clever satire in these three answers may be found
in the creed which Melanchthon makes Cain repeat: "Credo unum
esse Deum, omnipotentem conditorem totius mundi quem colendum
esse censeo sacrificiis, propter quae foecundat agros nostros-Sed an
exaudiat invocantes, an peccata remittat, ambigo. De immortalitate
etiam tunc videro cum ex hac vita discessero. Sentio autem bonos
mores colendos esse, ut vita tranquilla sit." Hereupon God blames
him because, forgetful of this, he does not obey the injunction of
the creed.

4.
　　　" Mein Bruder Abel ist wohl zu Hof,
　　　　Er ist worden unser Bischof,
　　　　Der Herr treibt mit ihm grosse Pracht,
　　　　Uns sonst all verspott und veracht,
　　　　Solln wir uns alle vor ihm biegen
　　　　Und ihm unter den Füssen liegen !
　　　　Es wird uns gar hart kommen an."

5. The piece bears the date of September 23, 1553, which was
most probably the day chosen for the representation. In the edition
we have consulted (Nuremberg, 1589, Bd., i. s. 14), the former
piece has only the date of the year, 1553. Godeke (*Grundriss z.
Gesch. d. deutschen Dichtung*) gives the plays in the following order :
—*Spil von Adam's kindern*, 23d September 1553; *Comedi Die
ungleichen kindern Evä wie sie Gott der Herr anredct*, 6th November 1553. In this case *Eve's Unlike Children* would be the later
piece, and it must be allowed that it is possible that Hans Sachs
was led, for some theological purpose, to develop a complete comedy
from the simple and more suitable form of the rhymed jest.
Melanchthon's story contains the basis of both plays, but he accords
no preference on account of age to the children in either set. Eve,
on looking through the window, sees the Lord arrive unexpectedly
while she is busy washing the children, because, the next day being
a festival, they are to attend a sacrifice which Adam intends to offer
and to accompany with a sermon. The children whom she has not
finished putting to rights she hides in the heaps of hay and straw.
We have here the source of the shorter piece. But God, who can
see that which is concealed, causes the hidden children to be called,
the eldest in particular. Cain appears not only with the hay sticking
in his hair, but in defiant mood, and he repeats his bad unbelieving
creed. Then God makes the good children, Abel and Seth, a priest
and a king, while Cain shall be only a peasant and a serf.

6.
　　　" Wenn der Herr kömmt herein,
　　　　So ziehet ab eure Schepplein fein
　　　　Und thut euch alle gen ihn neigen,
　　　　Thut ihm all Reverenz erzeigen,
　　　　Biet't ihm die Hände nach einander,
　　　　Dann knieet nieder—
　　　　So wird er euch den Segen geben."

7. When our Lord comes out to look for Peter, He remarks—

　　　" Ich glaub Petrus wird sich beweiben
　　　　Und unten auf der Erden bleiben,

Hat gar vergessen seinen Zusag,
Nun ist ja heut der neunte Tag,
Dass niemand ist beim Himmelsthor,
Ich glaub es stehn viel Seelen davor,
Die allsamt gerne wären rein,
Wie mag er nur so lange sein !—
Dort kommt er mit seinem schweren Gang—
Petre, Petre, wo bist so lang ! "

8. Eine neue schöne und geistliche Comödia, darinnen nicht allein die Lehre, Leben und Wandel des letzten deutlichen Wundermannes, Lutheri, sondern auch seine und zuvörderst des Herrn Christi zweier vornehmsten Hauptfeinde, *Pabsts* und *Calvinisten* vielfältige Rath- und Fehlschläge, auch endlicher in Gottes Wort offenbarter und gewisser Ausgang bis an den nunmehr bald zukünftigen jüngsten Tag, beides nach schöner poetischer und verblumter Art wie auch historischer richtiger Wahrheit abgemahlt und aufgeführt. Agiret vom Gymnasio zu Eisleben *post ferias caniculares*, 1613.

9. Cap. 45. [According to Mr. Herttage in his introduction to *The Early English Versions of the Gesta Romanorum*, published for the Early English Text Society, 1879, the *Gesta* must have been compiled some years before the *Decamerone* was written, as several of the tales in the latter are borrowed from the former collection. Hence the work cannot have been composed later than 1348. According to Warton, i. p. 241, " The work is compiled from the obsolete Latin chronicles of the later Roman or rather German story, heightened by romantic inventions from legends of the saints, oriental apologues, and many of the shorter fictitious narratives which came into Europe with the Arabian literature, and were familiar in the ages of ignorance and imagination. The classics are sometimes cited for authorities ; but these are of the lower order, such as Valerius Maximus, the favourite author of the mediæval period, Macrobius, Aulus Gellius, Seneca, Pliny, and Boethius. To every tale a moralisation is subjoined, reducing it into a Christian or moral lesson." The name *Gesta Romanorum* was properly applied to Roman history in general, and is so used in these tales. Many of the stories are totally unconnected with the Roman people ; but the collector, in order to justify his title, " has taken care to preface almost every story with the name or reign of a Roman emperor, who at the same time is often a monarch that never existed, and who seldom, whether real or supposititious, has any concern with the circumstances of the narrative." The preservation of the collection is largely due to the use which was made of them in sermons. For

other questions connected with the *Gesta* see the authorities above cited.]

10. A later edition adds, "and he kissed him as he lay dead."

11. [*Wolfenbüttel Fragments*—papers left by Reimarus, a Hamburg professor, and published by Lessing without the name of the author.]

12. [Influenced by the consistory of Brunswick, the ministry forbade both the further publication of the *Fragments* and the continuance of the controversy.]

13. Thus runs the well-known story of the *Gesta Romanorum* (c. 89), and as I find the same version in one of the most correct of German literary historians, I ought to premise that it rests on a somewhat corrupt reading of the *Gesta*. In two editions which lie before me at this moment, belonging respectively to the years 1499 and 1509, the mediation of the wise elder is lacking, while the main idea is at once less harsh and more in keeping with historical fact. A knight at his death makes his eldest son his heir and gives him his lands. To the second son he gives a treasure, and to the third a ring of greater worth than all that he is leaving his brothers, to whom he has already presented rings of less value (*non tam pretiosos*). After the father's death each son asserts that he possesses the precious ring worn by him, and they determine on a trial of its efficacy. Sick persons suffering from various diseases are brought, and while the rings of the elder brothers have no effect, that of the youngest heals them. In the moral (*moralisitio*) this is thus explained. The knight is our Lord Jesus Christ, who has three sons, Jews, Saracens, and Christians. To the Jews he gave the Promised Land; to the Saracens the treasures of this world, Riches and Might; to the Christians he has given the precious Ring of Faith, which has power to heal all the diseases and infirmities of the soul.

14. *Le vrai anel,* "which cures all ills and even raises the dead to life, and which is no more to be confounded with the two other rings of false metal than it is to be allowed that we should take the Saracenic or Jewish law for the true law of Christians." The learned editor of one of the volumes of the *Histoire littéraire de la France* (*Ouvrage commencé par des Religieux Benedictins de la Congr. de S. Maur continué par des Membres de l'Institut.*, t. xxiii., Par, 1856, 4, p. 259) Victor le Clerc, has only given the above extract from the manuscript, while he somewhat too contemptuously reckons the story

itself among the allegorical pieces, of which even the shortest analysis would be *fastidieuse*.

15. *Cento novello antiche*, Nr. 73.

16. *Decamerone*, i. 3.

17. *Das Sirventes des Templers :* Michaud, *Hist. des` Croisades*, t. v. p. 38 ; F. Diez, *Leben und Werke der Troubadours*, p. 589.

18. Mansi, *Collectio Concill.*, t. xxiii. p. 79.

19. C. Schwarz, *G. E. Lessing als Theolog.*, p. 214, Halle, 1854. " In this play a dramatic expression is given to an integral trait of our German life, to the quality which leads us naturally to seek for depth and freedom in our religious convictions. It is not the en-lightenment (*Aufklärung*) of the eighteenth century with its mere tolerance that is here glorified. No! it is an ideal of religious sympathy which soars far above the thought of the day, and which the German people can never fail to recognise as its own and to claim as its peculiar inheritance." [*Duldung* is the word here used in opposition to *Toleranz;* but while our English "pati-ence" hardly expresses the meaning, "sympathy" perhaps is a little too strong a term.]

20. Schwarz, *Lessing*, p. 215. "The Patriarch and Dajah both represent the Christian *populace*. In the former we see the worst form which this populace can assume when moulded by the sacer-dotal spirit. It then becomes capable of political intrigue and even of plots of assassination, and sacrifices its whole moral sense to a fanatical belief in a religion in which alone salvation is to be found. In Dajah we see an example of the simple form of credulity common to nurses and children, and she displays all the crude absurdity and impulsiveness which belong to an uncultivated mind."

21. W. Wackernagel in his beautiful university oration, *Lessing's Nathan der Weise*, published in *Gelzer's prot. Monatsblättern*, 1855, b. vi. part 4. [Reprinted among W. Wackernagel's *Kleinere Schriften*, Leipzig, 1874.]

22. *Ad Nicodem* [p. 18]. But the merely heathen element, which is often found even *post Christum natum*, is seen in the sentence which follows, assigning a motive for such good conduct. "For it is more to be expected that the gods shall confer some blessing on such worshippers, than on those who offer them many sacrifices."

23. In opposition to the general impression that the first representation of *Nathan* took place 28th November 1800, Devrient has shown (b. iii. p. 71, f.) that in 1783 Döbbelin undertook to produce the drama in Berlin, but that the performance was a complete failure, and has thus been forgotten.

24. Wackernagel alludes to this somewhat ironically : " Has not a schoolmaster of North Germany, Edward Niemeyer of Crefeld, quite recently affirmed it to be a very natural circumstance, most easily to be accounted for, that *Nathan* should even be used as a book of instruction, and has he not caused a whole volume of commentary to be printed especially to promote this employment of it in schools ? "

25. Gervinus, *Gesch. der poet. National-Literatur.* " This book is, next after Goethe's *Faust,* the most thoroughly German and entirely indigenous of the creations of our modern muse. Who has not felt his heart beat at the clear straightforwardness of the moral, every stroke in the delineation of which is masculine and noble ? And what man is there in these later days whom we should like to take as a model who has not adopted this cheery yet earnest faith as his form of creed ? And what better hope could we cherish for future ages than that this beauteous code of religious and secular morality should more and more strengthen its hold on the hearts of our nation, whose pre-eminent gift it seems to be able to believe without superstition, to doubt without despairing of the truth, and to be liberal in thought without becoming frivolous in act ? "

26. It will hardly escape the notice of an attentive student of the Bible that these words are spoken by Peter (Acts x. 35) to confirm God's willingness to receive the Gentiles also as followers of Christ. At the same time we may discern in the text the great primitive idea that, even apart from the religion of the Bible, Righteousness and the Fear of God, the Biblical terms for morality and piety, find favour in the sight of God.

NOTES TO LECTURE VI.

—•◦•—

1. [The first authentic record of the appearance of female actors on an English stage belongs to the year 1629. In France and Italy the practice had prevailed for some time. Coryat, whose *Crudities* were written in 1611, mentions that he had seen female performers in Venice, and that *he had heard* that women had been known to exhibit in London. The performers of 1629 were members of a French company, and seem to have met with very little public favour. See Collier, *Hist. Eng. Dramatic Poetry*, vol. i. p. 451, f.]

2. C. F. Ständlin, *Geschichte der Vorstellungen von der Sittlichkeit des Schauspiels*, Göttingen, 1823.

3. Nicole, *Essais de morale*, ed. 6, à la Haye, 1689, t. iii.

4. *Œuvres complettes, Melanges*, t. iii., Deuxponts, 1782.

5. *Supplement à la Collection des Œuvres de J. J. Rousseau*, t. i.

6. See the decree of the "*Comité de salut public*" for 25th January 1794.

7. It is said that the clerical orators of the day were in the habit of studying Tertullian, the most eloquent of the Latin fathers, and of introducing passages from his writings, for which reason they were called Tertullianists. If this were really the origin of the theatrical term, there is an unconscious irony in the circumstance that a portion of the theatre should have derived its name from the most zealous of the early antagonists of the stage (see p. 1).

8. Again in 1751 a collection of indictments against the theatre was published in Salamanca: Ramire, *Triumpha sagrado de la conscientia.*

9. In a censorship of the existing dramas at a special sitting of the Cortes, it was forbidden that more than one new comedy per week should be produced on the stage, so great was the literary wealth of the period. Only married women were to act, and the performance was to begin not later than two o'clock in the afternoon in the winter and three o'clock in the summer.

10. The occasion of this declaration lay in a complaint which had been made to the ministry, that the religious and political controversies of the time had been represented on the stage. Lord Burleigh commissioned the Lord Mayor to institute an inquiry into the causes of this complaint. After this is it surprising that Shakespeare should now lie open to the charge of having possessed neither faith nor creed ? See *New Facts regarding the Life of Shakespeare,* by Payne Collier.

11. The title runs, *" Histrio-Mastix. The Player's Scourge; or, Actor's Tragedie,* wherein it is evidenced by divers arguments, by the concurring authorities of Scripture, of the whole primitive Church, of 55 Synodes and Councels, of 71 Fathers and Christian writers, and of our owne English Statutes, Magistrates, Universities, that popular stage plays (the very pompes of the Divell) are sinfull, heathenish, lewde, ungodly spectacles, and most pernicious corruptions," &c., &c.

12. The Star Chamber ordered that his writings should be burned by the executioner, that he should be deprived of his academical honours, should pay a fine of £5000, and after being exposed in the pillory should be imprisoned for life. [Prynne wrote besides the *Player's Scourge,* a very large number of violent political and controversial works. His condemnation took place immediately after publication of the *Histrio-Mastix,* and was made to rest on a libel on the Queen contained in that work. In 1640 he was liberated and elected member for Newport. In spite of the violence of his opinions, he never became a warm adherent of Cromwell, and having joined in the restoration of Charles II., he was appointed under that monarch keeper of the records of the Tower. He died in 1669.]

13. Foote is said to have caricatured Whitfield at the Haymarket, but the caricature was overdrawn and not easily recognised. This reminds us of Aristophanes' picture of Socrates.

14. Luther's *Table Talk.* " Dr. Cellarius asked Dr. M. Luther for his advice, saying, " There was a schoolmaster in Silesia, by no means unlearned, who undertook the performance of a comedy of Terence ; but many were offended thereat, finding it unbecoming

in a Christian to meddle with any such light diversion as is found in heathen poets. What, then, might be the opinion of Dr. M. Luther?" Dr. Luther replied, "The performance of comedies in schools ought not to be hindered on account of the boys, in the first place, because they may be thus exercised in the Latin tongue; secondly, because the characters in these comedies are so cleverly imagined, pictured, and represented that the audience may derive much instruction therefrom, and every one may be reminded of his own office and calling, and admonished of what is befitting to him as a servant or a master, a youth or an old man; and before our eyes, as in a mirror, every rank, calling, and occupation is so displayed that every one may learn how to behave in his own position. Moreover, in these comedies the cunning plots and deceptions of pretentious persons and such like are described and represented, and we are shown the duties both of parents and young persons; and how these latter should be trained and brought to the estate of matrimony when the time for that shall arrive, &c. Such things as these are represented in comedies, and instruction in them is good and useful."

15. Luther's *Briefe*, in the edition by de Wette, b. ii. p. 626, and b. iii. p. 567.

16. See the preface to the Book of Judith : "It may be that they represented such histories, even as at the present day the Passion and other sacred stories are represented amongst ourselves; their purpose therein being that the youth and the common people might be instructed, as by a popular picture or spectacle, to trust in God in every time of need." Preface to the Book of Tobit : "We may presume that such beautiful tales and spectacles were common among the Jews, and that they exercised themselves therein on their feast-days and Sabbaths; so that by this means their young folk were inspired with delight in the words and the ways of God. In Judith we have the material of a righteous, solemn, and noble tragedy, and in Tobit of a delicate, graceful, and pious comedy." Luther even supposes that the Greeks may have borrowed from the Jews their custom of acting tragedies and comedies.

17. In *Henno*. The comedy referred to was in five acts, and was acted for the first time in the House Dalberg on Shrove Tuesday, 1497. It was printed the year after.

18. G. Grabovie, *Judicium de hodiernis comoedii aliisque theatricis spectaculis ex sanctissorum Patrum nec non probatissimorum Theologorum nostrae Ecclesiae judiciis conscriptum et a Lipsiensi Theologica*

Facultate comprobatum.   Francof., 1689. At that time Spener was still court preacher at Dresden.

19. O. Schade, *Das Puppenspiel Faust*, published in the *Weimar Jahrb.*, 1856.

20. Devrient, i. p. 386. The widow Veltheim, as late, however, as 1701, published a defence of the theatre which has been often reprinted by stage-managers : "*Curieuse und wohl erörterte Frage, ob Comödien unter den Christen geduldet und ohne Verletzung ihres Gewissens von denselben besucht werden können ?*"

21. In the preface to M. Gottfr. Hoffmann's *Lyc. Laub. Rectoris*, Lpz., 1696, the question is put, "Whether the performance of sacred dramas is to be permitted?" And it is argued that in Proverbs'(viii. 31) even the Almighty is represented as "rejoicing ;" also since the composition of sacred allegories and parables is allowed, it must also be fitting that additional force should be given to these parables through their representation by living persons.

22. *Dramatologia antiquo-hodierna*, Hamb., 1688.

23. The King was, however, induced to modify this despotic command, so far as to allow the younger Francke to pay instead a fine to the poor-box.

24. First in the *Hamburg. Nachrichten aus dem Reiche der Gelehrsamkeit.*, 1786, No. 102. Again in opposition to the *Defence of Pastor Schlosser*, &c., published by Professor Nolting, Götze wrote a pamphlet with the heading "Theologische Untersuchung der Sittlichkeit der heutigen Deutschen Schaubühne, überhaupt wie auch der Frage : ob ein Geistlicher, insonderheit ein wirklich im Predigtamt stehender Mann, ohne ein schweres Aergerniss zu geben, die Schaubühne besuchen, selbst Komödien schreiben, aufführen und drucken lassen, und die Schaubühne, so wie sie jetzo ist, vertheidigen und als einen Tempel der Tugend, als eine Schule der edlen Empfindungen und der guten Sitten anpreisen könne?" Hamburg, 1769.

25. In a discourse at a public session of the "Churfürstlichen deutschen Gesellschaft," held at Mannheim in 1784.

26. *Ueber das gegenwärtige deutsche Theater.* (Würtemburg, *Repertorium der Literatur*, 1782.)

27. From 1806 he frequently acted the part, and it was his last on the 5th December 1813.

28. Bremen, 1815.

29. Devrient, iii. p. 384.'

30. By F. C. Paldamus, "*Das deutsche Theater der Gegenwart,*" Mayence, 1857. But the mode of cure suggested is likely to prove very imperfect, *i.e.*, the elevation of the Theatre to the rank of a public institution, and "the most frank and decisive veto of the Church" against the Theatre in its present condition; which is insisted on, while at the same time much regret is expressed at the absence of all existing connection between Church and Theatre. On the other hand, some theologians, distinguished by breadth of culture and elevation of thought, regard the Theatre as so absolutely unchristian, that it is not so very long since a German theological paper (*Allgemeine Kirchenzeitung*, 1858, p. 82), gave it as its opinion that a government in so far as it subsidises the Theatre and assumes the direction of it, becomes Paganised and loses its claim to the support of the Church.

31. *Oratio de pace.*

32. R. F. Eyler, *Charakter-Züge u. hist. Fragmente aus dem Leben Fr. Wilh. III.*, Magdeb., 1846, b. iii. part 2, p. 315.

33. Saint-Marc Girardin (*Du Drame religieux en France; Revue des deux Mondes*, 1858, Jan. 1), has taken this view and shown that it is not the lack of intellect in religious matters in France which causes the religious drama to form so small a part of modern French literature.

34. The same, p. 211 : "Les passions humaines sont mal à leur aise dans le drame religieux, dont le principal héros met sa gloire à étouffer ses passions. A quoi donc nous intéresser ? Au triomphe de la règle et de la virtu, triomphe qui, pour être conforme au caractère du héros, ne doit pas même avoir les agitations du combat et les incertitudes de la lutte ? Le plaisir de voir triompher la vertu sans efforts ne peut pas nous retenir longtemps au théâtre, où nous n'allons plus, comme nos aïeux du XV. siècle, chercher l'edification : nous allons y chercher l'émotion. Le saint se dépouille de sa patrie et de sa famille pour ne plus songer qu'au ciel. Les affections du monde, les tracas de la vie, les intérêts terrestres, les embarras, les soins, les contrariétés, les travers, les ridicules, les vices, tout en lui

s'efface et disparait devant l'ascendant de la foi. Est-ce un personage dramatique, celui que la tragédie ne peut point prendre par
ses passions, ni la comédie par ses ridicules ? "

35. The representation of Werner's *Luther* in Weimar on the
eve of the Reformation festival of 1857 was rendered possible because the superintendent of the theatres, Dinglestadt, whose comprehension of the requirements of the stage was at once practically
clear and yet poetic, cut out from the piece the greater portion of
the superabundant mysticism. But this process of selection neces-
sarily caused much of the action to appear inconsequent, and however consistent with himself the principal personage might have
become, yet the impression which remained was a very mixed one.
Before that date, in the Jubilee year 1817, a drama named *Luther's
Eutscheidung*, by Heinrich Schorch, a former professor of Erfurt,
was being got ready for production, when some considerations were
suggested which prevented the representation of *Luther* on the
stage. Pevcer, the director of the consistory, had written a prologue for the intended performance.

36. *Los cabellos de Absolon*, the argument of which Calderon borrowed, with but slight alteration, from Tirsa's *Venganza de Thamar*.

37. [Hanswurst—Jackpudding ; the German clown.]

38. [Professor Hase has already (Lecture V.) referred unfavour-
ably to the ultra-orthodox Lutheran school. Vilmar, whose ideal
was placed in the ages of faith, and who looked on modern German
literature as a declension, belonged to this school.]

39. From Lope de Vega's *El niño inocente de la guardia*, and
Shakespeare's *Merchant of Venice*, down to Gutzkow's *Uriel Akosta*
and Wolfgang's *Osternacht*.

40. Schiller to Goethe, 5th January 1798 : " I should much like,
after I have had some success as a dramatist, and thus thoroughly
ingratiated myself with the public, to do something rather shocking,
and carry out an old idea of mine with regard to Julian the Apostate. In his surroundings we have a whole definite historical world
of a quite peculiar character, from which I should have no difficulty
in levying a poetic contribution ; while the solemnly affecting interest
which the subject itself offers, would be heightened by the force of
the poetic representation."

41. These student choristers received a trifling fee. Herder

appealed to the duke ; but it was not till 1818 that the practice was superseded by the employment of a professional chorus. Heiland, p. 18.

42. Richard Rothe, *Die Anfänge der christlichen Kirche*, Wittenb., 1837, p. 45 : " The original shyness, hostility, and natural repulsion which exist between art-life generally and religious worship, are first softened down into the antithesis of sacred and profane art ; and the longer these run on side by side, the more unsubstantial becomes the difference between them. The turning-point of the whole question lies in the relation between what is essentially human or natural and what is religious ; and the opposition of these two it is the great work of the Redemption operating in history to remove. As long as they are external to each other, the stage and the worship of the Church are also external to one another, or rather are opposed to each other. But if what is essentially human and what is religious are truly merged, then worship and the stage also become one. Common art-life in its perfect development is in itself common divine worship ; or, inversely, common divine worship is in itself the whole organism of common art-life."